The Brains Behind
Great Ad Campaigns

The Brains Behind Great Ad Campaigns

Creative Collaboration between Copywriters and Art Directors

MARGO BERMAN

AND

ROBYN BLAKEMAN

ROWMAN & LITTLEFIELD PUBLISHERS, INC.
Lanham • Boulder • New York • Toronto • Plymouth, UK

ROWMAN & LITTLEFIELD PUBLISHERS, INC.

Published in the United States of America
by Rowman & Littlefield Publishers, Inc.
A wholly owned subsidiary of The Rowman & Littlefield Publishing Group, Inc.
4501 Forbes Boulevard, Suite 200, Lanham, Maryland 20706
www.rowmanlittlefield.com

Estover Road
Plymouth PL6 7PY
United Kingdom

British Library Cataloguing in Publication Information Available

Library of Congress Cataloging-in-Publication Data:

Berman, Margo, 1947–
    The brains behind great ad campaigns : creative collaboration between copywriters and
art directors / Margo Berman and Robyn Blakeman.
        p. cm.
    Includes bibliographical references and index.
    ISBN 978-0-7425-5550-1 (cloth : alk. paper) — ISBN 978-0-7425-5551-8
(pbk. : alk. paper)
    1. Advertising campaigns. 2. Brand name products. I. Blakeman, Robyn, 1958–
II. Title.
  HF5837.B47 2009
    659.1'15—dc22   2008055414

Printed in the United States of America

∞The paper used in this publication meets the minimum requirements of American National
Standard for Information Sciences—Permanence of Paper for Printed Library Materials,
ANSI/NISO Z39.48-1992.

CONTENTS

ACKNOWLEDGMENTS

THIS WORK is a direct reflection of all the selfless people who helped us create it. We would like to take this time to individually acknowledge their support. Although most people listed below may believe they don't need to be thanked, we would respectfully argue the point. If we accidentally omitted someone, we apologize.

First, I (Margo) would like to thank my husband, Jack, who waited patiently for my attention while I was researching and writing. Next, I would like to recognize Jennifer Minnich, creative director of M2Design, for her suggestions and cheers of encouragement and suggestions. Third, I would like to acknowledge Ronni Alexander, my niece, who has always been my North Star. I would also like to send a warmhearted thanks to Monica Hudson, executive assistant, for her faithful commitment to my ongoing research efforts, book after book.

We must also thank two people at Rowman & Littlefield Publishers. First, Niels Aaboe, executive editor of communication and journalism, who maintained his enthusiasm throughout the process, and Asa Johnson, editorial assistant, who patiently handled the details.

We wish to thank all of the creative talents and various executives at ad agencies (in alphabetical order) who repeatedly interrupted their busy schedules to assist us by arranging interviews, obtaining visuals, and sharing pertinent campaign information.

At Crispin Porter + Bogusky: Steve Sapka, manager of agency communications, for tirelessly responding to every request, from overseeing ongoing correspondence and image acquisition to gathering information, permissions, and content approval; Elizabeth Harper, content supervisor, for handling the review and approval process; and Michele Conigliaro, assistant content manager, for coordinating final permissions. More thanks go to the following executives for lending images and granting approval: Andrew Cutler, MINI communications manager for MINI USA; and Clark Campbell, motorsport manager, Public Relations Department for Volkswagen Group of America, Inc. We are especially grateful to Tiffany Kosel, associate creative director/

art director, and Scott Linnen, vice president/creative director/copywriter, for their candid comments and image selection.

At DDB: Pat Sloan, media relations for DDB corporate, for arranging the initial steps in setting up interviews in the Chicago office; Amy Cheronis, U.S. communications director, for her unwavering attention to detail in interview scheduling and image acquisition; Mia Sisek, senior marketing communications associate, for arranging to have the final Budweiser image in the appropriate format. Special thanks go to the creative team of Adam Glickman, creative director/art director, and Craig Feigen, creative director/copywriter, who shared their ideas about the creative process.

At Deutsch: Scott Lahde, vice president/associate director of corporate communications at Deutsch Inc., for his persistence in arranging interviews, acquiring images, and double-checking all the tedious details. Additional thanks go to Eric Springer, executive vice president/group creative director at Deutsch L.A., for freely discussing collaborative conceptualization, and to Matt Jarvis, director of account planning at Deutsch L.A., for insight into the overall creation of the GM Robot campaign.

At Euro RSCG: Ron Berger, executive chairman, RSCG Worldwide, for facilitating communication and granting final permission; Earleen Surujballi, executive assistant to Ron Berger, for scheduling interviews and overseeing all of the follow-up correspondence; and Phil Silvestri and Rich Roth, both managing directors/executive creative directors, for their candor about being part of a creative team for more than twenty years.

At The Escape Pod: Vinny Warren, creative director, for his thought-provoking interview and diligence in image selection.

At Goodby, Silverstein & Partners: Christine O'Donnell, public relations director, for her perseverance in arranging interviews; Paul Charney, senior copywriter, for his indispensable interview and thoughtful comments; and creative team Sara Rose, senior copywriter, and Lea Ladera, senior art director, for their engaging interview and stimulating remarks.

At Laser Advertising: Tracy Datlen, owner, for her insightful interview, relevant images, and permission; and Natalia Rodriguez, graphic designer/ illustrator, for her focused dedication in setting up the interview, obtaining images, and gaining approval.

At The Martin Agency: Lauren Tucker, senior vice president/group planning director, for offering insight into strategic planning and for securing permissions; Andy Azula, senior vice president/creative director, for revealing the innovative thinking behind the UPS "Whiteboard" campaign; Theresa Dunn, account executive for media relations, for being so responsive to my multiple requests for specifically formatted images, as well as gaining permissions and content approval.

At Saatchi & Saatchi: Shannon Evans, creative ideas coordinator, United Kingdom office, for her efforts to obtain images; Derek Lockwood, worldwide director of design, for his assistance in coordinating correspondence and image acquisition from the New Zealand office; Tom Eslinger, worldwide creative director of interactive, for brilliantly orchestrating the acquisition of detailed information, permissions, and final images for the New Zealand Army and Answer Seguro Insurance Company online campaigns. Heartfelt thanks go to many executives at the New Zealand office, including Nicola Harvey, group account director; Campbell Moore, account manager; Richard Montgomerie, interactive producer; and Louise Dun, office manager, for their swift response in obtaining approvals, images, and permissions for the New Zealand Army campaign. Special thanks also go to Major Eugene Whakahoehoe, director of recruiting, New Zealand Army, for granting his final approval, and Patricia Martin, chief operating officer in the Del Campo Nazca office, for final caption and image approval. We are also grateful to the following people in the Del Campo Nazca office: Josefina Scasso, public relations director, for her assistance in image acquisition, and Paula Gambardella, account director, and Valeria Magrini, account executive, for their clear explanations and reference images for the Answer Seguro Insurance Company campaign. We would like to thank Heidi Young, executive vice president, general counsel, in the New York office, for her overall guidance regarding various comments and images.

At TBWA\Chiat\Day: Marianne Stefanowicz, U.S. public relations director, for her heroic effort in orchestrating interviews, gathering images, supervising approvals, identifying photographers to be credited, and being so methodical; Marissa Serritella, senior art producer, for assisting in every tiresome phase of image acquisition, plus ensuring that all of the PEDIGREE® campaign images were correctly formatted. At Arthaus, the agency's in-house photography studio: Arielle Viny Jr., photo producer, for obtaining specific, requested images and verifying which photographers shot which images; and Josh Withers, for allowing us to use his photographs. Additional thanks to the following photographers who shot various images in the PEDIGREE® campaign discussed in this work: Laura Crosta, Peggy Sirota, and Sharon Montrose. Special thanks go to the creative team of Margaret Keene, art director, and Chris Adams, copywriter, who openly shared their thoughts on creative partnerships and campaign development.

At Think Tank 3: Sharoz Makarechi, creative director, for her explicit comments, exciting visuals, and granting permission; Harris Silver, president, for organizing the agency's line of communication; Judah Stevenson, design operative, for diligently arranging interviews, acquiring images, and obtaining permissions.

At Two Parrot Productions: Jessica Kizorek, managing director, for offering her online video expertise.

At Young & Laramore: Tom Denari, president, for his continued support and final consent; Donna Unland, administrative assistant to Paul J. Knapp, David Young, and Jeff Laramore, for conscientiously coordinating all correspondence and final image releases. More thanks go to Carolyn Hadlock and Charlie Hopper, creative directors, for their well thought-out comments and wonderful array of images.

At Zubi Advertising: Andrés Ordóñez, vice president/creative director, for providing vital information on idea generation; and Frank Morales, senior account executive, for conscientiously coordinating all correspondence, arranging the interview, and facilitating the permission process.

Additional thanks go to Andy Carrigan, graduate of The Creative Circus, writer and creative director at various agencies, for her interesting comments.

For assistance from different creative centers of learning, we would like to thank the following people for their generosity.

At The Creative Circus: Norm Grey, executive creative director, for his continued encouragement and help reaching graduates.

At Florida International University: Lillian Kopenhaver, dean, School of Journalism and Mass Communication, for her unrelenting encouragement; Cathy Ahles, former department chair, Advertising and Public Relations, for her ongoing support; and Fernando Figueredo, department chair, for his appreciation of Margo's research interests.

We would also like to thank our students, colleagues, and seminar audiences, who continuously stimulate our intellectual curiosity and fuel our creativity. Last, we'd like to thank each other for the combined effort it took to create and execute our shared vision.

CHAPTER 1

The Brains behind the Campaign

The Strategy and the Brief

Unless your advertising contains a big idea, it will pass like a ship in the night.—David Ogilvy[1]

Defining a Creative Strategy

Creative describes a unique and individual idea. *Strategy* is a plan to accomplish that creative idea or concept. A creative strategy is all about sending the appropriate visual/verbal message to the right target audience, through the right media, in order to achieve the overall communication objectives.

A creative strategy is an integral part of the marketing communication process. Once you know the goals or objectives of the client, you can begin developing an effective creative strategy that will accomplish them. Effective strategies are the slippery yet essential monsters that define advertising direction. Determining the right ones requires research. You are not looking at ideas, describing a creative look, or solidifying media outlets at this point; you are looking at a solution to an advertising problem. These solutions will produce a concept or theme that can be consistently executed both visually and verbally within multiple media without losing substance or focus.

A successful creative strategy is developed from information found in the client's marketing plan (business plan) and is written from the consumer's point of view. It needs to ask, on behalf of the target, What's in it for me? How will it solve my problem or make my life better? The answers should ultimately lead to an idea that will make the product or service stand out from the competition and influence the target to act on the message.

The creative strategy will define your campaign's visual/verbal tone and is the foundation for the product's or service's communication phase. The creative strategy affects every aspect of creative development and will ultimately give the product its image and voice, and define seller-to-buyer contact.

Who Develops the Creative Strategy?

The creative strategy is usually developed by the agency account executive (AE), but it can also be developed jointly with the client. Representing the business side of advertising, the AE acts as the liaison between the client and the agency and the client and the creative team. This team of "creatives" will use the creative strategy to develop the overall concept or idea. Their interpretation of the creative strategy begins the construction phase of message development.

The Look of a Creative Strategy

Creative strategies can take many different forms, depending on the agency and the overall size and scope of the project. The longer, more explanatory form has two main areas: The first looks at the communication objectives and the second dissects the creative strategy directive into four main sections: the target (primary and secondary), the competition, the key benefit, and the proposed promotional mix. Let's take a brief look at each one.

Communication Objectives. Creative strategies must accommodate a specific set of objectives, or what the client needs the communication efforts to achieve. Objectives are determined by problems the target or product category may have and any market opportunities the product has to solve or overcome these problems.

Objectives describe what it is you want the target to think, feel, and do after exposure to the message and should answer the target's question: "what's in it for me?" Some of the most common objectives include creating brand awareness, or what you want the target to think or know about the product or service after exposure to the advertising message; defining a need the product or service can fulfill, such as improving how the target feels or demonstrating how much can be accomplished using the product or service; encouraging action on the part of the target such as making a purchase, visiting a showroom or website, or calling for more information. Determining how these objectives should be addressed is the first hurdle the creative team must clear before a creative direction is determined.

Creative Directive. Each of the following sections should be addressed in no more than one or two sentences. A successful strategy requires the creative team to have a thorough understanding of the target audience, the competition, the product, and media options.

Primary and Secondary Target Audience Profiles. The primary target is identified by research as the most likely prospect to buy the product or use the service. Secondary audiences are often influencers whose opinion the primary target audience member trusts or seeks out for advice. Take, for example, a campaign for iPod. Advertising efforts may focus on a primary target of fifteen- to twenty-eight-year-olds, with a secondary audience of parents or grandparents of the primary target. Messages targeted to the primary audience may focus on image and features, while advertising targeted to the secondary audience may add information on price or purchasing options.

A thorough understanding of both audiences will help the creative team determine the answers to some important questions: What do the targets want? Are they aware of the product or service? What will influence their decision to purchase? How will the product be used in their daily lives? Are they currently using a competitor's product? If so, what do they like or dislike about that product? What will it take to convince them to switch brands? Are there any major influencers, or secondary target audience members, who also have to be reached?

Advertising to a single target audience no longer has the impact it once had to deliver the brand's image and promise. Many purchases require little or no thought, while others, especially high-dollar purchases, or those that reflect a target's lifestyle, the need to fit in or be the first to own, are influenced by other individuals trusted by the primary target. These individuals are known as outside influencers.

In his book Strategies for Implementing Integrated Marketing Communications, Larry Percy identifies roles individuals play that can positively or negatively affect their decision or another's decision to buy:

1. **Initiator**: the individual who originally decides to purchase a product or use a service.
2. **Influencer**: an outside person or group of people who recommends or discourages the purchase of a product or use of a service.
3. **Decider**: the person who ultimately determines what will be purchased.
4. **Purchaser**: the individual who initiates purchase or use of the product or service.
5. **User**: the individual who in fact uses the product or service.

It's important to remember that advertising is directed not to a target audience, but to a single individual within that audience. Every time members of the target audience consider a particular type of purchase, they assume a mindset or play a role. That role will determine the type of message they receive. Initiators must be made aware of the product or service and the benefits that come with ownership or use. Influencers, such as family and friends, salespeople who may or may not recommend the product or service, and professional influencers such as doctors or financial advisors, must understand the reason a product or service should, or should not, be recommended. The decider must have the answer to "what's in it for me?" before deciding whether or not to purchase. A user must not only use the product but also be willing to recommend and repurchase the product or reuse the service.

The Competition. This is not a list of competitors, but rather a look at what competitors are doing and saying in their advertising and a statement regarding what the client's brand must do to compete within the product category, stand out from the competition, and attract the target's attention. Knowing how the product is positioned in the mind of consumers, or what they think about the product or service, will help determine a unique and individualized concept direction. A new product will need to have a 1) brand image and position created for it, 2) an established product will need to have its image and its position supported, and 3) a mature or reinvented product may need its position altered in the target's mind, or its image rebuilt or reestablished. It's important to know what leaders in the product category are doing so your message can address or challenge them with its own unique image and voice, avoiding a "me too" approach. It is also important for the target to know why your product is better than the competition.

Key Benefit. The key benefit is the answer to the target's question "what's in it for me?" It is the one product or service feature and benefit combination that research has shown to be the most important to the targeted audience. All communication efforts will focus on this feature and corresponding benefit.

It's important that the creative team know enough about the product or service to be able to understand, define, and highlight the key benefit's inherent drama. The successful translation of this drama into a meaningful benefit tailor-made to the target's self-image and lifestyle will make the product or service memorable and help it stand out from the competition.

Advertising must be memorable in order to obtain the stated objectives. Memorable advertising will present a key benefit that solves a target's problem or reflects a creative concept or idea that resonates with the target's lifestyle or self-image. For an ad to be memorable it must:

- Tell a visual and verbal story that can hold the target's attention.
- Push one strong idea of special interest or emotional benefit to the target: one that is important to the target, fulfills a need or want, and can be delivered both visually and verbally.

- Clearly repeat the product name throughout the copy and represent the product visually.
- Use an appeal that matches the benefit and target audience profile.
- Have a creative element or benefit that makes the ad stand out from those of competitors in the brand category.

Promotional Mix. Once you have a thorough understanding of what you need to accomplish, who your target is, and what their motivation is to purchase, it's time to consider the best promotional mix to reach your target.

This section should give the creative team an idea of where the message will appear, since media choices often affect the overall message to be delivered. Choices beyond—or even instead of—traditional advertising outlets can make it easier to reach your target audience members during each step of their decision-making process.

How will you know which media within the promotional mix to use? Ask yourself the following questions:

Public Relations

- Is there something newsworthy about the product or service?
- Is it a new product launch?
- Is the product or service sponsoring any charitable events or opening new production facilities?
- How does the company fit into the local community? Are relations good or bad?

Sales Promotion

- Why do you need to give something away?
- Do you strategically need to increase short-term profits?
- Is this a new product launch, where samples or "try me" opportunities would increase awareness and/or sales?

Direct Marketing

- How well does the company know the target audience?
- Will addressing the target personally increase awareness or induce purchase?

- Is there access to a computer database of target names, interests, and past purchase history to make a personalized message relevant or motivational?
- Is this a product or service that lends itself to creating a long-term relationship?
- Is there a target or prospective target niche that has been overlooked by previous communication efforts that fit the target profile?

Internet

- Do members of the target audience have a computer? If so, do they use it to seek out additional information and compare products?
- Is this a rational or life-sustaining purchase, like clothing or food, or a purely emotional or fun purchase?
- Is this a product that requires interaction with customer service or technical representatives?
- Does this product offer upgrades? Is there a need to update the consumer on any product changes or uses through personalized e-mail notices?
- If dealing with multiple targets, can alternative information be delivered with greater frequency and with less expense electronically?
- The Internet takes a product or service global—is the company able to handle this volume of consumers and keep customer service initiatives high and delivery timely?

The creative strategy should engage appropriate tactics to successfully integrate all messages throughout the promotional mix into one unified strategy.

Creative Strategies That Get to the Point

An established client making minor changes in describing a product's performance or image does not require the same amount of research as a new product or client. Existing knowledge about the target and competition can be easily reexamined and reused to coordinate message and media needs. This type of situation will often require a simpler and more informal creative strategy that is usually no more than two or three sentences long and includes:

- The objective or purpose of the message
- The target audience

- The key benefit
- The support statement (why buy)

Some creative strategies developed for corporate advertising may not use any of the above options and instead rely solely on the company's mission statement as a place to begin idea generation.

There is one more kind of strategy that needs to be considered: the creative strategy statement. This is a one-sentence formula that outlines the main objective of the campaign. It's simple; all you have to do is fill in the blanks:

> The brand is advertising to say something _____ (VERB—to persuade, convince, inform, educate) the audience (SPECIFIC CONSUMERS) that this _____ (PRODUCT, SERVICE, OR BRAND) will _____ (STATE THE BENEFIT) because _____ (SUPPORT STATEMENT, OR FEATURES THAT EXPLAIN WHY THE AUDIENCE SHOULD BELIEVE IT).[2]

Scott Linnen, vice president/creative director/copywriter for Crispin Porter + Bogusky, explains the creative strategy's role in the creative process this way, "whenever a strategy can be a bigger message and not just so small a focus, it helps a lot for coming up with ideas."[3]

Let's take a look at how a creative strategy is executed in a creative brief.

The Elements of a Comprehensive Creative Brief

Defining the Business behind Creative

Creative doesn't just happen. It's the result of months of research, planning, and preparation. When it's time to develop an idea, your direction will be based on a multiphased business plan started months earlier.

Young copywriters and art directors often believe they get to do anything they want creatively. Nothing could be further from the truth. The budget and the client's marketing initiatives most often challenge creative ingenuity. It's important to understand that you do not design for yourself; you design to sell a product or service to a predetermined target audience.

Most of us think of advertising as the creative work. However, the creative aspect is only one small portion of the process of advertising. Advertising is a business first and a creative outlet second.

The road to effective creative is well defined. It begins with the research of the product or service, often called the brand. Then it moves on to the client's creation of a marketing plan, and ends with the development of a creative brief by the agency.

Figure 1.1. This magazine ad was designed to highlight the privacy and serenity, as well as the excitement and exhilaration of private yachting.

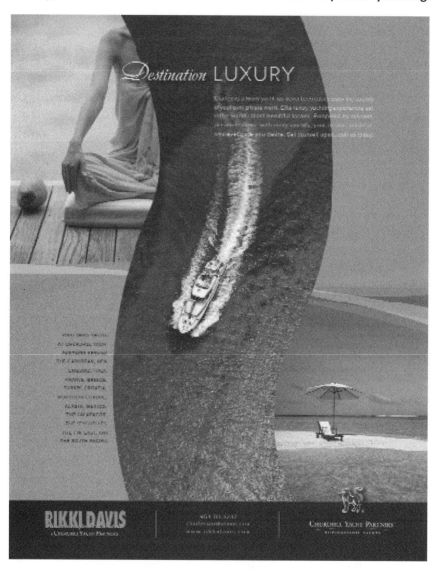

Image courtesy of Laser Advertising[a]

The Big Influence inside a Small Document

The creative brief, also known as a copy platform, creative work plan, creative plan, or copy strategy, is the next step in the evolution of the marketing plan. Creatives—that is, art directors and copywriters—will use the creative brief during concept development. It is the only document that outlines the brand's objective for the creative team and helps to keep them both on target and on strategy, moving toward accomplishing the varied communication-based goals. Information found in the marketing plan is used in the creative brief to outline the communication plan of attack.

A small internal document created by the account executive or the agency's account manager, the creative brief should dissect the product or service for the creative team. It should redefine the target audience, introduce the key consumer benefit, describe individual features and consumer benefits, define communication-based objectives, address the competition, and outline tactics. It is the main reference the creative team will use to define the message that needs to be communicated. Think of it as a set of building blocks providing the foundation for the concept or idea, which will become the visual/verbal message.

The creative brief is not a document that speculates or generalizes. It needs to be detailed and concise enough that a creative solution can be developed for the client's communication goal. A creative brief also ensures that the creative team, the account team, and the client all have a thorough understanding of exactly what objectives the promotional communication needs to accomplish.

First and foremost, the creative brief is a strategic plan that provides the guidelines for developing the creative message. It's not a creative outlet. It does not define or determine what creative should look like. It's a road map for idea generation and visual/verbal development.

There is no prescribed length for creative briefs, but they are usually no more than one or two pages long. It must contain all the information the creative team needs to develop ideas and remain focused on what communication problems need to be solved, in the shortest version possible.

What Makes Up a Creative Brief?

Overall length, information content, and format vary by agency, but most creative briefs contain at a maximum the following:

1. Target Audience Profile
2. Communication Objectives
3. Product Features and Benefits
4. Competition

5. Product Positioning
6. Key Consumer Benefit
7. Creative Strategy
8. Tone
9. Support Statement
10. Slogan or Tagline
11. Logo

Target Audience Profile. The target audience consists of those consumers determined through research to be the most likely to buy or use the product or service. The more you know about who will be using the product, the better you can target your message directly to them. This section of the brief breaks down the intended target audience according to the following market segments: demographics, psychographics, geographics, and behavioristics.

Demographics breaks down groups based on personal attributes such as sex, age, income, marital and professional status, occupation, education, and number of children, to name just a few.

Psychographics looks at personal attributes that affect lifestyle such as cultural, emotional, family, health, and social issues, as well as hobbies, overall beliefs, and attitudes.

Geographics defines where the target lives. Geographics can be broken down regionally or by city, state, or ZIP code. Where people live often influences the type of product they will buy and where the product should be advertised. It also affects their ambitions and how they process information. For example, a city dweller will not necessarily need the same products as someone living in a rural environment. They are also exposed to different media. As a result, they each require different messages.

Behavioristic profiles look at why a person buys: Is it because of loyalty, social acceptance, brand name, or need?

When determining the correct target audience for products or services, any one or combination of the above segmentation practices could be used. Answers found within these segments will determine both message content and media choice.

Once the appropriate profile has been determined, we still need to take our study of the target audience one step further, by isolating target attributes in an even more personalized way.

Left-Brain versus Right-Brain, a Thought

By understanding how consumers think, act, and feel, we can more accurately target our message to meet their needs. These needs are controlled by the brain, which is divided into two halves, the left side and the right side.

The left side of the brain governs reading and verbal skills, as well as the logical and rational thought processes that make an individual's outlook more conservative. This is the side that tells you not to step in front of a moving vehicle, and that you need a parachute when jumping from an airplane.

The left side of the brain is also responsible for math skills and your ability to memorize facts, names, and vocabulary.

The right side of the brain is the more creative, liberal, emotional, and visual side. Its strengths include a vivid imagination, musical and artistic abilities, and a more open-minded or unrestricted outlook. Many right-brained people need to see a message repeatedly, in multiple forms of media, before reacting to that message. Often left-brained individuals will respond to a message by researching a product or service more thoroughly, calling customer service departments, reading annual or consumer reports, or surfing the Web.

Most of us use a little of the abilities from both sides of our brain. We avoid that moving car. We love music or books, but hate math.

It is critical that people's left- and right-brained attributes be taken into consideration when creating visual/verbal relationships in advertising design. A left-brained individual relies on facts to make a decision, making copy more important. The right-brained individual relies more on the visual aspects of the ad. The overall creative message needs to appeal to both kinds of individuals within your target audience.

Initially, the basic needs for each of these individuals differ. If, for example, you are advertising a car, the left-brained consumer will be more interested in facts such as gas mileage and safety features, whereas the right-brained consumer will be more interested in seeing the car and learning about color choices. It's not that right-brainers don't care about safety or that left-brainers don't care about what the car looks like, they're just not the first or most important things they consider.

One way to create a strong visual/verbal relationship that immediately attracts the attention of both learners is to have a strong headline explaining a consumer benefit, accompanied by an answering visual. In other words, attract the left-brainer with words and the right-brainer with copy that paints a visual picture of them experiencing the car. This will also work for the left-brainer, if you intersperse relevant facts within the visual copy. This type of approach is particularly important for new product introductions, additions, and/or upgrades.

In addition, people primarily process information one of three ways, often referred to as neurolinguistic programming (NLP) or more recently as neurolinguistic conditioning (NLC). People absorb information in these three ways: 1) visually, 2) auditorially, and 3) kinesthetically. This is equally important in the message development phase and the client pitch presentation. Why? Because you need to include words that specifically speak to the way people process information. For the visual person, you would include words like "see," "picture," or "imagine." For example:

> See what I mean?
> Get the picture?
> Can you imagine this?

For the auditory person, you would use language like "hear," "sound," and "listen." For example:

> Hear what I'm saying?
> Sound good to you?
> Listen up!

For the kinesthetic person, you would integrate words like "feel," "touch," and "handle." For example:

> How's that feel?
> Does it touch you?
> Do you have a handle on that?

Knowing that people process information differently enables you to create messages that speak directly to them. People actually clearly demonstrate the way they process by their language and actions. For instance, the visual car buyer would want to see the paint colors, look at the dashboard, and examine the car's overall lines. The auditory buyer would have to hear the engine, listen to the stereo system, and check the sound of the horn. The kinesthetic shopper would have to feel the interior, kick the tires, and test-drive the car.

The more knowledge you have about your product, client, target, and competition, the more ammunition you have for creative ingenuity.

The goal of advertising is not only to inform, but also to find just the right way to inspire your target to act. When developing a creative direction it's important that the creative team never lose sight of who the target is. Your target audience is the reason you are developing communication efforts. You must know how it will react to your message in order to successfully advertise any product. Just knowing what the target thinks, what he finds important, and how the product or service can fulfill his needs and wants makes creating the right message a lot easier. You can strike out by communicating to the masses with a generalized message or you can hit the ball out of the park with an individualized consumer-focused message.

Communication Objectives. Communication objectives, or goals, clearly define what the communication efforts need to accomplish. Objectives should pinpoint what you want the target to think about the product or service, what you want the target to feel when using the product or toward the product in general, and what you want the target to do, such as make a purchase or request additional information.

There is a limit to what can be accomplished with one ad or even one campaign. On average, no product or service should have more than one to three obtainable objectives. Each objective needs to focus on communication-related issues. Communication-based objectives give consumers usable, personalized information, as opposed to marketing-based objectives, which are sales related. Primarily, creative efforts will focus on positioning objectives that educate the consumer about the product or service. It's important when determining objectives to know your target's level of knowledge about the product or service. A look at the product or service's life cycle stage will also be beneficial when determining what needs to be said or shown, what needs to be introduced or modified, and what needs to be overhauled completely. This is true whether it is a new product launch, maintenance advertising, or the reinvention of an existing brand. All of these considerations will affect whether objectives can be accomplished over the short or long term. Let's take a quick look at each of the life cycle stages.

New Brand. A new product will need an image that matches the target market's self-image and reflects its lifestyle. New products are a blank canvas that will, over time, need to develop brand equity and earn consumer loyalty. In order to create a competitive advantage, a new product must immediately distinguish its advantages from those of its competitors.

Determining which product advantage to promote will depend on the target, what the competition is doing, what needs to be accomplished, and the creative strategy used to influence the target. Considering these factors, a product's advantages may be implied, found among its features, presented as benefits, based on price, showcased as high-end, or seen as meeting emotional or rational needs. It is beneficial if the product can introduce a fad or reflect a trend. Creating brand awareness is critical to the success of a new product launch.

Brand Maintenance. Once a brand has been established, communication efforts must work to consistently maintain awareness, reinforce quality and reliability, and continue building a relationship with the target.

Reinvented Brand. Reinvention can occur when a brand is in need of a new or updated image. This can be the result of a damaged reputation from past indiscretions or erroneous scandals. A product's reinvention may also mean eliminating outdated approaches that directly affect image and ultimately target perception. Products that are reinvented, no matter the reason, will have to prove themselves over time in order to rebuild lost equity and regain brand loyalty.

Figure 1.2. One of a series of product demo TV spots for stuff that doesn't exist yet, dramatizing the fact that new sports and outdoor gear technologies are always being invented—and Gaylans will have them as soon as they're available.

Image courtesy of Young & Laramore[b]

SCRIPT STARTS HERE

"Hydroguard":30 Script

(With clouds gathering and his dog at his side, an outdoorsman leaves his remote campsite and hikes through a wild, beautiful landscape of mountains and rivers. Far from shelter, the two are caught in a downpour. Our mountaineer calmly pulls the hood of his advanced Hydroguard® coat and activates a technologically-advanced rain-deflecting shield, which creates, in effect, an aura of dry space around him. His dog hurries to his side, taking advantage of the shelter the Hydroguard® creates.)

VO: This coat is not available. Yet. If it ever is, we'll be the first to have it, Gaylans Sports & Outdoor Adventure. What's next?"

SCRIPT ENDS HERE

Think of it this way: If you have a new product launch or are reinventing a brand, a relationship must be built first on image and then on trust. So, the first thing you need to do is to position the brand in the mind of the consumer, while working to build brand awareness. Over time, the objective would be to achieve loyalty, and eventually, brand equity. This type of traditional or mass media advertising is known as brand image advertising. To be successful, all objectives must translate to results.

Product Features and Benefits. The features and benefits section looks at a product's varied features and attaches them to target needs and wants. A feature is a product attribute important to the target or that is beneficial to his or her lifestyle. One mistake young account executives or creatives often make is to sell a product's features and not its benefits.

Features are lovely, but have no intrinsic relevance. The point that needs to be hammered home is what the feature can offer the consumer. Determining a benefit for each of your product's features helps break down the product information into smaller, more manageable bundles, giving concept development a visual/verbal starting point.

The example below shows the features and benefits of a toaster.

Feature: It comes in five different colors: red, green, blue, yellow, and orange.

Benefit: Makes coordination with your kitchen color theme easier.

Feature: Comes in two-, four-, or six-slice models.

Benefit: No matter how many people in your family, there is a toaster size that makes feeding them faster and easier.

A third consideration is the product's value. This answers the question "what's it worth to me?" Consumers will buy products because they think they're worth the price.

Research gathered on the target audience might suggest to the creative team that the target is upwardly mobile and might have just bought a new home, is on a budget and will be remodeling, or is trendy and just likes to keep up with the most current looks in decorating. A benefit informing the target that the toaster comes in colors that match any decorating scheme or accommodates family size with its two-, four-, or six-slice models talks to the consumer's current needs.

Features can be inherent in the product (e.g., ingredients) or become a benefit by implying that the status or image of the brand can affect the consumer's personal image or lifestyle (e.g., Rolex).

Competition. This section should briefly discuss the brands that represent direct competition to your client's brand. Knowing what the competitors are doing with their advertising and product development is the difference between being a product category leader and being a follower. Compare and contrast each product to your client's brand. Then ask yourself how your target audience sees each brand. Rate your client's brand against its direct competitors based on brand image, position, and so on. Describe any advertising messages used currently or recently for competing brands. Understanding the similarities and differences between a product and its leading competitors is crucial for a product to stand out from the competition in the mind of the targeted consumer.

The creative team will use this section to avoid duplicating what competitors are saying and doing with their promotional efforts.

Product Positioning. Positioning relates to how the consumer thinks about and rates your product or service against the competition. Positioning requires highlighting target-relevant benefits for the product's features. Benefits must be tied to uses that will enhance the target's lifestyle or image.

Positioning is effective only if fully researched. You must know—not think you know—how the consumer thinks and feels about the product or service. Ask yourself a few questions: Who is most likely to use the product or service? What are the benefits to your target of using the product? How does the product stand up against its competition? What makes it unique? What features are duplicated? What is the perceived value of the product within the marketplace? How will the product be made available to the target? Does it come in different sizes, colors, or price ranges? Is it relevant to the target?

It's important to understand that your client's product is probably not the only product of its kind. It is most likely one of many virtually identical products in the category. To make it stand out from the crowd you must carve out a niche or position for it.

A strong position is a direct result of a strong brand. This position is built up over a period of time based on reliability of performance. Branding gives a product or service an air of exclusivity and a distinct identity from its competitors.

Key Consumer Benefit. The key consumer benefit is the one feature/benefit combination that either is unique to your client's product or can be positioned as big or important. The key benefit will be the point that screams from every ad, either visually or verbally, positioning the product as the one that meets your target's internal and external needs. It will become the one voice of your promotional message and should be chosen because research has determined that it's relevant to the target audience. Therefore, it will speak directly to their interests and lifestyle, encouraging some sort of desired action.

There are three types of key consumer benefits: a unique selling proposition (USP), a multiple selling proposition (MSP), and a big idea. Analysis of the target market determines which key benefit can accomplish the stated objectives. It will be the glue that holds all advertising and promotional efforts together. Along with the strategy, the key consumer benefit will help determine the visual/verbal direction the communication efforts will take. Let's take a brief look at each one.

A Unique, Big-Selling Idea

Determining whether to use a USP, a big idea, or an MSP depends on what the product or service has to say about itself as compared to the competition and whether the target audience members think its benefits will enhance their lives. If the product or service speaks of uniqueness, or is the first to introduce a feature, the best key consumer benefit to use would be a USP. Products that have no outstanding characteristics to differentiate them from the competition will need a big idea. A big idea takes the product's trait and turns it into a memorable idea that sells.

A USP showcases what is unique or exclusive to the brand. USPs are also used in promoting a commonplace feature as unique. Differentiation can highlight the target's particular interest, fulfill a need, or create a status symbol.

Although USPs are giving way to multiple selling propositions and permission marketing, it is good to focus first on one main point before branching out to meet or interpret individual target needs and wants.

An MSP is better suited for use in a campaign, since multiple messages based on the same product trait can be used to reach the target in the same media. USPs concentrate on running a single ad multiple times, which is sure to bore or cause the target to tune out the over saturated-message. MSPs, on the other hand, concentrate on the rotation of several ads over the same amount of time. The rotation of multiple ads is better suited to reach today's active, inattentive, factionalized, competitor-savvy, and advertising-avoidant consumer.

The Big Idea

A big idea is a creative solution that sets your product apart from the competition while solving the client's advertising problem. This does not mean your competitors don't have an identical feature, only that they're not pushing it in their advertising. Big ideas that are consumer-focused or based on lifestyle will have more longevity than product-oriented ideas. This is because concepts based on lifestyle are more difficult for the competition to duplicate. When using a big idea, creativity is the key to success.

Finding inspiration for a big idea is a little more difficult than determining a USP. The big idea most often has to establish something unique out of nothing in order to attract attention and create a relationship with the target. By focusing on consumers and their lifestyle, you can make even a generic product feature alter a target's existing view of a product. The key is to shape it into an unusual, different, or interesting benefit that will catch the target's attention. There are several places to look for a big idea:

◇ ◇ ◇

Where to Find Big Ideas

- Life (your imagination)
- Creative Strategy
- Product Name
- Product Use
- Product Appearance
- Product Features
- Product Comparison
- Pop Culture (book, movies, music)
- Historical Reference

A product or service will never stand out amongst the competition or build brand loyalty if the USP or big idea has a "me too" or "been there, seen that" message. A product must 1) have an identity, 2) offer personalized benefits, 3) be relevant to the target, 4) provide a reason to buy it, and 5) answer the question "what's in it for me?"

Creative Strategy. The creative strategy is the foundation for the creative direction or concept. Strategy tells the creative team how it will talk to the target and accomplish the stated objectives, and the best way to feature the key consumer benefit. The strategy's main objective is to discuss how advertising and promotional efforts will position the brand, and how it will compete against other products in the same category. Your client's product must be distinguished from the competition in a way that is important to the target. If research, media, and creative efforts reflect the strategy, a successful outcome is within reach.

Two of the most common types of strategy are positioning and branding. A positioning strategy focuses on how the product is perceived relative to its competition. In order to favorably position the product in the mind of the consumer, you must determine what factors are important to your target and build your message around them. Branding develops a personality for a product or service that creates a favorable relationship between product value and target need. Building brand loyalty through quality or reliability ensures the product is the only purchase option in the mind of the consumer, leading to repeat purchases.

Many factors can affect the creative strategy. One of the most important is the life cycle stage of the product or service. Many communication obstacles can be overcome and many opportunities can be exploited by considering and using this information. For example, during a product launch, building brand awareness is one of the most important steps. As interest in the brand grows, increasing awareness plays less of a role and the need to create brand-loyal consumers increases.

There are several decisions you need to make before choosing a strategic direction. The first is what approach will be used to strategically determine how the product or service will be positioned, and the second is what kind of appeal will be used to reach the target.

The approach can focus on either the product or the consumer, while the appeal looks at whether the product or service will fulfill an emotional or rational need. Let's take a brief look at each one.

Product- or Consumer-Oriented Strategic Approaches

There are several different ways an ad's message can be approached. Most can be categorized as having either a product- or consumer-oriented focus. The appeal will be based on the approach:

1. A product-oriented approach focuses on one or more features of the product.
2. A consumer-oriented approach focuses on shaping consumer attitudes about new and existing products and demonstrating how the product can solve a problem.

Product-Oriented Approach

A product-oriented approach can focus on four different areas: generic claim, product feature, USP, or positioning.

1. **Generic Claim.** Pushes a product category rather than a specific product.
2. **Product Feature.** Pushes one specific feature of the product—ideally one unique to the product—in all advertising and promotional efforts.
3. **Unique Selling Proposition (USP).** Pushes a unique product benefit important to the target market.
4. **Positioning.** Focuses on how the target should think about the product or service as compared to the competition.

Consumer-Oriented Approach

A consumer-oriented approach can focus on three major areas: brand image, lifestyle, and attitude.

1. **Brand Image.** Creates an image or builds a personality for the product.
2. **Lifestyle.** Affiliates the product with the lifestyle of the target.
3. **Attitude.** Affiliates the product with feelings, attitudes, and overall benefits of use.

It's not uncommon to use multiple approaches. Strategies under each approach can be used individually or in combination.

The strategic approach you decide to use will depend on the product or service, the target audience, the key benefit, the overall objectives, and the appeal and execution package employed.

The Appeal of the Message

Once you have determined whether you will be using a consumer- or product-oriented approach and its strategic focus, the next step is to determine the appeal.

An ad's job is to persuade. Whether it is successful or not can depend on the type of appeal used. There are two types of appeals: emotional and rational.

Emotional needs include lifestyle enhancers such as cars, iPods, jewelry, and fashion. Emotional appeals target image and are used for status-related products. These ads appeal to the target's need to fit in, be a trendsetter, or stand out from the crowd.

Rational needs are life-sustaining, like food and clothing. Rational appeals are information-based, using facts, charts, or expert opinions to back up claims. These are meant to educate the consumer on the product's use, quality, and value. Many advertising efforts will employ both appeals.

Appeals are used to attract consumer attention and influence the perception of need for a product. The focus is most often placed on the consumer's need for, or use of, the product and how it will affect the consumer's lifestyle. Message content reflects the product's features and benefit to the consumer. Often emotional appeals will work better on brands that have little or no differentiation from competing brands, since communication efforts are more creative and memorable and build image based on the target's psychological and social needs.

Since emotional appeals deal with the target's own self-image as well as his or her image of the product or service, both the strategy and message content can be more creative and less rational, focusing on personal pleasure. If the message will focus on lifestyle, consider the following options: achievement, affection, ambition, comfort, excitement, fear, happiness, joy, love, nostalgia, pleasure, pride, safety, security, self-esteem, sentimentality, or sadness. Strategies focusing on status-based emotions might make use of acceptance, approval, belonging, embarrassment, involvement, recognition, rejection, respect, and social status or class.

Rational appeals can take several different forms: feature, competitive, price, news, and image appeals. Feature appeals focus on the most important trait of the product or service. Competitive appeals make comparisons to other brands in order to point out important or differentiating features. Price appeals use a product's price as a differentiating feature. News appeals give some kind of update about the product, perhaps information about a new and improved version or a technological advancement or upgrade. Image appeals stress a brand's status or popularity within its category or among other users. Some of the most common rational motives for purchase include comfort, convenience, dependability, durability, economy, efficiency, health, performance, and quality.

If the product or service doesn't fit snugly into either the rational or emotional appeal categories, consider reminder or teaser advertising as alternatives. Reminder advertising is used to maintain brand awareness for more mature products. Teaser advertising is used mostly for new product launches, but can also be used for reinvented products to increase curiosity and build interest before launch or relaunch. Basically, this type of promotion is used to tease or build curiosity about the product, without showing it.

Tone. An extension of the creative strategy section, the tone, execution style, or technique defines the personality and overall voice or style you want your advertising message to have. The only rule is that the tone should reflect the key consumer benefit.

Once the strategy has been nailed down, it's important to determine how the information will be delivered. The tone is the development of the visual/verbal voice of the ad or campaign—how it will look and sound, as well as how the ad will be presented to the target.

The tone should be outlined as a list of adjectives that describe the product's personality and the attitude, mood, or spirit of the promotional message as presented in the key consumer benefit and strategy sections. This personality can be either stated or visualized in the advertised message. It is important to remember that the style of language, whether based on quality, fun, or status, flags the consumer's attention as much as any visual.

Questions to consider when determining tone:

Will the overall visual/verbal message be emotional or rational in tone?
Will the focus be on the product or the consumer?
What role, if any, should the competition play?
Where is the product or service in its life cycle?
Should the tone of the message be hard sell, soft sell, or more visually enticing in nature?

The visual/verbal tone used to address the target audience has to be very accurate because if the target audience does not connect with the product, there is a good chance they won't buy it. By now the creative team should be able to determine how that connection can be developed and how the target will respond to humor, facts, or testimonials. Is the product or service newsworthy? Can it teach the target something? Or will consumers be more interested in a demonstration? Whatever tone you take, it should work toward creating or supporting the brand's image, promoting the key consumer benefit, and advancing the strategy.

The technique chosen should be the tie that binds the approach and appeal together. In order to visually and verbally get your key consumer benefit across, the right tone is crucial.

If you choose a rational appeal then consider one or more of the following rational tones:

- Factual
- Technical
- Scientific
- Educational
- Instructional
- Authoritative
- Medical
- Logical

If you choose an emotional appeal then consider one or more of the following emotional tones:

- Humorous
- Testimonial
- Whimsical
- Challenging
- Intimidating
- Sexy
- Reprimanding
- Threatening
- Teasing
- Loving
- Compassionate
- Gracious

Support Statement. The support statement is one feature/benefit combination that can be used to directly support or advance the key consumer benefit. Consider the toaster example used earlier. If the toaster's flexibility regarding kitchen décor becomes the key consumer benefit, then the support statement for the two-, four-, or six-slice toaster could address how much counter space is required for use or how its stylish design is contemporary enough to complement any decorating scheme. The toaster's overall appearance is one of the main reasons why people choose this product.

Slogan or Tagline. The slogan is married to the logo and must appear near it. A slogan deals with a company or corporate philosophy. A subslogan, sometimes called a tagline, refers only to a specific campaign.

Logo. The logo is the product or corporate symbol. It can be a simple graphic, a line of text, simple initials, or a combination of both a graphic and text.

When all is said and done, the job of the creative brief is to help the creative team build the image of the product or service and project its visual/verbal voice to those most likely to use the brand.

The next step is the visual/verbal development of the idea, or brainstorming, followed by the development of copy and layout.

Notes

1. David Ogilvy, *Ogilvy on Advertising* (New York: Vintage Books, 1985), 16.

2. Margo Berman, *Street-Smart Advertising: How to Win the Battle of the Buzz* (Lanham, MD: Rowman & Littlefield Publishers, 2007), 109.

3. Scott Linnen, personal communication, August 31, 2007.

Image Credits

a. "Destination Luxury" magazine ad created by Tracy Datlen (Copywriter), and Natalia Rodriguez (Art Director) of Laser Advertising for Rikki Davis at Churchill Yacht Partners.

b. "Hydroguard" TV spot created by Young & Laramore (Writer David Nehamkin; Art Director Jeff Morris; Creative Director Charlie Hopper; Producer Char Loving; Strategy Tom Denari) for Galyans Sports and Outdoor.

Creative Strategy Template

1. *Communication Objectives*

2. *Creative Strategy Statement.* Each section should be answered with no more than one or two sentences.

   a. Primary and any secondary target audience profiles

   b. Competition/Positioning

   c. Key Benefit

   d. Promotional Mix

Sample Creative Brief

Product: _____ Date: _____

Creative Director: _____

1. *Key consumer benefit*

2. *Consumer problem the advertising solves*

3. *Advertising objective(s)*

4. *Competition—who are they?*

5. *Target audience (To whom are we speaking?)*

6. *Creative strategy*

    a. Prospect definition:

    b. Principle competition:

    c. Consumer benefit:

    d. Reason why:

    e. What's the big idea? (stated in a short slogan-like phrase)

7. *Mandatories and policy limitations (if necessary)*

CHAPTER 2

Brainstorming
The Marriage of Visual and Verbal to the Strategy

The creative process requires more than reason. Most original thinking isn't even verbal. It requires a groping experimentation with ideas, governed by intuitive hunches and inspired by the unconscious.—
David Ogilvy[1]

The Creative Process: How It Happens

Every creative team is looking to develop a message that speaks directly to the target and delivers a relevant, on-strategy message. But just how is this accomplished? Although there is a variety of idea-generating techniques that may be used, it doesn't appear that there is a specific formula to finding creative solutions. Clients explain what they're looking to accomplish, but that still may not be enough information to direct the creative course. Creative teams, after absorbing the clients' briefs and digesting their overall goals, must translate that information into a *creative strategy*. There is a difference between clients' objectives, which Rich Roth, managing director and executive creative director from Euro RSCG, calls the *business strategy*, and the *creative strategy*. He explains the difference this way:

> First of all, there's always a business strategy that the clients create, along with the advertising agency. But it's much more of a strategy about what

they would like to accomplish and achieve for their product. I call it a basic business strategy. Then, it's handed to the creative people and they come up with what I call a creative strategy.

This distinction between the business strategy and the creative strategy may more clearly explain how the creative team is able to come up with a creative direction that embraces clients' goals and achieves them in a unique way.

Roth further clarifies how the creative teams actually come up with these creative strategies:

> It's interesting because we come up with strategic ideas the same way we used to come up with creative ideas, which is you absorb all this information and then something clicks in your brain, and you have an idea. It's the same thing. You're still absorbing all this information, and you're trying all these things. Then, all of a sudden, there are connections that appear and lead to an idea.

The *creative strategy statement*,[2] as discussed in chapter 1, needs to be reviewed before the creative team moves toward the advertising solution. This simple one-sentence formula focuses the creative team on the main overall campaign objective, reminding team members to become fully familiar with the audience, the product's deliverable benefit, and reason why people should buy it.

Matt Jarvis, director of account planning on the GM account at Deutsch L.A., offers a lucid definition of the role strategy plays in the idea development process and how it helps to ensure each client's goals are met.

> What the strategy provides is a clear sense of the objectives of the communication, how we want to use the brand to advance our client's needs, and it also provides the creative department with a sense of context in which the communications need to operate. Within that context, we would need to include key business issues, target assumptions, the cultural context in which the brand needs to operate, and an understanding of the target.

How Strategy Focuses Teams

To shed light on the creative solution and overall campaign objective, Tiffany Kosel and Scott Linnen at Crispin Porter + Bogusky (CP+B) return to the brief as a beacon to keep them on course. The brief gives the creative teams a map with coordinates to check against as they're brainstorming. First the brief leads to the creative strategy. Then, a specific direction is set. Kosel explains it this way:

That's where strategy also starts to help. It's kind of like a track where you can keep going down. Sometimes, we take little detours and maybe go too far. Sometimes, the detours are good and they get us to a better place and [provide] a short cut or whatever. Sometimes, we can go too far off that track and end up being not relevant to what the brand is or the product. So, that's where strategy helps. It's like, "Oh, let's wait and go back and look at that brief again and make sure we're in the right area." It's something to kind of keep us flowing. There will be little keynotes, and highlights, and points within the brief that you can use as a basis to start brainstorming on, which are kind of nice.

For years, the creative development of on-strategy ideas was left to the creative teams, who would absorb the research provided by the account planners. Now, during brainstorming sessions, creative talents are integrating the ideas from their account and media teams to help tweak the main strategic direction.

Planners Do More Than Plan

More and more often, agencies include the planning department in the creative strategizing process. Planners can assist by explaining cultural trends, adding brand insight, and providing additional research. Tiffany Kosel, associate creative director/art director from Crispin Porter + Bogusky, says that at Crispin Porter + Bogusky, "our account planners are called Cultural Anthropologists. So, they're COGs for short. The COGs really immerse themselves in what's going on in culture and whatever the culture of a certain brand is. They really help us out."

Her creative partner, Scott Linnen, vice president/creative director/copywriter, describes in more detail how the COGs help refine the overall direction of the campaign:

They work with us to talk about things, and we go back and forth with why we think a strategy might work or why it doesn't work. And, then they'll do research for us. They really work closely with us to help develop the strategy, especially when it's new clients.

He continues to say that when the project is for a client they've had for a long time, the COGs are less involved because the creative team is so much more familiar with the brand. Instead, they develop smaller strategies with the content manager, who is part of the account service team.

Creative directors at Young & Laramore (Y&L), Carolyn Hadlock and Charlie Hopper, explain that they engage members of the account team when they all get together to discuss creative strategy. They find that by being inclusive and not exclusive in the idea-generating process, they get even stronger ideas from group collaboration. By including the account group, creative teams in many agencies are able to gain a new perspective and glean deeper insight into the client. Hadlock expounds on how the alliance works to support strategic thinking at Young & Laramore.

> I think a lot of the creative people sometimes approach the account people with some sort of apprehension and even contempt at times, if they aren't real deft. If you have a smart account person, they will help you come up with creative solutions that you then get to absorb all the credit for. So, it's almost like having a secret weapon, if you have a good account person who can . . . enunciate [the creative solution] simply.

Sometimes teams start speaking in vague or unclear terms about the strategy and need someone to clarify what they're trying to do. In that case, Hadlock explains, having someone outside the creative team "boil it down to one simple statement" that they can work with really helps move the creative process forward. She adds:

> That's where the team aspect comes. You can come up with a good idea by yourself. But, the more smart people you're with does it sometimes.

At Young & Laramore, as well as at other agencies today, the tension that once existed between the creative talent and the account planners has been alleviated. Now, there are great campaigns that were codirected, or at least mutually agreed upon, that serve as evidence of the value of including the planners. The relationships and interactions between the creative and account teams differ from agency to agency. Hadlock explains how Y&L has tried to remove any barriers between the creative and planning teams:

> We've worked so hard to keep the wall between the creators and the account people down. That's a difficult task because they are such different sorts of talents, that it attracts such different people. There tends to be that little gulf, that little wall between the account side and the creative side.

Although Hadlock says some creative talents at agencies consider the account side "the suits," at Y&L they welcome the account team because they not only help clarify, troubleshoot, and present the work, they also in many cases improve the work, as they did for the "Beet" ad.

In one ad, they showed a tomato with the headline: "What Makes a Good Beet?" (fig. 2.1). Another ad included a coupon along with the truthful

Figure 2.1.   Ad for Redpack Tomatoes, which leverages the fact that unlike many brands of tomatoes, this company specializes. The implication that specialization results in more care, more expertise, and more pride in the product is intensified when we turn mere specialization into "obsession." And it's a short hop from being obsessed to being monomaniacal—an engaging brand position the big brands can only envy, which has been effective for tomatoes in all the markets in which it's appeared.

Image courtesy of Young & Laramore [a]

Figure 3.2. Coupon for Redpack Tomatoes, which takes a possible limitation—being a smaller player—and turns it into a benefit: if we're not as big and have no interest in packing other vegetables, then naturally we take way more care to make our tomatoes the best they can be. Our limited but extreme expertise is highlighted in the coupon section by the little sub-feature of a pair of wax beans and the copy, "These are wax beans. We don't know if they're good ones or not. Tomatoes? Tomatoes we could talk about all night."

Image courtesy of Young & Laramore[b]

headline: "We Have No Other Vegetables to Fall Back On" (fig. 2.2). Just admitting that Redpack didn't have a plan B if it didn't get tomatoes right showed the company's commitment to quality. Hadlock shares the importance of including the account team in this campaign:

> I worked on that with an art director. We had a lot of ideas. That "What Makes a Good Beet" line was pulled out by the account person, who said, "This should be the headline." We sat there and said, "All right. You're right. Sure. Yeah, that is fun." And I think in another situation, where you have such a chilled relationship between the two, you don't have people who are open-minded to that kind of suggestion.

Even with all the brains behind the campaigns working together, sometimes an idea is so strong, it pushes past all the research, the planning, the strategizing, and can't be ignored. It just breaks through. Here's a little insight into how this happens.

How Breakthrough Ideas Happen

At TBWA\Chiat\Day, the creative team of copywriter Chris Adams and art director Margaret Keene told how often its gut instinct paired with insight from Lee Clow, the worldwide creative officer, can create the inspiration for a breakthrough idea. Although the planners sometimes come up with amazing suggestions, Adams describes how creative teams come up with their insights and ideas during the creative process:

> Sometimes it's really talented people's gut instincts about a brand, and what that brand can be, and what it means that end up being the impetus of the entire brief. It doesn't have to come out of a focus group or a planner's brain or the account team's strategy. I think it's really important that the creatives be involved in that process, too.

At times, the idea is so powerful, it actually redirects the strategy. Sometimes it's so creative, it can take the campaign off-strategy because it is such an entertaining or humorous idea that it leads to other off-strategy ideas. At that point, the team might even reevaluate the entire direction. Eric Springer, executive vice president/group creative director from Deutsch L.A., says about the strength of a great idea:

> Sometimes an idea can change the strategy. Sometimes we've seen creative work that we say, "Oh, that's so much smarter!" And it's slightly on

strategy. But what it does is it just digs a little deeper into whatever you were trying to say. We can always tie it back. And that's always a good thing. That's a healthy thing. We've rewritten many strategies once the creatives have started working on stuff.

One of the most important aspects of strategizing is making sure that the message is relevant to the brand and to the audience. If it is, this solution can provide a super sticky solution that resonates as truth to the target audience and develops an emotional attachment to the brand. CP+B copywriter and creative director Scott Linnen explains it as tension.

> What happens is we'll have what we call the "at-a-glance." It's the thinking that's relevant to the idea of the brand, and from that we'll try to come up with: What's the tension? What's the cultural, psychological, and social thing that makes this potentially sticky? We use that word "sticky" to describe that. The tension's really important.

Critical to every successful campaign is understanding exactly what that consumer needs, wants, and values. The most brilliant messages are only effective if they speak directly to a specific audience in a relevant way. That means they must sound authentic to be internalized.

Gaining Consumer Insight

Matt Jarvis, speaking from the account planning side at Deutsch L.A., details how the strategy marries the business objectives. The communication must meet the brand's goals and be delivered with a message that resonates within and connects to the target in a meaningful way:

> A lot of how strategy works here at Deutsch is a combination of looking at the business issues and exercising that muscle, and really identifying how we need to use communications. But it's also bringing culture and humanity to the business situation and gaining a deeper understanding of the target, so that we can connect with them. And that's what it's all about.

If the message discusses the objectives but doesn't resonate with the target audience, it becomes invisible. It doesn't deliver because it's not relevant to the consumer. Therefore, the message must present the key benefit in a way that connects with the audience so that it will ultimately be internalized and digested.

Jarvis added that it also has to be delivered in an appropriate media environment, one that will engage the target's attention and allow for interactivity.

It is this combination of the correct message in the right medium that produces optimal results. This is what causes strategic messages to be "appropriately internalized, and socialized. That's the path to effectiveness."

Sometimes a brand is rejuvenated because consumer insight inspired the creative team to develop a fresh new campaign slogan that was so relevant, it not only resonated with the consumer, but, even more significantly, became integrated into the fabric of American expression.

Creating Memorable Campaigns

Every agency wants to develop unforgettable, sticky campaigns: those that are talked about, quoted, and even adopted in everyday speech. When Clara Peller barked "Where's the Beef?" it resounded around the country. That Wendy's slogan, created by Dancer-Fitzgerald-Sample in 1984, was even adopted that same year by Walter Mondale in his presidential bid against Gary Hart. The phrase was so catchy, it appeared in everyday banter and countless comedy acts, as well as on T-shirts, underwear, and other merchandise. In addition, eighty-four-year-old Clara Peller recorded the slogan on a 45-rpm record with music composed by Coyote McCloud, preserving it for posterity on Awesome Records, Wendy's own recording label.[3]

More recently, the Chicago office of DDB Worldwide created the Budweiser "Whassup" campaign, which was created from actual footage of regular guys taking to each other. The campaign first ran in the 2000 Super Bowl and was inspired by the audience that was being targeted. In 1998, film director Charles Stone III captured his old college buddies' favorite greeting, fifteen years later. Although they favored the unfinished pronunciation of "Whaazzaah?" with their tongues hanging out, both versions are extremely funny because they portray a real scenario of guys calling each other, admitting they were "just chillin' and havin' a beer." Their response to each other was "True, true."[4]

The agency's strategists saw the "True" film and instantly knew they had discovered a cultural gem. They grasped the authenticity of Stone's two-minute film, knowing it would resonate with their core audience everywhere.

Other campaigns that fall into everyday speech are the "Got Milk?" campaign, created in 1993 for the California Milk Processor Board by Goodby, Berlin & Silverstein, renamed Goodby, Silverstein & Partners the next year. The slogan has been so broadly adopted into America culture that there are "Got Ripped Off" posters you can download from www.gotmilk.com.[5]

Finding that magical phrase, that on-target, on-strategy message that is embraced by the targeted audience and enjoyed by an even wider audience is the aim of every agency.

"Group Think" Creates Solutions

Eric Springer, a group creative director at Deutsch L.A., can't pinpoint where ideas come from either. But including members of the interactive or planning teams in the creative mix strengthens the results.

> It's all about collaboration. And now it's gotten to the point where it's not just the art director and the writer sitting in the room coming up with ideas, it's the interactive person or the direct person, or it's the designers. It's everybody.
>
> A big idea or great ideas come from anywhere. Sometimes flying on a plane back from New York, sitting next to one of my account directors, they'll say, "Did you think about this?" And then I'm like, "Oh, that's fun." As long as you're open-minded, anybody in any part of the agency can have a great idea, especially nowadays because they're just getting inundated with all these new mediums and ways of communicating. And they're creative people, or they wouldn't be in the same building as us.

Springer succinctly adds that ideas simply come from someone saying "What if?" "What if you did this? What if you did that?" The more collaboration the better. At Deutsch, the collaborative culture enables everyone to walk into anyone else's office and throw out an idea. That person could even be a client. For Springer, "That's the healthiest part or the most exciting part of what drives me to come to Deutsch, but also to be in this business every day."

Matt Jarvis, who works with Springer as account director on the GM account, went into more detail on the way different departments collaborate like a think tank, refining and molding the strategic direction as the various teams work in tandem. Jarvis explains that "strategies are part of our process. They're not the end result themselves." If the strategy doesn't spark a response in the creative department or fails to solve a business problem, it is reviewed and revised:

> In the strategic process, we're constantly going back and forth with the creatives, brainstorming, and pitching them approaches, so that by the time you "land" on a strategy, it's already been vetted, and all the creatives have a sense of ownership of the strategic platform.

He states it best when he says, "It's very infrequent that someone comes down from the mountain with an idea that doesn't have multiple parents." Once everyone's arrived at the creative briefing and everyone's agreed on a strategic direction, they move on to deciding on the tactics or communication executions, whether they will be online, out-of-home, on-air, and so on. The creative team doesn't run solo even at this juncture because the account planners continue to add insightful ideas. Jarvis summarizes that they "continue to be partners by commenting and contributing, as appropriate to the ultimate end product."

Mike Lescarbeau, group creative director at Ogilvy & Mather, whose work has been recognized in the One Show, D&AD, and CA Annuals, as well as at the Cannes Advertising Film Festival, says this:

> Not everything works, however, and I'd say that for me, the real key to producing good work has been editing out the bad. Co-workers can help. Partners can help. And whether you want them to or not, clients can help. It's amazing how dumb a great line can get between six o'clock in the evening and nine o'clock the next morning.[6]

Insights into Teamwork

According to Lauren Tucker, senior vice president/group planning director for The Martin Agency, there are five principle departments that cohesively work together to develop creative ideas. This internal structure serves as the underlying foundation for each strategy-planning session.

> At The Martin Agency, our core belief is in ideas and the power of inventive thinking—ideas that help clients prosper, make consumers talk, and make the people who work here proud. How we work, how we think, and how we deliver ideas is based on our structure consisting of 1) the ownership team, 2) a unique marketing philosophy, 3) a game–changing process, 4) one brief, and 5) synchronized media development.

Tucker further explains how these different teams collectively search for a holistic approach, making sure each element of the campaign works as part of an integrated, well-orchestrated whole. Each execution reinforces the strategy, driving home the main idea to the consumer. Here's what Tucker says about how the creative process at The Martin Agency differs from that of other agencies:

> We have people from different areas meet together, so we come up with an integrated plan. The question is: How do we take the way we work and then translate that into how we think? In most agencies the account planner comes up with the strategy and sends it to creative, then interactive media. Then, PR and relationship marketing get involved.

We don't work that way. I'm into sweating it out in a room and asking: What's the business problem we are trying to solve? How can communication provide a solution? We then look for a creative idea that unifies the entire campaign and provides that solution.

Unrestricted Creative Participation

At Crispin Porter + Bogusky, the creative team of Tiffany Kosel and Scott Linnen explain how all departments of the agency have creative talent and all contribute to the generation of ideas. Kosel and Linnen describe the search for ideas as a creative free-for-all, with unrestricted participation. Linnen says that everyone at the agency, not just the creative teams, is highly imaginative, from the media or content distribution people (the COGs) to the content management teams. Kosel concurs:

> Each of these ideas has come from every type of position at the agency. Someone will just throw an idea out and it doesn't matter whose it is. If it feels like it fits within this branding idea, or whatever, it will happen.

The trend today, as validated by similar comments from several creative teams, is that many agencies involve everyone who is working on the account to generate ideas, not just creative teams. That being said, the final creative solutions still end up in the hands of the copywriter and art director. This is why the relationship between the two has to have that creative spark. It's not enough to be brilliant individuals; they have to be creatively compatible.

It's All about Chemistry

Most creative teams agree: If there's no chemistry, there are no great ideas. According to Scott Linnen, "There's no real formula or science to it. It's more like, when it happens, it just works. It's about communication and chemistry between teams." He continues, "Sometimes we will work independently and come together and share ideas. That seems to work pretty well." Even though they spend time apart to come up with ideas, there's some inexplicable magic that happens when they collaborate. Kosel confesses, "there's something about being in the room together, and just sitting there, and having a good time together, and laughing. And throwing ideas out, both bad ones and good ones, and watching that process happen live."

Copywriter Chris Adams and art director Margaret Keene from TBWA\Chiat\Day agree. Without chemistry between them, nothing happens. It doesn't matter whether you're friends. A great friendship doesn't guarantee a strong, creative working relationship. Chemistry, which is critical to idea generation, can't be explained. It's either there or it's not. Keene shares these insights:

> A powerful working relationship is like a creative marriage. Endless hours are spent together working on solutions. The truth is creative teams often spend more time together than they do with their respective spouses, partners, and other family members.

Although they need to respect each other's feelings, team members still must be able to have a free exchange of ideas without holding back their true opinions. That happens more easily the longer teams work together.

Adams stressed the importance of being able to give and receive criticism. If an idea isn't working, each member of the team has to be able to let it go, so they can move ahead together. If either one of them clings to an idea that's not working, the team gets stuck in a creative stalemate. Adams adds,

> At some point you have to be comfortable enough just to say, "We don't have to fix this tonight, let's just go home and we'll come back in the morning and we'll have some better ideas."

Eric Springer, a copywriter by craft, explains how teams at Deutsch L.A. work together as they share everyday experiences. If the chemistry is there, ideas flow out of a relaxed, easy exchange during the long hours they spend together. Here's what he said about chemistry and how it affects collaboration:

> You go to lunch, or you hang out, or you share an office. You know you really put aside the time to do concepting, come up with big ideas. So, that relationship is everything. You throw out a lot of dumb ideas, but from a dumb idea out of my mouth, Mike might go, "You know, that wouldn't be stupid if you did it this way," and have a whole other take on it, and suddenly it becomes, "Oh well, that's cool, I didn't think of that."

The Fun Factor

Teams often talk about having fun and laughing when they're concepting ideas together. Being playful and genuinely enjoying the process enhances the idea generation. Forcing an idea or overthinking the path to the solution just doesn't work. Scott Linnen describes this relaxed state as being in flow.

He explains how fun makes it easier to concept: "If you're having fun, it's light and filled with laughter; that's when the good things happen." David Ogilvy says it best: "When people aren't having any fun, they don't produce good advertising."[7]

Demanding Exceptional Solutions

It's particularly challenging to develop fresh campaigns with long-standing accounts. Creative teams take different approaches to breathing new energy into these ongoing brand relationships. Young & Laramore has a creative bar against which all work is measured, regardless of how many different teams work on the account. Hopper further explained that regardless of how small the assignment in relation to the entire campaign, team members never feel as if they should just get the work over with so they can go home. People will stay until midnight over a table tent card when they could have easily just gone home at five. But they just don't settle for average work. They set the bar high for themselves. If it isn't "smart or engaging," they'll keep working. Even though more than twenty teams have worked on Steak 'n Shake, he said that every creative wanted to be proud of the work.

> Everyone takes it on again [because] the next new project could be the one that we always talk about, that we always show. And [the one] that keeps self-perpetuating.

Handling Products with a Niche Market

Some products have a very narrow market. That means the message only needs to target that specific audience. One example would be luxury yachts. With companies that produce this kind of product, print ads are just the beginning of a conversation with the high-end niche consumer. According to Tracy Datlen, founder/owner of Laser Advertising, "The ads are just a place to start part of a dialogue with the person who wants to purchase a twenty-million-dollar yacht. That person isn't going to decide to buy that by looking at a magazine ad."

So how, exactly, does the agency come up with a way to communicate with this narrow audience? Datlen explains it this way:

> A multimillion-dollar yacht is a very big, very complicated product. A one-page ad or an eight-page brochure can't tell the whole story. Our challenge is to highlight the key points that would make a potential client take interest. We're always trying to make the match between what our clients are trying to sell and the kind of person who would want to buy it.

With buyers of varying interests and requirements, Datlen says the agency has to determine "what the unique feature is that would make their yacht experience compelling for the buyer."

With luxury yachts, the higher the price point, the narrower the audience. That means the message needs to speak directly to a small number of qualified buyers. How can you differentiate one yacht builder from another when members of this audience can have any design they desire? When a budget limitation is not even a discussion point? With such limitless design possibilities, even a 100-page brochure couldn't begin to describe every single attribute. So the question is, how to best utilize any advertising space? Datlen reiterates what creatives continue to say: you need to focus on the one key idea that will resonate with the audience. She shares these insights into the strategic thinking behind the creative development for the Outer Reef campaign:

> A unique feature of the Outer Reef Yacht is that you can really go places and have an adventure. This type of buyer is someone who will want to go somewhere (or at least think they want to go somewhere).

To exemplify the idea of going somewhere, the creative team focuses on including destination shots, especially those that can tie into the name. That approach helps to convey the message and the product with maximum information and minimum words.

> The name of the company is Outer Reef. So, we showed a picture of a reef. Then we had a headline that said, "Go Beyond the Reef." The idea is that you can go beyond the shoreline and get way out there. Then we have the little destination shots.

Ultimately, with so much to say and so little room to say it in, Datlen concedes, "all you can do is initiate the awareness and stimulate desire on the part of the reader." An example of the "Beyond the Reef" magazine ad by Laser Advertising is shown in figure 2.3.

Messages created for high-end products, which target a very small market, must do one thing: pique the audience's interest to call up and gather more details. Multimillion-dollar purchases are not made because of a quick look at an ad, no matter how well executed the ad might be. The best these advertisements can do is attract attention and convince the buyer to take the initiative and investigate.

Targeting a New Audience, Creating a Fresh Approach

What about messages that need to create a paradigm shift in the audience? How can an advertiser change the audience's preconceived idea about a product? For

Figure 2.3. This magazine ad was created to reinforce the brand name and emphasize that this boat can take you where you want to go.

GO BEYOND THE REEF

60' | 65' | 70' | 73' | 78' | 80' | 85' | 105' | 115'

fort lauderdale | 954.767.8305
annapolis | 410.315.8156
seattle | 206.957.4664
antibes, france | +33 (0) 492 91 59 25

OUTER REEF YACHTS
www.outerreefyachts.com

Image courtesy of Laser Advertising [c]

example, how did Cadillac go from appealing to a sixty-five-plus market to a thirty-plus market with "the Caddy that zigs"? That language alone targeted a much younger audience. What sixty-five-year-old wants to be zigging and zagging all over the highway? Not only did the styles change drastically, but the Cadillac language also spoke in a fresh, new way. Like the models themselves, the tone of voice diverged sharply from what had been used before. Now there are Escalades, XLR Roadsters, SRX Crossovers, CTSs, V-series, and more. Because of the exciting new models paired with dynamic language, the Caddy gradually became cool.

Another example of a campaign that transformed brand perception is California raisins, which used a hit song and Claymation dancing raisins to convert a boring food into a fun, cool snack. The campaign was created in 1986 by two Foote, Cone and Belding ad agency copywriters, Seth Werner and Dextor Fedor. The San Francisco–based agency was hired by the California Raisin Advisory Board to revitalize sagging raisin sales. The copywriters used Marvin Gaye's song "I Heard It Through the Grapevine" and paired it with raisins packed with hip personalities and dressed in sunglasses. The raisins were created by Portland-based Claymation artist, Will Vinton, who had already won an Oscar for *Closed Mondays*, a short film.[8]

There is no question that one clever, catchy idea with a fun twist can rejuvenate or reposition a declining or forgotten brand. Likewise, taking a novel stance and going against a current trend can increase awareness of a relatively new or barely known brand. Yet another example of infusing the cool factor into a brand was the MINI Cooper reintroduction campaign. Created in England in 1959, and originally launched in the U.S. in the 1960s, it was reintroduced under BMW in 2002, when big vehicles were the rage. So how did small become chic when SUVs were in such high demand?

The creative team at Miami-based Crispin Porter + Bogusky developed innovative marketing that involved the audience in its whimsical, fun approach. When looking at all the things people stored on the top of their cars, the creatives realized that all the fun stuff was up there: skis, kayaks, and surfboards. So, they put the MINI Cooper on top of a Ford SUV and drove it all over town. Instantly, small become cool. It appeared as a 2002 *Playboy* centerfold, was a $16,996 kiddy ride (in quarters only), and appeared inside an oversized model toy box in shopping malls. The car was even up on billboards. This campaign created new media and showed new ways to use traditional media. It was even okay to create fictional characters like the Robot campaign and to invent hoaxes like the myth of "fakes" on the market.[9] They really reminded everyone how much fun advertising could be, while generating endless buzz about the "new" cool product.

Some agencies follow a formal, structured process, which enables them to examine critical factors and core brand strengths before any strategic direction is determined. Developing a detailed outline for each account helps ensure against overlooking crucial components in the strategic-thinking and idea-generation processes.

◇ ◇ ◇

Any of the talented people writing in this book will tell you that coming up with ideas is not so much a step by step process as it is a silent, lonely vigil interrupted infrequently by great thoughts, whose origins are almost always a mystery.—Mike Lescarbeau[10]

The more people trust you, the more they buy from you.—David Ogilvy[11]

How do you create a haven for creativity? First, get rid of negativity. "No" is not a part of the language of creativity. "No" breeds fear.—Mark Oldach[12]

Four Areas That Need to Be Examined

As mentioned earlier, group planning director Lauren Tucker from The Martin Agency emphasizes that myriad teams work together to develop the strategy that ultimately drives each of the creative solutions. She describes four main areas that demand the teams' focus, starting with what the brand stands for and ending with a marketing opportunity in which the agency can leverage that recognition and translate it into a relevant message for the consumer.

Our first step to finding this solution is to identify the opportunity for the brand. We look for four key leverage points that will lead to the opportunity definition—the brand's current equity, the business dynamics, the brand's core competency, and key consumer insights. We start by identifying the brand's core equity. What is the brand known for and respected for today? We then analyze the business dynamics affecting the brand.

This gives context to understanding the next leverage point, the core competency. What is the core competency that makes your equity ownable and credible? Finally, we focus on consumer insights. Who are your core consumers and how can we find others that look like them or who are poised to love the brand? What insights do we have that will help us define the opportunity for the brand? The ultimate goal is to identify the opportunity that will give the brand new relevance in the marketplace while expanding the brand's current equity and market demand.

Another team needed to change public opinion before consumers could love the brand. The client was Goodwill, the agency was Young & Laramore, and the creative team was Carolyn Hadlock and Charlie Hopper, whom we discussed earlier in this chapter. What would make shoppers go there for clothing if they weren't in one of two groups most often assumed to be Goodwill's core audience? The problem was to alleviate the guilt shoppers felt when they made Goodwill purchases because they could have easily afforded to shop somewhere else. They believed they were preventing other people who couldn't afford to shop elsewhere from buying items that they may have needed.

Probably the main nugget for us was when we first started working on the campaign strategy, we all felt validated in thinking that you shop at Goodwill if you are one of two people: 1) you can't afford to shop elsewhere, or 2) you're a college student, and you just don't want to spend a lot of money. We felt as if there was almost this sense of inherent guilt for somebody who does well, to go shop there: "Am I taking something nice from somebody else when I can afford to go out to Ann Taylor and buy the real deal?" And what we found was [that] we had to make it permissible for somebody to do that.

A solid, well-thought-out strategy is at the heart of all effective campaigns. This why agencies spend countless hours developing the brief, defining the strategy, and rechecking that the creative solution answers the overall objectives, offering a key consumer benefit and a relevant, on-target message. A highly imaginative creative idea that doesn't meet the strategic direction cannot deliver successful results.

Notes

1. David Ogilvy, *Confessions of an Advertising Man* (New York: Atheneum, 1981), 20.

2. Margo Berman, *Street-Smart Advertising: How to Win the Battle of the Buzz* (Lanham, MD: Rowman & Littlefield Publishers, 2007), 109.

3. www.tvacres.com/admascots_clarapeller.htm, accessed January 30, 2008.

4. www.tvacres.com/admascots_whassup_guys.htm, accessed January 30, 2008.

5. Berman, *Street-Smart Advertising*, 98.

6. The Designers and Art Directors Association of the United Kingdom, *The Copywriter's Bible* (Switzerland: RotoVision SA, 2000), 96.

7. David Ogilvy, *Ogilvy on Advertising* (New York: Vintage Books, 1985), 45.

8. www.tvacres.com/admascots_california.htm, accessed February 1, 2008.

9. Berman, *Street-Smart Advertising*, 110–11.

10. Mike Lescarbeau in *The Copywriter's Bible*, 96.

11. Ogilvy, *Ogilvy on Advertising*, 149.

12. Mark Oldach, *Creativity for Graphic Designers* (Cincinnati, OH: North Light Books, 1995), 61.

Image Credits

a. "Good Beet" coupon advertising created by Young & Laramore (Writer Charlie Hopper; Art Director Pam Kelliher; Creative Director Charlie Hopper; Strategy Ann Beriault) for Redpack Tomatoes.

b. "No other vegetables to fall back on" coupon advertising created by Young & Laramore (Writer Charlie Hopper; Art Director Pam Kelliher; Creative Director Charlie Hopper; Strategy Ann Beriault) for Redpack Tomatoes.

c. "Go Beyond The Reef'" magazine ad created by Tracy Datlen (Copywriter), and Natalia Rodriguez (Art Director) of Laser Advertising for Rikki Davis at Churchill Yacht Partners.

Interviews

Paul Charney, personal communication, March 6, 2008.

Tracy Datlen, personal communication, July 10, 2007.

Carolyn Hadlock and Charlie Hopper, personal communication, May 5, 2007.

Matt Jarvis, personal communication, May 22, 2007.

Margaret Keene and Chris Adams, personal communication, January 4, 2008.

Tiffany Kosel and Scott Linnen, personal communication, August 31, 2007.

Rich Roth, personal communication, July 3, 2007.

Eric Springer, personal communication, May 2, 2007.

CHAPTER 3

Brainstorming
Techniques to Get to the Big Idea

Imagining a Great Idea

Idea generation, or brainstorming, takes place when copywriters and art directors sit down with the creative brief and consider visual/verbal solutions for a client's advertising problem. Hundreds of good, bad, and even wild ideas are tossed out for discussion. Most will be discarded, but many will be worked on and developed further.

Members of a creative team must be open-minded and well versed in social behaviors, technology trends, current issues, politics, movies, music, and the classics. They should be able to use anything from historical references to present-day slang to sell or represent a product or service. These brainstorming sessions are critical to release stale ideas and predictable clichés in order to find the new, unusual, and eventually successful ideas. New ideas set a product apart from its competitors and can be the catalyst to building lasting brand images and an indelible positioning in the mind of the consumer.

The key to a good brainstorming session is to never be afraid to look stupid or to come up with a really, really dumb idea. It's a humbling process, but necessary in order to ignite ideas in others in the room: One really lousy thought, voiced aloud, can spark another, hopefully better, idea in another.

Stale advertising begins and ends with stale ideas. Most young creatives believe their first idea is their best idea, but it's only their best idea because it's their *only* idea. Test the waters, stretch your legs, and you will be surprised where you end up.

The creative cylinders that must be firing to be a successful, imaginative copywriter or art director include the following:

1. Be able to see what is not there. If a product comes in six colors, what does that represent? A canvas, an oil spill, a sunset?
2. Never linger in one place too long. A creative solution is often elusive and must be singled out amongst the clutter of one's own mind. Staring off into space, role-playing, or reviewing the actions of the guy on the subway might evoke new ideas.
3. Know your profession. What is old can be made new again, but not if it's already associated with a similar product. Using retro images in your message can make a point; copying a competitor can be confusing.
4. Be a student of media. Watch TV. Go to mainstream and independent movies. Pick up a book, newspaper, or magazine and read up on current and historical events. Watch for fads and trends. Notice fashion changes. Listen to a different radio station. By knowing and interpreting what's going on in society you set new trends rather than follow them.
5. Watch the human species. We're interesting, we're unique, and we can read each other's body language and mannerisms, from eye movement and hand gestures to personal style and unique personalities. We can even categorize people in myriad age groups by how they move, eat, sit, and interact.
6. Know your product. If you haven't used the product, do so. If you're unfamiliar with competing products, use them and compare. You can only successfully sell a product you are intimate with. Knowledge is power, so empower yourself and you will be able to ignite action and stimulate interest in your target audience.
7. Understand that advertising is a business. Creative is based on a business plan. It must be on strategy by meeting the stated objectives, on target by speaking in relevant terms, and on budget by sticking to a fiscal plan. You will never get to do what you want. Accept that great ideas are not hindered by limitations, but challenged by them.
8. Excellence should come with the territory. If you can't spell or use grammar correctly, copywriting may not be in your future. If you are artistically limited and cannot easily visualize ideas, art direction may not be the pro-

fession to pursue. Clients pay large sums of money for advertising expertise. Because of this, the competition is fierce, the life span short, and the stress high. It's what makes the profession a compelling one.

9. Cry a little. Laugh a lot. The creative process is a tough one. The chance of anyone liking your ideas in their original form is slim to none. Revisions are a fact of life. Regular rejection of ideas is right up there with death and taxes. Get over it. When an idea does take form and fly, it's like birthing a baby. Initially you don't want to do it again, but once you see its first smile, you can't wait to start all over again.

A Brilliant Idea Can Come from Anywhere at Anytime

To jumpstart idea generation creatives use many different techniques such as taking regular breaks, working on a hobby, or going out to lunch. Staring out the window is still motivational, as is throwing darts or playing a round of Nerf basketball in your office. Still others will rely on looking at the exceptionally imaginative work of others for creative inspiration, including those found in annuals like the One Show, Creative Annual Awards, and American Design Awards. They will also read graphic arts publications like *HOW*, *PRINT*, *Communication Arts*, *Dynamic Graphics*, *Graphis*, *AdWeek*, and *Advertising Age* and review winning entries in the CLIO Awards Festival, Cannes Lions International Advertising Festival, Webby Awards, Art Directors Club, International Film Festival, John Caples International Awards, and other prestigious award competitions.

Sara Rose, senior copywriter, and Lea Ladera, senior art director at Goodby, Silverstein & Partners, described how they use visual stimulation by other creative teams to feed their imagination. "In the creative process," said Ladera, "I think it helps to immerse yourself in art, and in music, and in things that inspire you. I think that's how we try to keep it fresh." Rose concurs, believing that inspiration comes by "just seeing other people's ads, and the creative work they do, and being jealous of it, and wanting to do great work like that because there are fresh ideas out there."

People not working in a creative field sometimes think it's not a problem to stay inspired. But the truth is that many talented art directors and copywriters actually work at staying creative. Ladera confesses, "It's a continual challenge."

Scott Linnen, vice president/creative director/copywriter at Crispin Porter + Bogusky, goes on to say, "It's tough; when you're working so much, you can deplete your reservoir of creativity. You've got to go out and see a movie, a concert, or a play. You've got to read magazines and books. Go to the supermarket and really look around at everything. Be a sponge and absorb culture."

Figure 3.1.   This ad humorously points out how we are naturally born fast swimmers.

Images courtesy of Think Tank 3 [a]

An Idea Can Come When You Least Expect It

Even the most creative copywriters and art directors need inspiration, so it is important they keep their eyes and ears tuned to what is going on around them at all times.

Andrés Ordóñez, vice president/creative director at Zubi Advertising, believes the best ideas happen while you're going about your everyday life. Being highly observant and able to connect those random observations to a current project can be the source of wonderful creative solutions. Ordóñez goes on to say, "I believe this is the way the creative process happens. You've got to learn you have always got to be watching what's going on around you because ideas are right in front of your face."

To illustrate this, Ordóñez explained how one great idea hit him while he was in Puerto Rico, waiting in line to buy tickets for a movie. The lady ahead of him asked if the film had subtitles and the ticket agent said it didn't. So she walked away without buying a ticket. He was amazed to realize that there were Spanish-speakers who could speak English, yet wouldn't sit through a movie without subtitles. When he returned to BBDO, the agency he was working for at the time, he asked the research team to find out how many people read subtitles in English-language movies. He learned that 70 percent of people would read subtitles, even though they speak English.

What happened was an epiphany. He created a trailer for *X-Men 2* that would run in the movies with subtitles. But the subtitles had no relation to what the person on screen was saying. At the end, he explained, it read, "You know, you've been reading these subtitles and losing the rest of the movie. You should learn." Instead of being offended, people were laughing. The spot was for Berlitz, a company that produces language-learning materials. Here's what he said the result of the campaign was:

> Sales went up about 30 percent in two weeks. It worked perfectly. So, part of the [creative] process is always being aware that anything that happens in your life could be brought into your work.

A second, equally funny campaign came to Ordóñez when he realized that people the world over, regardless of language or country, tell their dog to "sit" in English. So when he asked his dog to sit, the dog sat. He realized the dog could understand English. Here's how he explained another campaign for Berlitz:

> I said it's incredible that I could say sit to someone who speaks only Spanish and he won't understand what I'm asking him. And I say that my dog knows more English? So what I did is I filmed the dog. I asked my dog to sit and we put a super, "Do you feel this dog knows more English than you? Then call us."

As the examples above illustrate, a great idea can come from anywhere, at any time, from anyone. Being responsive to those serendipitous moments is what separates great creative minds from ordinary thinkers. Their right side is always on, even when it's in "sleep mode."

Once that great idea is conceived, it will take long hours and a lot of reworking before it can be presented, first internally to the team and then eventually to the client. Because the creative process takes place toward the end of the advertising process, time is limited. Brilliance may have as little as a few hours, or as much as three to four weeks, to show itself. Any creative team member must be able to turn on the creative juices at a moment's notice and for long hours at a time. You must be willing to fight for what you believe in, but also to let go of those ideas that just don't measure up—to go and live to fight another day. Stress should be considered a creative catalyst, not a paralyzing force.

Because of these unique challenges, creatives are pretty well left alone to come and go as they please, and to work in as creative and individualistic an environment as possible.

The Creative Concept

Creatives have a wide-eyed view of the world that marketers or others in advertising don't. They see the world as an imaginative canvas that a bit of imagination, grit, drive, and competitive difference can reinvent.

Frustration and exhilaration define the range of emotions that any creative can experience on any given day for any given product, not because he or she cannot come up with a good idea, but because there are too many ideas. Finding one great concept or idea that both creatively and memorably solves the client's advertising problem and can be effectively used across varied media is the goal for every creative team.

A creative concept is an idea that imaginatively solves the client's advertising objective. Coming up with a brilliant and effective idea takes hard work. Before you can isolate one great idea, you must pursue many mediocre ones. Conceptual development, or brainstorming, is a process that starts when you kick your imagination into overdrive and discover the "unthought-of."

Brainstorming Is Your Brain on a Freewheeling, Chaotic Journey

Brainstorming is your imagination in high gear. In the process, good ideas, partial ideas, and bad ideas are considered, explored, revised, or thrown out.

Brainstorming is still done the old-fashioned way—from a thought, to discussion, to example. Brainstorming sessions may include a creative team of copywriters and art directors and possibly even a member of the account team and/or media department, or they may be solitary sessions in which you allow your thoughts to marinate. Nothing is set in stone apart from the product's features, so don't number ideas.

There Are No Brainstorming Rules

There is no set way that creatives brainstorm ideas. Their main goal is to discuss the creative brief and imagine a way to solve a problem. Within the key consumer benefit lies the product's inherent drama. What makes it tick? What aspects are interesting or unusual? How will it benefit the target audience? Brainstorming isolates that benefit and places it within various scenarios that have meaning to the target audience. The result should cause the audience to think. Most people don't pay attention to abstract ideas. They pay attention to truth, and they want to know "what's in it for me?" In other words, how the product or service can solve their personal problem or need.

A traditional brainstorming session may begin with a copywriter throwing out a headline to promote the key consumer benefit while the art director, either at the computer or with drawing pad and marker in hand, quickly roughs out a visual that supports the headline. On average, a creative team can come up with anywhere from fifty to one hundred ideas per session. Of course, not all of these ideas will be brilliant. Some ideas are weak, some too complicated, some useless. But each one inspires another direction or even the possible combination of ideas.

The next step is to search for quality in the quantity. Ideas with potential will eventually be reworked and narrowed down to three to five concepts that are presented to the client.

How Do I Know a Creative Idea When I Think of It?

That's a good question. The short answer is that if you've seen it done before, it's no longer creative. It's that same old worn-out thing again. Once an idea becomes mainstream, it won't hold the target's interest the same way a new and innovative approach will.

You will recognize a good idea when it comes along because it will be dead-on strategy, feature the key benefit, and meet the goals laid out in the objectives. But, more importantly, it will be just as good days later as when you first thought of it.

Remember, ideas can come from anywhere. You might witness something relevant on the street or overhear a devastatingly good conversation on the bus or at a coffee shop. You could remember an enlightening cocktail conversation, recall an exciting experience, or engage in a stimulating product discussion. Talk about it, think about it, question it, position it, brand it, place it in a relevant setting (or even an irrelevant one), let it stand alone, compare it to the competition, show before-and-after results, twist it or bend it—but make it your own. When the Eureka! moment finally comes—and it will come—pounce on it.

All those daydreams come out as ideas, many of which will be rejected. Others may stand the test of development. All are worth sharing. It is important when you have an idea to present it to others. Don't worry about whether you think your ideas are stupid. We guarantee that you will excel in the realm of the ridiculous, or be teased, or never live it down—but you will inspire ideas in others by sharing your not-so-fabulous thoughts as well as those brilliant ones. There are several ways to jump-start a brainstorming session. Let's take a look at what they are and how they will help inspire your creative imagination.

Idea-Generating Techniques

Let's begin by taking a look at how a few creative teams work together.

Some creative talents like Paul Charney, senior copywriter at Goodby, Silverstein & Partners, still concept the old-fashioned way and brainstorm by kicking ideas around. Their technique, according to Charney, is to "just talk with people, sit with them, and just come up with ideas."

Other teams use different techniques, several of which will be discussed in greater detail later in this chapter, such as creating product-benefit lists, randomly choosing words on a page, cluster writing of loose ideas, listing imaginative uses for a product, referring to creative annuals for inspiration, taking breaks to let the mind rest, or inviting other team or agency members to offer up ideas.

Andy Carrigan, writer/creative director formerly at Saatchi & Saatchi, likes to walk away from the problem for a while, revisiting it only after something he calls mental marination™ has taken place. He explains the first step of the technique this way:

> You sit down together as a team and just start concepting and batting ideas around. It varies from team to team, but really, this is a pretty free-form process. There is no right or wrong way to approach a new assignment or brief, and this initial process of concepting helps you understand what the business problem is.

He goes on to explain how they rough out ideas for several days, and possibly even a few weeks. Then, if there's time, they can put them aside and keep on brainstorming. After letting the ideas sit, they go back and revisit them. Time is the ultimate litmus test for ideas. Exceptional concepts are just as powerful the next day, the next week, and even the next year. Creatives often like to sleep on an idea and see how they feel about it when they come in the next day. Sometimes the most exciting ideas the night before lose all their appeal in the light of dawn. Mike Lescarbeau, group creative director at Ogilvy & Mather, concurs.

> Not everything works, and I'd have to say that for me, the real key to producing good work has been the editing out the bad [work]. Coworkers can help. Partners can help. And whether you want them to or not, clients will help. What works best for me is the overnight test. It's amazing how dumb a great line can get between six o'clock in the evening and nine o'clock the next morning.

Where Ideas Come from

When asked if she knew where her team's creative ideas originated, art director Tiffany Kosel on the MINI Cooper creative team at CP+B talked about how randomly shooting ideas out can lead to solutions. With so many ideas being tossed out at once, Kosel explains, it's hard to tell whose idea was whose in the end.

The best ideas that you come up with, you never know where they originate. There's a process of kind of bouncing ideas off each other, back and forth. At some point, you get to a good idea, and you don't really know how exactly you got there, and who said what to get you to that point.

She confessed that after all the bantering back and forth no one can remember who said what. But ultimately, one idea leads to another and "by working together, you get there."

Team member and copywriter Scott Linnen, who worked with Kosel on the MINI Cooper project, concurs, believing copywriters and art directors should always be open to exchanging roles in order to keep ideas fresh and inventive. "Tiffany is the art director of the team, and I'm the copywriter," says Linnen, "but sometimes Tiffany does the writing and I come up with the visual idea." Kosel goes on to say, "Yeah, we definitely cross over. Being creative we can kind of do both things." For example, says Linnen, "We did an outdoor board when we launched the convertible. I had the visual idea to do one of those sensually suggestive motion neon Vegas strip signs where the top goes up and down. And Tiffany turned to me and said instead of "XXX"—"XXS," for extra small, being MINI. Done. The highlight of that was seeing it huge and all lit up in Times Square" (fig. 3.2).

Figure 3.2.   This motion neon outdoor board reminiscent of Las Vegas strip ads appeared in downtown night club areas in cities like New York, Miami, San Francisco, and Los Angeles. It celebrated the arrival of MINI's new convertible with the line, "Always open."

Other Techniques to Kick-Start Creative Concepting

Word Lists

The best place to start when trying to develop a great idea is with a word list. A word list gets your left and right brain working. It is important to realize that a great idea, for the most part, will not just pop into your head. It will most likely come in bits and pieces, such as in a word list, and come together at the most unlikely of times and places—in a business meeting, the subway, or the shower.

A word list is a great way to start the brainstorming process and to experience how consumers think, while at the same time helping to build your conceptual skills. A word list is composed of three columns or parts.

The left or first column represents the left brain. Here is where you list the facts about your product or service. Let's use an orange as an example.

Fact Column One: Orange
Round
Sour
Slice

In the second or middle column, choose a descriptive or visual word(s) to represent the product/service fact used in column one (a thesaurus works well for assistance with column two). This column should lead in previously "unthought-of" directions. Here is where war-worn ideas go to die.

Fact Column Two: Sunshine
Navel
Face Contortion
Saw
Knife
Teeth

The third or right column is where you describe how the combinations of these two words might be used in an ad. Ask yourself questions. Consider the five Ws—Who, What, When, Where, and Why—and don't forget How. Create a scenario for use either visually or verbally.

Fact Column Three: HOT, HOT, HOT, TASTE.
Show a human navel, talk about connection to Mother Earth.

> Show varied people's reactions to their first bite of
> an orange.
> No matter how you slice it. . . . Show the options
> being used on an orange.

The third column, representing right-brain, or sensory traits, should create something we can feel, taste, or just genuinely experience. Set up your word list so the words are aligned across the page from left to right; one or more ideas can be expressed in any column for any word.

1. Orange	Sunshine	HOT, HOT, HOT, TASTE.
2. Round	Navel	Show a human navel, talk about the connection to Mother Earth.
3. Sour	Face Contortion	Show varied people's reactions to their first bite of an orange.
4. Slice	Saw	No matter how you slice it. . . . Show the options being used on an orange.
	Knife	
	Teeth	

Now you try it. What product or service do these words impart to you?

1. Safety	Tranquil	How would you describe it?

Remember, a good ad should contain elements needed for both left- and right-brain consumers.

Are Word Lists Really Useful?

Why make a word list? It opens up your imagination and teaches you to think visually and relate verbally. Word lists help you reenergize your imagination while at the same time building your word power. This is a way to communicate to both sides of your consumer's brain. A good word list should include twenty to twenty-five words and visual representations.

The goal of all creative is to develop an image or express an idea that is unique to your client. Stale creative is eliminated when you explore your infinite options. That means conservative views must sometimes step aside and let the wild ideas step up. For instance, how many of you would have chosen a duck to sell insurance or used Frankenstein's monster to sell joint cream? How many of you would have chosen instead to use a pitchman talking about protecting your family or a bunch of athletes sitting around complaining about pain? Exercising your infinite options really puts a new spin on "never been there, never done that," doesn't it?

Breaking concept ideas down to one or two words helps you to focus on the point you're trying to solve. One way to break out of old hat thinking—the conservative approach to advertising—is to create and work out both good and bad ideas inside your word list.

Another good brainstorming technique involves going after the quantity of ideas before determining quality. A freethinking technique we like to call Posting-it requires coming up with as many ideas as you can—good, bad, or mediocre. The idea here is to create volume, not quality.

Begin by having the creative team throw out ideas. Each idea will be written down on a Post-it note, or a moderator could record ideas on a flip chart. Connect them together to create a sticky ladder of ideas or post the flip chart pages around the room. Set a time limit for the exercise.

The next step requires the team to sift through the quantity, identifying one quality idea and tossing the rest. Repeat the process until you have three or more quality ideas to develop further.

180-degree Brainstorming

Nancy Vonk and Janet Kestin in their book *Pick Me: Breaking into Advertising and Staying There* offer another good brainstorming technique they call "180-degree thinking." This creative exercise requires the team to "think of the worst possible way to sell the product ('Use this shampoo and your hair will dissolve'; Buy this mattress made of solid ice')."

This type of brainstorming technique startles the imagination into seeing the product in a new way, triggering a unique solution to traditional been-there-done-that ideas.

Vinny Warren, creative director of The Escape Pod, approaches problem solving in yet another way, believing that brainstorming is intuitive, but that it should happen after you've spent time analyzing the problem. Determining the message and the medium happens after you've fully familiarized yourself with the problem you're trying to solve. Warren goes on to say,

> Most of your time should be spent thinking about the problem, rather than coming up with ideas. The problem comes first. A lot of the problems, sometimes, they're not neat. Not round, perfectly shaped circles. So you have to first feel around the problem before you know what the shape of the solution is.

Exaggerations, Interruptions, and Failures

In their book *Bang! Getting Your Message Heard in a Noisy World*, Linda Kaplan Thaler and Robin Koval suggest using the following techniques to boost idea generation: exaggeration, interruption, and creative failure. Exaggeration is a great way to compare your product to the competition. Interruption allows people who are not working on a creative problem to interrupt a meeting, often bringing in fresh thinking. The creation of a safe environment in which creatives can make mistakes without fearing ridicule can often result in new thinking.

Kaplan Thaler and Koval also integrate other techniques, including improvisation, forgetting the problem, and restricting the thought process. With improvisation, people let go of preconceived ideas and culturally expected responses. Instead, they learn to fully listen to everyone else and jump in with any idea that comes to mind to move the story forward. Secondly, by forgetting the problem, people can give the problem to the subconscious, permitting the mind to relax and be open to a Eureka! moment. And finally, restricting the thought process eliminates past influences and forces writers to compress ideas down to their core, much the same way that haikus restrict the creative process with a specific syllabic count.

Mindmapping and Cluster Writing

Other brainstorming techniques like mindmapping, cluster writing, or the use of think bubbles all begin with a central word that describes the problem the team is trying to solve. The central word is the hub of a wheel or the trunk of a tree from which other words or ideas are expanded and developed. The overall result will look like the spokes of a wheel or the branches of a tree—ideas, connected by a line, spin out to create additional ideas.

Each of these very visual techniques allows the team members to see how their initial ideas grow and mature. For more ideas on brainstorming, check out the following books: *A Whack on the Side of the Head*, by Roger von Oech; *The Writer's Block*, by Jason Rekulak; and *The Do-It-Yourself Lobotomy*, by Tom Monahan.

So where does the creative brief fit into the brainstorming process? Eric Springer from Deutsch describes how the creative process utilizes the brief to develop myriad ideas that are first presented to the client, then tested for audience response, and finally refined into the creative message delivered to the audience.

We take the creative brief and sit down with a creative team, an art director and a writer, and brief them on the assignment. We go over the creative brief, make any changes we feel need to be done, which has the—sometimes it's called—unique selling proposition. Every agency seems to have its own terminology for this nugget of truth that's on the creative brief. Next, all the creatives get briefed and have a couple of weeks to go off, concept, and come up with TV, radio, print, and all the mediums. And you come up with a big idea that will transcend all those mediums.

Then we look at all the ideas internally. Put them all on the wall. We have three or four buckets of work. Three or four campaign ideas that for one reason or another say what we need said, slightly differently. And we'll probably take one or two—sometimes it's one if we really love it, or sometimes it's a couple—and we'll take them back to the client.

Brainstorming does not end the creative session once a few brilliant ideas are isolated. It just kicks it into overdrive. The next step: copy and layout.

Notes

1. Denis Higgins, *The Art of Writing Advertising: Conversations with the Masters of the Craft* (Chicago: NTC Business Books, 1965).

Image Credits

a. "Fastest Swimmer" ad for Total Immersion created by Sharoz Makarechi and Harris Silver at Think Tank 3.

b. "XXS Neon" billboard created by Scott Linnen and Tiffany Kosel of Crispin Porter + Bogusky for MINI Cooper.

Interviews

Scott Linnen, personal communication, August 31, 2007.
Andrés Ordóñez, personal communication, March 13, 2008.
Sara Rose and Lea Ladera, personal communication, June 10, 2008.
Eric Springer, personal communication, May 2, 2007.
Vinny Warren, personal communication, August 31, 2007.

CHAPTER 4

How Campaigns Tell the Brand's Story

◇◇◇

Unless your campaign is built around a great idea, it will flop.—David Ogilvy[1]

The Visual/Verbal Voice of a Campaign

Campaigns tell a product or service's story through multiple media, employ one unifying message and image, and talk to a specific target audience. An effective campaign focuses on long-term results that build brand image and brand equity, and works toward building a brand-loyal consumer. To effectively reach your target, your campaign must talk to an individual via a two-way dialogue, creating interactive opportunities to connect directly with the targeted individual. Finally, it is important that all members of the promotional mix, beyond advertising, are working as a team to strategically accomplish the same objectives, rather than as individual contractors.

A campaign can be defined as creative execution that uses diverse media to deliver a strategic, cohesive, centralized collection of planned messages that focus on a single idea or concept. Campaign development can be broken down into four distinct steps: 1) planning the campaign, 2) isolating a single idea or key benefit, 3) developing a cohesive visual/verbal message, and 4) selecting the appropriate media.

Planning the Campaign

The planning, construction, and launch of a campaign don't happen overnight or in a vacuum. It takes a team of dedicated individuals working across many disciplines to launch each phase on time, on budget, and with the right message, to place it in the correct media (or medium), and to address the right target audience.

In the planning stage, the account executive and the client will look at the marketing plan and review several key areas, including the target audience, the features and benefits of the product or service, the competition, and the communication objectives.

Target Audience. Knowing what the target needs and wants from this product category, and how your client's product fits into or addresses those needs, is critical. In order to develop a consumer-focused approach, you must know as much about the target as you do about the product or service. Their personal experiences, individual ideas, and ultimate uses for the product are what will assist with message direction and positioning.

Features and Benefits. It is important to know more about the product or service than just the key benefit. Knowing the product's attributes, capabilities, and limitations makes it easier to find a creative direction.

Questions you will need to ask include: How is the brand currently perceived? How does its current image affect what needs to be accomplished? Does the brand need to be strengthened or corrected? How many features does the product have? How is it manufactured? What is the quality of materials used, and how is it reflected in the price, packaging, store layout, and so on?

Today's educated consumer is armed with enough product knowledge to compare brands and make purchasing decisions based on more than just price. The product must offer some kind of tangible benefit either not offered or not identified by the competition. It is important to know the answers to the questions your target audience will ask before they compare products. Individuals are not attracted by a great idea alone; they are looking for concrete answers that offer a relevant benefit or solve a real problem.

Competition. As with target and product knowledge, you can't know enough about the competition. How do your client's products measure up? Do competitors have studies or professionals backing up their claims or recommending the product? Do you? What is their image, slogan, concept, or theme, and is it different from your own? Does the competition offer accessories to go with the product? How long have they been in business? How is their reputation? How well does their product perform as compared to your product?

Knowledge is endless when used to support a concept. Use this knowledge to build the product's image, develop a strategy and concept, and determine how the product should be positioned.

Figure 4.1.   As a high-end faucet brand that brings fashion to the home, Brizo partnered with designer Jason Wu, who created dresses to complement Brizo's faucets for kitchen, bath, and shower. Finally, dancers wearing Wu's dresses were photographed underwater by acclaimed photographer Howard Schatz. The resulting, otherworldly images encouraged Brizo's target audience to—in a word—dream. Pictured here and on pages 68 and 71 is Brizo's Venuto model for kitchen.

Communication Objectives. Once the target, the product, and the competition have been reviewed, the next step is another look at the communication objectives, or what the client wants to accomplish with its communication efforts. Communication-based objectives concentrate on what you want the target to think, feel, or do after exposure to the message. These objectives should be clearly stated, measurable, defined as long- or short-term in nature, and related to the product's position in the product category.

Isolating the Key Benefit. Determining the key benefit is easier once you know the product, the target, and the competition. With product knowledge, you can determine how your product or service—as opposed to the competition's—can affect the target's lifestyle. This critical decision, which feature/benefit will be used as the key benefit, will define the campaign.

The key benefit is the target's motivation to buy. It should fulfill a want or need, create excitement, or make the target feel better or more relaxed. The key benefit becomes the voice of the entire campaign. How it is delivered will depend on the strategy and the choice of tone, approach, and appeal used to define the visual/verbal message. Together, these will lay the foundation for the positioning of the brand and the development of the brand's image. And of course, the key benefit should explain "what's in it for me?"

Developing a Cohesive Visual/Verbal Message

Campaigns must appear and speak with one consistent tone of voice across the promotional mix. The visual/verbal message is the common thread that will bind all the communication efforts together. A key benefit alone, if clearly stated and properly targeted, should be enough to bind a campaign together but does not create a lasting visual/verbal identity on its own.

The ability to create a visual/verbal relationship between campaign components not only assists with brand-name recognition and image development, but also attracts both left- and right-brained target members. The diverse choice of visual/verbal ties should reflect both the strategy and the brand's image and may include typeface style, layout style, headline and body copy style, color usage, spokesperson or character representative, jingle, package design, logo, and slogan and/or tagline.

Whatever is used to bind the advertising/promotional messages together, it must become synonymous with the product or service—the first thing that comes to mind when the product is mentioned. If a product or service is associated with a catchy statement or phrase that becomes a part of mainstream conversation—like "Whassup?"—or a catchy jingle consumers can't get out of their heads—like the Oscar Mayer Wiener song—that raises awareness and gives lasting impact to a campaign.

◇◇◇

What Unifies a Campaign?

1. Every campaign is driven by a key benefit in the form of a big idea, unique selling proposition (USP), or multiple selling proposition (MSP).
2. Strategically, all advertising executions (ads, billboards, etc.) work to accomplish the stated objectives.
3. A campaign's message speaks directly to the target audience's needs and wants.
4. Overall appearance may be based on a specific message or idea, layout or headline style, layout templates, graphic icons, character or spokespersons, typeface style, visual element, or colors.
5. Each of the above-mentioned ad components are placed consistently.
6. The campaign has a visual/verbal identity that is clearly recognizable in all advertising and promotional devices.
7. The concept direction creates a unique brand identity to set the product off from the competition.

Why Multiple Execution?

By this point you may be wondering why you need a series of ads: Why won't just one or two do? Repetitive visual/verbal ties are what differentiate a campaign from a single-view message. Single-view means the message is seen one time and is not associated with any other advertising used currently or previously. One ad with one message, or even a once-in-a-while ad, is not a campaign and does not offer a synchronized message. A message delivered just once has no repetitive identity reinforcement and does not build or strengthen an existing brand image.

Because consumers are exposed to so many messages, a single-view ad does not create a memorable impression. It takes consistent visual cues and a repetitive message in order for the viewer to give an ad more than a passing glance. Without repetition, the experience goes into short-term memory and is quickly forgotten. For a message to be stored in the target's long-term memory, it must be repeatedly seen or heard.

So why use single-view ads at all? There are several reasons why an ad may only be seen once, but the two most common reasons are poor planning and overstock or sales-related opportunities. Poor planning is a problem that can and often does affect brand loyalty and brand equity. If the consumer does not receive the correct information, if stock is not available, or if the message is placed in the wrong media, both the target and the product are affected. Overstocks, on the other hand, provide a great incentive to purchase. Additional stock usually means lower prices are passed on to a motivated consumer.

No matter the reason for the ad, the goal is to use the unifying devices that were implemented in previous advertising and promotional efforts to make a single-view ad fit within the campaign pattern seamlessly.

The Promotional and Media Mix

Once you know to whom you're talking and what needs to be said, determining the correct promotional and media mix will be more effective. It is important that campaign ideas translate well from one medium to another. Once the concept is solidified, the final promotional and media mix will be critical to the visual/verbal message.

The ability to reach the targeted audience with the appropriate promotional and media mix is crucial to campaign development. The promotional mix includes public relations, advertising, direct marketing, sales promotion, and alternative or new media options such as out-of-home, mobile, interactive, the Internet, and guerrilla marketing.

Communication efforts are often directed at different audiences, each requiring its own message and promotional mix. Determining which combination of promotional vehicles to use often depends on the target's overall knowledge of the product or service. For example, those unfamiliar with a brand will need a different promotional mix than regular users.

The media mix breaks the promotional mix down to specific media vehicles such as newspapers, magazines, direct mail, out-of-home advertising, digital media, and so on. Like the promotional mix, the type of media mix employed will depend on budget, overall objectives, and the target audience and its degree of brand knowledge and loyalty. In whatever medium (or media) a piece appears, it must consistently use the same tone of voice and visual/verbal template that is used to represent the key benefit throughout the campaign.

Before we can decide the best promotional or media mix to reach our target market, we need to know a little more about the choices.

Public Relations

Public relations is a free form of communication and is often used in campaigns as a launching pad for new or reinvented product introductions. Public relations can be informational, educational, or promotional in nature. Its purpose is to reach the media with a message. Unlike paid advertising, the content of a news video, article, or press release is uncontrollable, and is not guaranteed to reach the public in its original form.

Advertising

Advertising is a paid form of targeted, but not necessarily personalized, mass media traditionally consisting of newspaper, magazine, radio, television, and billboards, which has recently branched out into a wider arena, from out-of-home advertising to digital messages and beyond. Advertising's strengths include its ability to reach large numbers of consumers, successfully build brand awareness, generate brand loyalty, and deliver a consistent message. Advertising uses persuasion to sell, inform, educate, remind, or entertain the target.

Personal Selling

Since this text deals exclusively with consumer promotions and personal selling is usually found in corporate environments, it will not be discussed in detail. However, as a member of the promotional mix, it is worth mentioning. Personal selling is conducted face-to-face, between a buyer and a seller—the ultimate interactive relationship. However, its very one-to-one nature makes it extremely expensive, relegating its use almost exclusively to the corporate environment.

Direct Marketing

Direct marketing is personalized and interactive and includes such things as direct mail, infomercials, and telemarketing. Direct marketing, which is very consumer-focused, may also include a direct response mechanism. Its ability to talk to individual consumers makes it a great relationship tool. Its core strength comes from the collection of personal information that is gathered and stored about the target in computer databases. The ease with which purchases can be made with credit cards and the dialogue that can be generated between buyer and seller through toll-free numbers and Internet sites are other advantages.

Sales Promotion

Sales promotion offers something to the public as an incentive to buy. These promotions can include coupons, rebates, giveaways, contests, or creative consumer content, to name just a few. Sales promotion can temporarily boost sales and is considered a support medium for public relations, advertising, and direct marketing. Like advertising, it is a nonpersonal form of promotion.

Figure 4.3.

Image courtesy of Young & Laramore [b]

Mobile Marketing

It won't be long before regular text messaging will be used more frequently in the United States to deliver advertising via the target's cellular phone. Mobile phones have evolved from just a social connection to a media device. Users can phone, text, browse the Internet, play music, watch streaming video, create a personal organizer, e-mail, take pictures, record video, play games, enter contests, change ringtones, and listen to the radio all in the palm of their hand. Potential customers can be targeted based on phone number, time of day, and location.

Interactive Messages

Interactive messages use media devices such as e-mail, viral marketing, weblogs, and streaming audio and video, to list just a few, to actively engage the target in the message. The more creative, informative, and interactive the message, the more likely consumers are to not only remember the message but share it with their friends, colleagues, and family.

Internet Advertising or Cybermarketing

The Internet is a relatively inexpensive information mecca. Consumers can go to a client's site or a competitor's site to look up information about a product or service and compare features and benefits. The Internet has created savvier consumers, who can take the time to forage through the clutter for the information they need to make a buying decision. Consumers can order products directly from a site or hear back from customer service representatives at their home or office, at a time that is convenient to them.

Guerrilla Marketing

Guerrilla marketing can be defined as the use of nontraditional promotional methods to attract attention, increase memorability, and make a sale. The more unique the techniques, or more unusual the locale or surface, the better. Surfaces appropriate for guerilla marketing campaigns include, but are not limited to, sidewalks, cars and other vehicles, parking meters, and bathroom stalls.

Its rise in popularity can be directly attributed to media-blitzed consumers ignoring most traditional advertising messages; however, when the message springs up where and in ways consumers least expect it, the message breaks through the advertising clutter and engages that same inattentive mind. Its nontraditional approach develops, introduces, and delivers pop culture directly to the target and extends message life through word of mouth.

The use of guerrilla marketing techniques was originally envisioned as a low-cost way for small businesses to attract consumer attention in a creative and unique way. Increasingly, however, Fortune 500 companies are investing big bucks to create extravaganzas rather than just small, but innovative, marketing/promotional events.

Synergizing the Promotional Mix Message

Synergistic visual/verbal development is the backbone of any campaign. Synergy happens when all messages to the target speak with one tone of voice and project an instantly identifiable image, giving the idea more impact than any single message could by itself. Without synergistic coordination you will not deliver cohesive, consistent messages to the target that repeatedly reinforce the key benefit. Multiple unrelated messages appearing in multiple media not only create confusion about what the product stands for, but also keep the consumer from retaining the main idea. For example, if the public relations team is unaware of the overall advertising strategy, an integrated campaign cannot be synchronized. Public relations may mistakenly announce a new product, highlighting one feature or benefit, months before advertising is ready to launch a campaign focusing on a completely different feature or benefit. Inconsistent messages can successfully erode a product's competitive edge and confuse the target. Consequently, brand image and brand loyalty are affected when sales personnel or customer service representatives are flooded with questions to which they have no answer.

Types of Campaigns

Campaigns typically fall into one of four distinct varieties: 1) national, 2) service, 3) corporate, and 4) retail. Let's take a look at each one.

National Campaigns. National campaigns use a diverse promotional mix and can be seen or heard across the country. Campaigns of this size are very expensive and are most often undertaken by the corporate giants. Established brands, large budgets, and a diverse promotional mix drive national campaigns.

Students of advertising often assume that large budgets are the key to making a campaign stand out and that campaigns with smaller budgets will languish or even fail. Nothing could be further from the truth. A big budget does not make a great idea; it can only help one along. Memorable advertising is idea-driven, target-focused, and audience-relevant to the key benefit. The most successful campaigns are on-target and on-strategy.

Figure 4.4.

Image courtesy of Young & Laramore [c]

Service Campaigns. Service campaigns are no different from product-based advertising. Although everyone needs and uses services such as health care, banking, and insurance, the goal is to make your client's service stand out from the competition as the one everyone wants. One of the best ways to do this is to talk about service benefits, such as good customer service, no health screenings, easy claim service, or no waiting, to name just a few. The key is to offer the same service as the competition but to make providing that service seem more important to your organization. Then when consumers open the phone book to find a representative or location nearby, they will see your ad and remember the visual/verbal message from television or the newspaper—and a bond is created. Your message may directly offer a solution to a problem they are having.

Service is about comfort. You cannot touch customer service, but you experience it every time you enter the bank or need compassionate health care. Giving your ads a similar appearance and tone reminds the target of who your client is and what it has to offer, every time they see an ad. Service campaigns need to emit "warm fuzzies" such as security, trust, and reliability. The very word "service" means more than one thing, so be sure to tie your key benefit to the overall corporate philosophy.

Corporate Campaigns. Corporate advertising is basically a company tooting its own horn. Here, a corporation takes the opportunity to let its target know what it has been up to, from its ecological commitment to its new product developments. Service to the community creates goodwill, contributes to a brand's equity, and tells environmentally-or-socially minded targets that this company is helping society or the environment in some meaningful way: an excellent key benefit. Corporate advertising can raise employee morale as well because it talks about the company's community and national contributions or involvement, which ultimately affects the employees.

When repositioning to address target needs or to compete with competitors, it is important that the campaign direction communicates not only externally, but internally as well. Internally, other shareholders, such as employees, often will be asked to adjust or adapt to corporate changes. Internal communication is an intrinsic contributor to the success of external advertising. For example, if the message to the public is "Avis: We Try Harder," employees with access to the public must understand this message. Nothing will kill advertising momentum faster than retailers or customer service representatives who don't know—and thus can't act upon—the corporate message.

The worst kind of corporate advertising results from bad publicity, after which a company must repair its image in the mind of the consumer. This is a very costly and time-intensive process. The corporation must redeem itself to the target in order to build back consumer loyalty. Politics also plays a big role in corporate advertising when corporations use advertising to influence political leaders on upcoming legislation.

Retail Campaigns. These can be divided into two categories: hard sell and image. Often referred to as the ultimate real estate sale, retail campaigns can push individual products but more often promote an entire store or company. The hard-sell campaigns are based on price, like those used by Wal-Mart. The image campaigns are based on reputation and quality, like those of Tiffany & Co. Each will approach its advertising differently: price versus image.

Retail campaigns rarely stand out creatively since price is the name of the game. Either way, uniformity is still critical to memorability. Because price plays such an important role and constant change is a fact of life, a sense of urgency is always present. Whether the sale lasts a weekend, a week, or a month, the goal is to get consumers into the store. Because image must be maintained, ongoing campaigns constantly promote status.

Unlike the other campaigns we will examine, both kinds of retail or name recognition campaigns have a lot to do. They must initiate attention, create interest, direct buyers throughout the store, demonstrate or showcase products, and encourage purchase through price or quality. Name recognition campaigns never stop selling, from the signage inside the store to the shopping bags carried out after purchase.

From Research to Message

Taking dry research and seemingly unrelated objectives and turning them into a message that speaks directly to the target across multiple media is not an easy task. The success of creative efforts will depend on how well it mimics and delivers the research found in the creative brief. Since the creative brief is limited to statistical information, it is up to the creative team to turn that information into a viable solution that is on-target and on-strategy.

Staying on-target requires finding an appropriate creative direction. For a good place to start, look at the brand name, the packaging, and the product's uses. It is the creative team's job to develop connections to the product or service. Consider doing the opposite of what the target expects—like a surprise ending in a movie, lead the audience in one direction before taking it somewhere else. Consider using a play on words. Although advertisers are often criticized for exploiting the English language for their own creative purposes, it can be a memorable way to present a message. The only limits are that you must not deviate from the brief, reach the wrong audience (be off-target), or talk to them about something they don't care about (be off-strategy).

The message cannot be implied, or it will not accomplish the stated objectives or receive the needed recognition and sales throughout all media. Consumers do not want to struggle to understand the message. If your message is not clear, they will choose a competing brand whose information is easier to digest and whose benefit is immediately apparent.

Tweaking the Message or Idea

Successful campaigns often run for years, continually striving to build both brand loyalty and brand equity. Change should be considered only when the product, company, or audience significantly changes. Today's advertised messages often change with the seasons, leaving little time for brand awareness or loyalty to emerge. The inconsistent repositioning of brands or repeated challenges to competing brands can affect the target's image of the product or service. Products that are patient and work at building loyalty over time will find competitors' constant message changes less of a threat in building and maintaining brand equity.

Concept Components

A campaign consists of two interrelated components that affect concept development and overall appearance: message consistency and visual and verbal uniformity.

Campaign uniformity means that the overall look and message are the same no matter the media outlet used or the final appearance of any creative piece. Visual uniformity means that all creative materials have a distinctive look and unique, uniform message. This happens when all layouts use the same graphics, images, slogans, typography, tone of voice, colors, and placement of ad components. Verbal uniformity takes place when all creative pieces promote one idea, or key benefit. For the campaign to be successful, it must strategically accomplish the objectives developed in the creative brief and spotlight the benefit. A diverse promotional mix using the same verbal tone of voice and visual appearance increases the likelihood that the target will see and remember the message, distinguishing your client's product from the competition's.

The components that affect campaign development emerge from the creative brief to form the campaign's overall creative foundation. Before any creative direction can be successful, it must be able to address and accomplish each of the following: 1) know what needs to be accomplished before you begin the design phase, 2) exhaust the brainstorming stages, 3) find the unique concepts, and 4) discard the been-there-done-that ideas. It is crucial that every campaign includes cohesiveness, consistency, and repetition. Does your campaign idea have all of these key elements throughout the promotional mix? If not, what component(s) will need to be adjusted to create the uniformity needed?

The Concept Develops the Visual/Verbal Ties

Verbal Elements

The verbal elements, with their own individualistic personalities, include headlines, subheads, body copy, slogans or taglines, and jingles. Each element has a distinct job to do in order to tell the product's or service's story. In order to define the brand's image, a distinct, coordinated tone of voice must express and identify the brand's personality. The voice, which can be exemplified as sound, can also unify a campaign through jingles or music, or the distinctive voice of a spokesperson.

Verbal elements should create a cohesive and consistent tone throughout the campaign and across all media. A campaign's message should be so intertwined that the consumer gets the feeling of a continuity of thought from one ad to the next.

Verbal elements include:

1. *Headlines*. Headlines are most often used to announce the key benefit. Each headline's tone of voice should match the tone, approach, and appeal determined in the strategy and should give the brand an identity. The choice of headline style should reflect the brand's image and bring the concept to life. The overall style should remain consistent throughout a campaign. For example, if you ask a question of the target in a newspaper ad, ask one in magazine ads, out-of-home messages, radio spots, television commercials, or online executions.

2. *Subheads*. A subhead should support the headline's main idea and benefit. The subhead's job is to keep the reader moving through the ad by offering tantalizing bits of information. Additional subheads can be used to clarify or explain in further detail what the headline is saying or to break up long blocks of text.

3. *Body Copy*. The length and overall voice of the body copy is also a great way to tie ads together. Body copy tells the product's story through its features and benefits, primary uses, and any additional or secondary uses that will help to demonstrate the product's importance in the target's life. The first paragraph should continue the discussion on the key benefit, the middle section should make the sale, and the closing paragraph should move the target to action.

4. *Slogan or Tagline*. A slogan identifies a corporate or product philosophy. Think of it like the foundation of a house. You may change the décor, but the foundation stays intact. A subslogan, which some people call a tagline, reflects the concept and key benefit used in a specific campaign. No matter

which one is used, it will always appear near the logo. If a slogan is spoken on radio or television, be sure the tone of voice matches the persona of the character representative or spokesperson.

5. *Musical Logo.* If you can sing the message in an interesting way, why bore the target by saying it? Musical references can get in a target's head and stay there; that's why jingles can be described as "catchy."

Visual Elements

Visual elements speak to the target in a different way. They help the target see or experience the product or service and how it will improve their lives. Visual images can show the product in use. The types of images chosen, as well as layout and typeface, can suggest the visual/verbal tone to be used. Color choices can set a mood, and specific placement of elements within an ad can help define the overall product image. Consistency and repetition is key to binding campaign pieces together. Nothing can be said or shown just once in any campaign series.

Visual elements include:

1. *Layout Style.* Layout style, or the overall way each component is laid out or placed within the ad, creates a consistent visual appearance between media. Use the same layout style for each printed piece. Layout styles can transfer to radio and television through the voice of the character or spokesperson delivering the message.

2. *Visual Images.* The choice of image depends on the concept. If using a nostalgic theme, think about using black-and-white photographs or a Norman Rockwell style of illustration that complements the concept. If the concept deals with making what is old new again, the use of spot color on a black-and-white photograph can highlight the product or logo by creating eye flow. Graphic images give a modern, stylish, or trendy feel to a product, while color photographs bring the product alive with rich colors, textures, and detail.

3. *Typeface.* The same typeface, type style, and type weight should be used on all ads in the campaign. Whenever possible, headlines, subheads, and body copy should be the same point size and length from ad to ad, as uniform size creates visual unity.

4. *Character or Spokesperson.* A representative, either animated or human, who can speak for and represent a product gives a personality or face to the product and should appear in all pieces. When at all possible, the image should reflect the same size, visual technique, and placement.

5. *Repetitive Border Treatments*. Repetitive border treatments can create a mood. Use of a decorative border, whether elaborate or simplistic, can isolate both the ad and the elements within the ad by pulling the viewer in, creating an air of exclusivity and elegance. Depending on the graphics used, borders with images within them or as an extension of them can create an illusion of playfulness or hominess, or give the ad a seasonal appeal.

6. *Color*. Color, or the lack thereof, can make an ad unique in the same way a particular illustrative, graphic, or photographic style can. Each color creates a psychological effect, so the choice of color should reflect both the corporate image and the overall key consumer benefit and strategy. Color choices can be used as design elements, to create specific emotions, or to set a mood or attract the eye. Color is also easier to remember than product names.

7. *Logos and Slogans*. The logo and slogan should appear in the same location on all pieces and should be the same size whenever possible.

Know Your Media

Know your promotional mix before finalizing concept direction. Knowing where the ads will be seen or heard will help determine the best way to show or tell the concept. For example, should the concept rely on a lengthy verbal message to get its point across, or will media restrictions allow only a few words to make the same point? Will visuals that show the product in use, in a certain setting, or through some kind of demonstration project the key benefit better?

Stand Up And Stand Out: It Pays to Be Different

Product categories with little or no product differentiation need a unique approach to set the product apart—not by features, but by status, image, or imagination. This is where the right strategic appeal creates difference among the masses. Targets will buy a creative image over the status quo. It just needs to fit their own image and their needs. What will be the tie that binds—a character or spokesman, a musical reference, or theme-related headline treatment, slogan, or layout style? The key to creative individualism lies in the research and brainstorming stages. Create a trend, connect the product to an existing trend, resurrect a trend, or create a voice or a statement that can be reinforced visually through photographs, illustrations, or graphic devices.

Campaigns and their creative imagery and messages allow you to continually remind the target what your product or service brings them over the competition.

Note

1. David Ogilvy, *Confessions of an Advertising Man* (New York: Atheneum, 1981), 95.

Image Credits

a. Print ad created by Young & Laramore (Writer Scott King; Art Directors Trevor Williams, Uriaha Foust; Creative Director Carolyn Hadlock; Strategy, Ann Beriault, Tom Denari) for Brizo.

b. Print ad created by Young & Laramore (Writer Scott King; Art Directors Trevor Williams, Uriaha Foust; Creative Director Carolyn Hadlock; Strategy, Ann Beriault, Tom Denari) for Brizo.

c. Print ad created by Young & Laramore (Writer Scott King; Art Directors Trevor Williams, Uriaha Foust; Creative Director Carolyn Hadlock; Strategy, Ann Beriault, Tom Denari) for Brizo.

Campaign Checklist

1. _____ Does each ad clearly state the key benefit?

2. _____ Does the campaign's message talk to the target audience in their language and in a way that holds their attention? (Is it "on-target?")

3. _____ Does the campaign's message address and answer each stated objective?

4. _____ Is the relationship clear between the key benefit, the headline, the body copy, and the visuals?

5. _____ Is this relationship reflected in the strategy?

6. _____ Does each ad or promotion's overall image match the tone, approach, and appeal stated in the strategy? (Is it "on-strategy?")

7. _____ Does the layout style reflect the strategy?

8. _____ If you created a jingle, do the music and words reflect the strategy?

9. _____ Is the concept as strong visually as it is verbally, regardless of the medium in which it appears?

10. _____ Is the concept unique to your product, and does it position itself away from the competition?

11. _____ Does the copy's tone of voice match that stated in the strategy?

12. _____ Does the first paragraph of the body copy continue the key benefit discussion begun in the headline?

13. _____ Does the middle paragraph of the body copy give enough information about the product to understand what it is, what it does, and how it will affect the target's lifestyle?

14. _____ Does the copy close with a call to action?

15. _____ Did you remember to include the detail copy, to make shopping or ordering easier?

16. _____ Is the message clearly consumer-focused?

17. _____ Do the visual components match the strategy?

18. _____ Do the visuals match the image created in the headline and copy?

19. _____ Are the visuals consistent throughout the campaign?

20. _____ Is the logo clearly seen in every message?

21. _____ Does the slogan or tagline appear in every message?

22. _____ If you used specific color combinations in the ads, do they appear in every message and do they match the tone, approach, and appeal used in the strategy?

23. _____ Is the typeface and style consistent on every ad?

24. _____ Is the layout style evident and verbal tone apparent on every ad?

25. _____ Did you keep the headline size and body copy length as consistent as possible on every ad?

26. _____ Can you see an identifiable template, in which all the components are in the same place and use the same typographic and visual treatment?

27. _____ If you are using a spokesperson or character representative, is he or she seen or heard in every ad?

28. _____ Is the cropping and image size as consistent as possible in every ad?

29. _____ Does the package's design match the brand's image?

30. _____ Does the campaign reflect a long-term focus, with enough time built in to build consumer loyalty?

31. _____ Are there interactive components built into the campaign?

32. _____ Does the promotional mix reflect the target's lifestyle and interests?

33. _____ Is the visual/verbal relationship so strong that if your campaign were next to many other competitors' campaigns, the target would be able to pick out your series of ads?

34. _____ Does your campaign have one clear benefit, a distinct appearance, and one tone of voice that is apparent across all media?

CHAPTER 5

How Copywriters Approach Strategy Verbally

> *I'm not saying that charming, witty and warm copy won't sell. I'm just saying I've seen thousands of charming, witty campaigns that didn't sell.*—Rosser Reeves[1]

The Writing Process: A Close-Up Look

How do different copywriters begin the writing process that will support the strategy? Do they have a mental preparation process they adhere to? With strategy driving the creative, copywriters often follow a multistep process before beginning to consider a creative direction. The creative process may involve some or all of these steps: They may 1) immerse themselves in the brief, 2) examine current cultural trends, 3) digest consumer-based research, 4) review the brand's past creative direction, 5) comprehend the target market, 6) reflect on the account and/or media planning teams' insights, 7) redefine the key consumer benefit, 8) glance at brand competitors' campaigns, and 9) examine award annuals for creative inspiration. After soaking up all the information and creative references, they can let the mind rest or "incubate." This can be accomplished by completely forgetting about the creative challenge, focusing on another project, taking a break, or even doing something relaxing like going to a museum or movie.

Before copywriters can write, they need to be totally familiar with the brand, the audience, and the overall strategic direction: the main objective discussed in the brief. Some people outside the industry may think creative talents just go off and create, but long before that, they have steeped themselves in critically important information. Otherwise they could not begin to determine the tone of voice—how they'll express the message—to drive home a key consumer benefit.

They must also understand what core values the brand and the audience share. What specifically do the brand and audience have in common? For example, if the brand is perceived as "cool," it has what's considered the "cool factor." The audience that perceives itself as "cool" would intuitively be attracted to that product. One example would be the iPod and the iPhone. It wasn't that other mp3 players and cell phones didn't exist and people didn't have other choices. It was that the Apple products portrayed "coolness" and millions of people want to be considered "cool." Apple's advertising, whether it was in print or on television, reflected the brand's personality as "cool." Even the TV spots that compared PCs to Mac computers from 2006 through 2008 showed Apple as the "cooler" choice.

Understanding what the audience wants is crucial to message development. Even Leo Burnett said he needed to know the product and audience before starting on a solution. When Denis Higgins asked Burnett if his problem-solving approach included certain rituals, Burnett answered:

> No. My technique, if I have one, is to saturate myself with knowledge of the product. I believe in good in-depth interviewing where I come realistically face to face with the people I am trying to sell. To try to get a picture in my mind of the kind of people they are—how they use this product, and what it is—they don't often tell you in so many words—but it is what actually motivates them to buy something or to interest them in something.[2]

After absorbing the brief and digesting the brand and consumer information, some copywriters just dive right in and swim past the analytical process. They begin with slivers of ideas or tiny bits of phrases, which may spark other observations or new realizations about the product or audience. Some use lists or words related to the product, audience, or benefit. Others open books and find words randomly and start tossing abstract ideas around. And still others start with fragments of unrelated ideas. TBWA\Chiat\Day copywriter Chris Adams shares how he begins:

> I think the important thing is to just start writing. In the beginning of the campaign, I just have sheets and sheets of paper with tagline ideas, sentences, phrases, you know, fragments of thoughts, and I just keep putting

it down. And then I go back and look at it all and just start highlighting or checking off some things that seem interesting to me.

Adams further discusses a manifesto, which we will come back to later, that is prepared to direct the team's general thinking about the brand and to explain the brand beliefs. Getting to the "what" of the brand and the "how" to communicate it helps focus the creative team on every account.

A Quick Checklist before Writing

There are several key points that need to be totally understood before any ideas can be generated. You must be fully aware of the answers to each of these questions. You must take the time needed to clearly define exactly what the brand means, what is being said, how it is going to be phrased, who is going to hear it, and why they need to know it. Take a look at this list each time you set out to develop a creative, on-strategy solution.

1) *What does the brand stand for?* What are its intrinsic attributes? What does it represent? If you described it, would you say it's trustworthy, fun, innovative, timeless, elegant, environmentally conscious, or unique? What, when drilled down to its essence, is the brand about?

2) *What is the brand's story?* What is its heritage? What is its history and growth? Was it created by two fun-loving guys like Ben Cohen and Jerry Greenfield, who opened Ben & Jerry's Homemade Ice Cream in 1978, developing a company that was "green" decades ahead of the current trend? Did it create entrepreneurial opportunities for artisans, tradespeople, farmers, and other native inhabitants of third world countries while preserving natural resources and respecting tribal cultures, like Anita Roddick's The Body Shop, founded in 1976 and known for its social consciousness and principle-based profits? What is the brand's life story?

3) *How should this be expressed?* What is the best way to state this? How can you encapsulate the heart of the company's story in a relevant message that is relatable to your audience?

4) *Can you identify common core values shared by both the consumer and the brand?* Core values are the personal beliefs that define our opinions and guide our actions. When Michelin reminded everyone how precious passengers were to drivers, it implied that it too, cared about their safety with the slogan: "There's a lot riding on your tires."

5) *What is the particular tone of voice of the message?* How will you speak to your audience? Will you be authoritative, compassionate, informative, intimidating, or truthful?

6) *What does the target audience want to hear?* If you were the consumer deciding between brands, what would persuade you to choose one over the other? Always remember to think like the consumer when developing any kind of message.

7) *How can we connect with the audience?* What can you say that will show the audience that you understand its needs and desires, while sounding genuinely sincere?

8) *What is the marketing objective set forth in the brief?* Be sure to go back time and again to be certain that the creative direction you're going in is not only on-target, but also on-strategy.

Back in 1991, Anita Roddick stated in her book, *The Body Shop*, that "the shared heritage of company and community should be emphasized; conversation should be generated with the consumer." This may be even truer at this time, when brands are trying to engage the audience with interactive games and websites to stimulate a participatory response.

Today at TBWA\Chiat\Day, copywriter Adams explains that before he and his creative partner, art director Margaret Keene, begin going in any creative direction, they create a "manifesto" or an "internal mantra" that states the brand's most important message. This document helps creative teams systematically refine their thinking.

> You start doing that and then you start developing a tone of voice. For me, I always think about who is the target or consumer? What do they want to hear? What's going to inspire them? What's going to motivate them? And then, once you develop a little bit of a perspective of what the brand believes, you can start communicating that to people.

He believes the brand "has a position in the world" and it has to be something more important than just creating a cool product and putting it on the market.

A Few Definitions for Promotional Copy

When you talk about the main message of the campaign, you're talking about the slogan, catch phrase, or theme line. Some use the word tagline to mean the same thing. Others consider a tagline a phrase used for a secondary campaign that is still part of the brand's main slogan. So if you had a slogan like "Gotta Get It" for the main campaign, you might use "subslogans" or taglines for different parts of the campaign. Let's say the product is a beverage and it has regional and national exposure. Then, for the regional campaigns, you might say, "Georgia's Gotta Get It," or "New York's Gotta Get It."

The headline works differently. The headline is the main idea for one particular part of the campaign. So each ad in a series could have a different, but related headline, while still keeping the same slogan and/or regional tagline. Notice the word "related" in the previous sentence. In order for a series of promotional messages, whether ads, brochures, billboards, or banner ads, and so forth, to work as a campaign, they all need to relate to one another under one big main idea.

So using the example above, with the main slogan being "Gotta Get It," New York's tagline would be "New York's Gotta Get It" and the series of related headlines could be:

1) "New Yorkers? Fuggetabout It. They Got It."
2) "The Big Apple? Yeah, Ya Got It."
3) "Hey, the City That Doesn't Sleep? Ya Got It."
4) "New York Yankees? Ya Got It."

You could use the vernacular of the area to regionalize it even more with all kinds of fun and whimsical headlines like:

1) "You Talkin' to Me? Ya It."
2) "Whaddaya Think? I Got It."
3) "Who Ya Kiddin'? 'Course I Got It."
4) "Ya Think I'm from Kansas? Yeah, I Got It."

To deregionalize the campaign, you could continue spinning out the concept without any geographic reference or local jargon and use commands (imperative statements) with headlines such as:

1) "Come and Get It."
2) "Face It. You're Gonna Get It."
3) "Don't Wait. You Gotta Get It Now."
4) "Listen. You Got It Comin'."

The first thing writers have to do is find that big idea that will spin out and be equally powerful in all media. It also has to work along with the one main slogan that will sit "under" every headline concept. Remember that slogans stay the same, but headlines, although interrelated, usually change with each advertising message and medium. Now, let's return to how the creative talents create their solutions.

A Shift in How Creative Teams Work

Eric Springer, executive vice president/group creative director, discusses the change initiated at Doyle Dane Bernbach in the 1960s, when creative talents began to approach solutions as teams, as they do today, rather than working separately. Springer explains the impact this had on the future of idea collaboration:

> Well, it used to be a kind of a line drawn . . . before great agencies like Doyle Dane Bernbach came around in the 1960s and changed the way creatives work together in the industry. Writers would sit at their typewriters and just create lines and come up with thoughts. And they would literally just slip it under the door of the art director or the artists at the time, and they would draw them up. There wasn't a big collaboration.

Springer continued to explain that after the 1960s, creative talents started to spend time working together and bouncing ideas off each other. In this way, the artist could not only visually portray what the copywriter's concept was, but also come up with an image that would strengthen the headline, making it work even harder to drive home the point.

The visual and the copy always have to work together. In fact, the message, in some campaigns, is so important that it has to be guarded against being weakened by an incongruous visual.

Immersing the Creative Team and Experiencing the Brand

At most agencies, the account, media, and creative teams become intimately familiar with the brands and their products. Sharoz Makarechi, founder and creative director of Think Tank 3, explains that the creative team must first experience the product or service before trying to find a way to share the information with the audience in a way that is interesting and relevant. For example, the team went to Total Immersion and took a swimming course to see what made this program different from other training programs. The team members' swimming strokes were even videotaped so they could be improved.

This program wasn't for the novice or nonswimmer. It was for the more serious athletes who wanted to swim with greater efficiency. By thinking about what would capture the audience's attention, the team had to focus on the key consumer benefit that would speak directly to swimming and fitness enthusiasts. Makarechi explains that they start the creative process by "figuring out what the core proposition of any product is, and how someone might benefit from knowing about it."

So what was the benefit for someone who already knew how to swim well? This specific technique allowed swimmers to swim for hours without feeling fatigued. For someone using swimming as part of a fitness routine or in preparation for a triathlon event, that would be a significant improvement over regular, everyday swimming. The whole focus of the program was to make people better swimmers by retraining their movement through lessons, books, and DVDs.

This campaign, which ran in triathlon, swimming, and running magazines, was designed for a narrow niche market, as discussed in chapter 2. Individuals in this selective audience, according to Makarechi, "were people who are already very active, and interested in being more active, and really want to push themselves."

She further explains how quickly the targeted audience could miss the message as they flip through a magazine, "They don't want to know everything. They just want to know why they should care." Doesn't that sum up the goal of almost all campaigns: to show the audience why they should bother to absorb the promotional message, regardless of medium? One ad had this interesting headline: "Only 71% of the World Is Water. What a Pity." Another ad that commanded the reader's attention showed a stream of sperm swimming and offered this provocative headline: "You Started Out as the Fastest Swimmer" (see chapter 3, fig. 3.1).

The slogan was simple and direct: "Just Add Water." You've heard that line many times before. But Makarechi explains how it came to life because of the product. "This was a total branding packet, so we went from logo development, to positioning, to essentially the line 'Just Add Water.' A pretty generic set of words, yet in this context, it's new all over again."

Even the logo, as shown in chapter 6 (fig. 6.1), is an abstract depiction in silhouette of someone becoming more "fish-like," with elongated arms that resemble fins. By moving more like a fish, the swimmer has less water resistance and more economy of movement, ultimately becoming more slippery in the water.

When Makarechi's team was developing the message for this campaign, it was focused on the copy, that is, what it should say. Then the team was careful to use a visual that wouldn't detract from the headline. With all campaigns, there always has to be a healthy marriage between the visual and the copy. Here's how she explains this part of the process:

> Visually you might ruin a great headline if you have the wrong visual approach. So you look around and see tonally what fits with the type of product you have. Then marry all of these elements, and make sure that they're not clashing with each other.

Campaigns with Multipurpose Slogans

Some slogans work harder than others. They can become part of everyday language like "Just Do It." They can appear on greeting cards, T-shirts, and posters. They can be rearranged into seemingly endless variations like "Got Milk?" "Got a Job?" or "Got Respect?" Or they can be the ever-present reminder of the brand's claimed superiority—"The Energizer Bunny Keeps Going."

One slogan, "Know Your Roots," created for Stone Ridge Orchard, another Think Tank 3 account, has multiple uses. It makes consumers really think about where their food is coming from and how making an informed decision affects their family's health. It refocuses the audience's understanding of "organic" and makes families aware of the importance of choosing a healthier diet. It ties the consumer back to one specific farm located in upstate New York and promotes the entire region surrounding the farm, reminding residents of the area's agricultural "roots." Makarechi, who has already used the line in ads (fig. 5.1), and on trucks (fig. 5.2), has continued using the phrase in myriad ways. She explains its versatility:

> We're very proud of that, and we're going to be doing a lot more with that line. It's one of those rare cases where the positioning is also the tagline. It works on many, many levels.

She explains that people all over use the word "organic," yet many of them do not have a clear understanding of what that word means. Some think it means that no pesticides have been used in the growing process. Others think organic produce is grown in a special, protected kind of environment. The point is, using the word "organic" adds value to products, leading people to buy them without understanding what exactly they are. Makarechi discusses how her company prides itself on informing consumers with clear, direct messages that lift the veil off "organic" and reveal to the public what it really means. Educating the public is, as she says, "part of the core of this brand." Just saying, "Oh, I bought organic," or having a vague understanding that organic is vegetable in origin isn't enough now. She says the campaign "further clarified the myth around the word 'organic'" this way:

> But there are a lot of things people don't know about organic. What does it mean exactly to be organic? It doesn't necessarily mean that food has not been sprayed. It means that it's sprayed with sprays that are considered organic by the USDA.

She states that as an advertising agency owner, she is responsible for delivering accurate, fact-based messages that clarify rather than conceal, especially in

Figure 5.1. This ad reminds readers of the importance of understanding exactly where their food comes from.

So, we're **Stone Ridge Orchard** and this is our new logo, to help us share our story and what we grow with chefs, grocers, foodies, and pretty much anyone with taste buds that have yet to dull. While we're here, please note that Know Your Roots™ isn't just our tagline, but also a rallying cry, a wake-up call, and the basis of our values. It's 2007 people. You really should know where your food comes from. And with us, you won't have to go very far to find out where that is.

..Know . Your Roots™.

Route 213 | Stone Ridge, NY 12484 | 845.687.2587
www.stoneridgeorchard.com .. •

Image courtesy of Think Tank 3 [a]

Figure 5.2.   This van wrap makes readers take another look at their definition of a tree.

Image courtesy of Think Tank 3 [b]

an era steeped in consumer skepticism. Makarechi shares a very revealing comment that sums up the importance of choosing exact language, not just using the word organic in a casual, off-handed way:

> And even though we're advertisers and we're helping people market themselves, we don't subscribe to just marketing terms for the sake of marketing terms.

The agency's goal is to allow the audience to make a fully informed decision on its diet.

Making the Mundane Magical

The transformation of a seemingly boring assignment into a "wow" happens when creative talents look beyond a restricted medium and seek an alternative solution. As we saw in chapter 2, brainstorming restriction, like the demanding structure of haikus, can compress the message into one that's even more powerful because of the limitation. When Carolyn Hadlock and Charlie Hopper, creative directors at Young & Laramore, had to design directionals (billboards that primarily state directions) for Steak n Shake, the general rule of thumb of including only five to seven words per board was particularly challenging because that word count had to include directions.

They took this daunting assignment and managed to create a headline that not only included the directions, but had immediate stopping power, capturing the attention of the driver: "Didn't _Nostradamus_ say something about Exit 160?" (fig. 5.3). Underlining the name "Nostradamus," setting it in a different font, and putting it at an angle made the word jump off the board. Usually long words slow the reader down, but in this case, it drew the eye to it, hastening the comprehension. To clarify the product, they showed a luscious-looking whipped-cream-and-cherry-topped chocolate shake.

Another directional in the campaign read "Exit 156A can't come _soon enough_" (fig. 5.4). Once again the words "soon enough" were underlined, set in a contrasting script font, and placed at an angle to strengthen the message. This time they showed the shake married to a juicy double cheeseburger with all the toppings.

Hadlock explained how the creative team came up with the directionals, sharing what a challenging assignment that was. Rather than just putting

Figures 5.3 and 5.4.   Two in a series of highway directional billboards for Steak n Shake restaurants, applying the restaurant's consistently quirky brand personality to the basic job of getting hungry drivers to the correct exit.

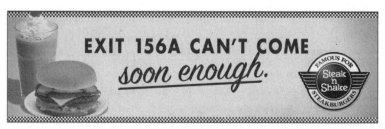

Image courtesy of Young & Laramore [c]

the directionals on the boards, they wanted to do something more exciting, as she explains:

> This team is a pretty nimble couple of guys. So they just took that basic idea of: Let's do a directional campaign that's engaging in its directional concepts.

They created several ideas and then selected the ones with the best concept and used those. Hopper describes the thinking behind developing a message on an outdoor sign this way:

> I think the main mission is just to engage people because getting personality into a billboard is one of the major challenges. And I think if somebody isn't engaged by something, then you haven't made it possible to understand. Or if it's not willfully obtuse or something, it doesn't have to abide by any set standard.

Other eye-stopping billboards in this attention-getting campaign included these ingenious headlines:

1. *"Weak-Willed Vegetarians, Look Away."* This overexaggeration of the power of suggestion was wickedly funny. Hopper shares what the team was thinking when they created this message: "Yes, that was done as a billboard also. It kind of depends on which direction you want to go with it. That one, actually, I think as a billboard, was kind of fun because it tells you to stop looking at the billboard." He continues to explain the humor in the line, "You know, that idea of them crumbling at the sight of this burger. And we're trying to help them by warning them away. There's a little bit of a skit in there that goes beyond just a simple line."
2. *"Run, Tofu, Run."* This line ran both as a single-message billboard and as a directional. Hadlock says, "It runs both ways. It's short enough that you can put an exit number on there. That's fairly uncomplicated, and we've done that. We've also run it just as an image board."

Even when creating coupon inserts, creative directors Hadlock and Hopper avoid commonplace solutions. They looked at the Steak n Shake logo, and pulled out the last two words, using that as the headline: "Hence the "n Shake" (fig. 5.5). This concept was so strong, it was also used as an ad.

To develop one big idea that would work (spin out) for a series of ads, once again they looked at the logo and noticed that it included the line "Famous for Steakburgers." Instantly, they found the answer for the series. They pulled

Figure 5.5.   One in a long-lived series of print executions for Steak n Shake restaurants, which approaches each basic task—this concept began life as a coupon insert—as a chance to engage its customers in a concept that respects their native intelligence, appealing to the sort of person who can appreciate the superiority of a Steakburger or real-milk Milk Shake over more pedestrian fast food fare.

out the words and bracketed them to compare their burgers and shakes with their competitors. This became another series of billboards with just type. In one, the billboard simply stated "Milk Shakes." They bracketed the single word "shakes" and typed "them" under it. They bracketed both words "milk shakes" and placed "us" under them (fig. 5.6). The comparison was obvious and only used four words. They used the same technique with "Steakburgers," singling out "burgers" for "them" and "steakburgers" for "us." The message was so clear that no image was necessary.

Because neither Hopper nor Hadlock consider small projects insignificant or unimportant, they consistently create excellent work. Hopper explains that even

> the "Steakburgers" and "Milk Shakes" ads were all ads for the ad planners, for people to just pick up and run in little yearbooks, or community

Figure 5.6.   Two print ads from the long-running Steak n Shake campaign, a campaign that has changed very little since its inception in 1991 and which uses wit to assert facts over vague claims: rather than saying "tasty" or "succulent" or even "delicious" (words which never appear in Steak n Shake advertising), Steak n Shake advertising uses provable facts such as "made with real steak" or "made with real milk" to allow consumers to conclude its food is superior to fast food competitors.

Image courtesy of Young & Laramore [e]

football programs, or whatever might come along. You know, the things that would typically be shunted off to the interns, while someone gets to work on the TV.

He further explains that all work deserves the best solutions, no matter how small the project. That even extends to placemats and yearbook ads. The fact is, there is no insignificant work. Hopper continues:

> Everything gets equal billing. As far as the collaborative process between members of the team, idea generation, and how concepts can get off strategy—all of that is the product of I'd say two things: One is just people not wanting to be the ones who came up with the boring Steak n Shake ads. And second, we try.

To create great work when given seemingly less-than-exciting assignments requires an uncompromising commitment by the creative team to achieve creative excellence despite the medium's space restrictions, like billboards, or its limited reach, like high school football programs.

Great Ideas Are Gender Neutral

Talented creative teams can write with an authentic voice for any product. They should be equally comfortable writing for products for either gender. Likewise, the audience shouldn't be able to tell if a guy or girl wrote it. One case in point is the Goodwill TV campaign, also directed by Hopper and Hadlock of Young & Laramore. The strategy behind the campaign was to present Goodwill as an ideal place to find fashionable attire. They wanted to change the perception that everything in Goodwill was secondhand to one that Goodwill offered fashion "finds." Hadlock describes going from the strategy to the creative solution, discussing the first two commercials they did for Goodwill: 1) "Label" and 2) the "Little Black Dress" spots. Although both the art director and the copywriter were men, the creative direction was to showcase Goodwill as a place to find beautiful, high fashion clothing, and not just second-hand clothes.

The research showed that people tended to frequent the same store over and over, getting into what she calls a "Goodwill rut." Goodwill is not centralized, so donations are not dropped off in one place and shipped somewhere else. They discovered that most people didn't know that the items remained in the store where they were donated. With that in mind, she describes how they proceeded to the creative solution: "We wanted to do something that introduced the idea of circuit, a Goodwill circuit."

The heart of the "Little Black Dress" spot boiled down to the hard-to-deny fact that every woman is always on a search for the perfect black dress, something to which men weren't privy. She explains how much fun it was to work with guys on this account and talk longingly about the little black dress. Ultimately, she says, this question was asked: "What if it was this sort of quest for the ultimate obvious thing: the little black dress?" Here's how she describes the male-female interaction in one of the sessions:

> They were saying, "Do girls really talk about that?" And we were like, "Yeah."

Just sharing how most women think about this one cherished item was a revelation to the all-guy team. The interesting fact was that the agency had more than fifteen different teams on this account, and all of the people in them were males, except for Hadlock. The "Little Black Dress" (LBD) spot demonstrated the hunt for the perfect LBD. The back of the truck opened up and there on a motorized mannequin was the quintessential little black dress, moving to 1930s Hollywood music. It highlighted the success of the quest, similar to finding the Holy Grail (fig. 5.7).

The second spot in the TV campaign, "Label" showed the Goodwill truck driver reading the designer labels on the clothes, but mispronouncing the names. He thought they were the kind of labels parents put in their kids' clothes when they sent them off to camp. The fact that the actor was unfamiliar with the designer labels made the spot all the more believable. The mispronunciations not only emphasized that Goodwill carried designer labels, they also endeared the actor to the audience. This also showcased guys who were lovably ignorant about brand-name labels.

To draw even more attention to the beautiful fashion that people can find at Goodwill, the logo was placed on the white paper of a wire hanger and trucks were painted with many colorful images of accessories like handbags (fig. 5.8). The whimsical headline highlighted the never-ending cycle of material accumulation in a lighthearted way: "Donate Shop. Donate Shop. Vicious Cycle, Isn't It?" The second message on the back of the truck, "Your Purses Create Jobs," reminded consumers that their purchases not only funded a charitable organization, but also supported salaries. The slogan encapsulated the Goodwill brand in a simple, yet direct message: "Good clothes. Good prices. Good cause." Visually, placing the name on the white area of a clotheshanger, and on both the side and back of the truck, reemphasized the shopping aspect of Goodwill.

Figure 5.7.   This TV spot reminds viewers that Goodwill is an affordable source of classically fashionable clothing—available at not just one, but many area Goodwill locations.

Image courtesy of Young & Laramore [f]

Touching a Touchy Topic

Sometimes creative teams develop campaigns for emotionally charged topics like abortion, drunk driving, smoking, drugs, pedestrian accidents, spouse abuse, and juvenile delinquency, among many others. The objective is to address the

Figure 5.8.   One of a series that highlighted items commonly available in Goodwill stores, this wrap converted Goodwill's highly visible trucks into colorful rolling billboards.

Image courtesy of Young & Laramore [8]

topic, take a clear position, and leave an indelible impression. If the attention is taken off the message and onto the inappropriateness of the campaign, the impact is diluted. Therefore, creative talents strive to address the issue and not get lost in the delivery.

When Sharoz Makarechi, founder and creative director of Think Tank 3, wanted to spotlight how children become lawbreakers, she exposed the family history and the horrific experiences of the children involved in crimes. Yes, they were guilty of these crimes, but they were also "guilty" of being born into families with histories of violence, drug abuse, and prostitution. That was truly circumstantial, totally out of their control. The copy in this poster, which sits under a police mug shot of young girl, says it all (fig. 5.9):

> Guilty of being born to a prostitute. Guilty of being raped by stepdad at 7. Guilty of running away at 11. Guilty of getting pregnant at 12. Guilty of prostitution at 13.

The call to action, which follows the logo and slogan, simply lists a phone number and website. The slogan, without sounding preachy, acts as a reminder that we have the power to enact change: "Breaking the cycle of abuse."

Figure 5.9. This ad challenges readers to rethink their beliefs about juvenile delinquents and youthful offenders.

Image courtesy of Think Tank 3 [h]

This visual was so powerful that the agency had a difficult time finding young models willing to pose with this and other equally disturbing headlines. The campaign never ran throughout the city because the models' parents objected to having their children's images associated with these authentic-looking mug shots. Makarechi explains how that resistance significantly influenced and thus severely reduced the media placement:

> It's difficult. There was very minimal exposure for those ads, partially because nobody wanted their children to be models for those ads. So, that was an issue. The campaign would have been a major one, all throughout the city, with large, bus-shelter-type ads, which did not happen because we couldn't get everyone on board with it because of the model issue.

Even though some of the models included kids from the United Nations school, who perfectly suited the campaign because they represented many nationalities and various races, the truth was, as Makarechi explains, "Nobody wanted to do it and no one wanted to pay for the media to have them blown up all over bus shelters." Despite that, the agency is frequently asked for the ads' republication rights because, she says, "they're touching and poignant." But also, she adds, because "it's the exactly right message." She continues:

> But, know you're doing something right when you're touching those buttons because it's a very sensitive issue. We felt very strongly about this being the right way to go and the notion of breaking the cycle of abuse.

Although each ad was based on a heartbreaking and true story, Makarechi did not struggle with the ad's message and it didn't seem shocking to her at all. How else can you get people to understand the problem and care about the solution? This honest, true-life approach showed precisely why they should care, story by story. She defends her creative approach like this:

> I had no problems calling it like it is. The strategy was essentially to break down why this happens. The reason it happens is because there are just generations of people who are going through hard times, and the children will suffer unless we stop them through organizations like Safe Space.

The fact that the content was so shocking that people didn't want to model in the posters showed the strength of the campaign. Makarechi realizes this and explains that she is always thinking about the message people will walk away with when developing solutions: "I'm very much interested in what people's takeaways are and I understand that. But the reality is that advertising that doesn't stand out might as well not be advertising."

Creating Unforgettable Controversial Messages

Another campaign that touched on a touchy subject was the one Makarechi created for an art exhibition featuring paintings of Jewish boxers. Most agencies would avoid using language that highlights ethnic stereotyping. Undaunted by what might be considered offensive, the headlines for the "Jewish Boxers" ads were so direct that they created resistance. One, in fact, never ran, even after the agency fought the publication, demanding the right to freedom of speech. Here are three of the headlines Think Tank 3 developed for the campaign. Which one do you think was pulled before it ran?

1. "Those Jews. Always Fighting for Money."
2. "Hey, you Want a Knuckle Sandwich on Rye with that?"
3. "Leave It to an Orthodox Jew to Be the Muhammad Ali of His Time."

If you guessed the first one, you were right. That ad was stating that, contrary to common belief, the only reason Jews boxed was that they were poor (fig. 5.10). The second headline, which invited you to order a knuckle sandwich, had a more whimsical, less controversial headline (fig. 5.11). You might have thought that the third ad would have been considered disrespectful, but that one ran, as did the second one. Makarechi, who says she wants to educate readers, further explains the thinking behind this campaign:

> If someone's going to take the time to read an ad, we should give them something for that time. A piece of information they could use, even if they're not going to come to the show. Now they know, there were Jewish boxers and some of them were cultural heroes of their era. At least become curious about it.

The intention was to stir enough interest that people would view the exhibition and learn something they might not have known. Unfortunately, the agency's educational objective didn't prevent the press from censoring that one ad. There have been other campaigns that weren't expected to generate a controversy either, yet they did. We'll take a look at a few of those now.

Figure 5.10.   The controversial ads seen here and on page 103 speak directly to the stereotypical attitude some people have about Jewish people. The brazen headline forces the audience to read the ad.

Image courtesy of Think Tank 3 [i]

An Unintended Controversy

Sometimes an advertisement can inadvertently strike a nerve and create a negative response. This is what happened when a creative team at Deutsch L.A. incorporated a light-hearted reference to a robot driven to suicide in a TV spot for General Motors. Of course, there's nothing humorous about suicide. Yet Eric Springer, group creative director at Deutsch L.A., explains that it was never meant to diminish the seriousness of this tragedy. The spot showed a robot that

Figure 5.11.

Image courtesy of Think Tank 3 [j]

dreamed it threw itself off a bridge after being fired because of poor performance on the assembly line. At the end of the ad, the robot wakes up from his
nightmare and realizes that he hadn't been fired after all. Although most people
enjoyed the spot, one group found it offensive: the Suicide Hotline.

The idea behind the spot was that GM's standards were so high, they caused
even robots to be worried about losing their jobs. It seemed like an obvious
humorous exaggeration. Springer says the main message was to highlight the
dedication of GM workers: "Everyone at GM is taking what they do very seriously, and that's why we're offering the 100,000-mile warranty." Here's how
Springer describes the public's reaction to this spot (fig. 5.12):

> The first time it ran as a sixty was at the Super Bowl and that was with the
> suicide ending. And it really became a hot topic where people were stick-
> ing up for it and saying, "No, this is nothing more than *It's a Wonderful*

Figure 5.12. This campaign was designed to convey the outstanding quality of GM cars and trucks today.

The ad opens with Robot working diligently as part of a GM vehicle assembly line.

Robot screws up and loses his job as a result. He understands perfection is the only option at this GM factory.

Robot yearns for his old job back as he works various jobs. He's ashamed he couldn't hold up the commitment to quality.

The Robot passes by a junkyard and is frightened by the terrible state of the vehicle as he watches it get crushed. Will he follow the same demise?

Robot is continually reminded of his former life as all of the beautiful, well-made GM vehicles he used to help build pass him by on the street.

The nightmare is brought to a end when Robot wakes up with a big sigh of relief. He is safe and sound in the GM factory.

Images courtesy of Deutsch LA [k]

Life where Jimmy Stewart jumps off the bridge." It was exactly the same thing, except it's a robot and robots don't dream and so it was even more facetious. But we loved it because it probably got ten times the amount of talk value on all the radio and TV stations, and Kelly and Regis talked about it.

The spot created free publicity because it had "talk value." He adds that he thought it was ludicrous for the Suicide Prevention organization, which he admitted does great work, to "jump on the GM bandwagon and get some free publicity for themselves." The truth is, he says, "No one wants to promote suicide. Nobody wants to make fun of those affected by it, of course."

There's a very endearing quality to the spots. People felt sorry for the poor robot who, after being fired, unsuccessfully tried his hand at other odd jobs.[3] Of course GM wasn't being unsympathetic to people who were fired, they were sharing the plight of this poor, dedicated, and heartbroken robot. Springer adds that the campaign also touched on other sensitive, almost-taboo topics:

> That spot was a huge production and was such a big thing, giving GM quite a bit of credit because it did take a lot of guts for them to do that spot, [which showed] firing an employee, and all the taboos that you normally never want to talk about. But the public didn't hold that against anybody. It wasn't like, "Oh my god, you're talking about firing employees. And you guys had to lay people off." No, they didn't bring any of that up. It got the message across, and it was an endearing little robot that people fell in love with.

The team ultimately changed the ending. In the new version, he imagines himself being tossed into a scrap metal pile. When you think about it, robots don't dream or feel stress, so they wouldn't have an emotional response to any situation. The spots anthropomorphized the robot, which is a technique that gives human emotions to nonhumans.

The Use of Anthropomorphism

Another brilliant campaign that anthropomorphized nonhuman characters was the Budweiser Clydesdale commercials by DDB. The first one, which aired in the 1996 Super Bowl, was called "Football" and showed the horses playing the game with a zebra as referee. The clever closing line, called a button, was a retort to this comment: "This referee's a jackass." The response was "No, I believe that's a zebra."

Originally, the Clydesdale hitch team was only used in commercials to show their grace and majesty. Gliding along a picturesque country road, set against the famous "Here Comes the King" jingle by Steve Karmen, the Clydesdales were introduced on national television in 1970, with their trusted companion, the Dalmatian, sitting beside the driver. Another commercial, the 1987 "Christmas Sleigh Ride," ushered in the holiday season. It showed the hitch team in a country setting and didn't include any spoken words, just a slowed down, music-only jingle that sent a message of holiday cheer from Budweiser.

But it wasn't until 1995 that the DDB team of creative directors Adam Glickman (art director) and Craig Feigen (copywriter) humanized the Clydesdales and the Dalmatian. Feigen explains the thinking behind the anthropomorphism:

> The strategy behind the brand really hasn't changed that much over the years. And it's really that Budweiser's an iconic brand, and they really wanted to make the brand fun again. That was kind of the overarching strategy. So ["Football"] was really the first Clydesdale spot we had ever done in this new strategy of just making the brand fun and contemporary.

The team continued to use anthropomorphism in these and other beloved Super Bowl spots: "Separated at Birth" (1999), "Snowball Fight" (2003), "American Dream" (2006), "Fake Dalmatian" (2007), and "Team" (2008).

In case you missed seeing any of these, we'll review them. In "Snowball Fight," the Clydesdales are horsing around in the snow, one group hitting the others with snowballs. In the end, one of the snowball-struck horses leans into a tree and shakes the snow onto the group of snowball throwers. The sound of one of the snow-covered pranksters coughing as if he had gotten snow up his nose or caught in his throat was comical. This and the following spots show how effortlessly Glickman and Feigen combine humor and anthropomorphism.

In the "Separated at Birth" spot two Dalmatian puppies were brought to the firehouse. When one was chosen to ride on the fire truck, he blew a raspberry to his brother. Two years later, when they pass each other on the road, the second puppy, which is riding on the Budweiser hitch team, sticks out his tongue to his sibling onboard the fire truck. This spot embodied sibling rivalry and one-upmanship, clearly showing the higher status of being on the Budweiser hitch team. Glickman explains how they decided to use the Dalmatian in other commercials:

> Since we had done so many spots with just the horses, we decided to bring in another character, which was the Dalmatian. And over the years, there have been more spots done with that Dalmatian.

Other spots show the lengths to which some animals would go to get on board with Budweiser. In "Fake Dalmatian," the Dalmatian didn't have enough spots, but when he got splattered with mud and suddenly had more spots, he was able to ride along in a parade. When a beauty pageant winner leans over to hug him, she ends up with dirt on her face.

Feigen and Glickman didn't just show the pride of joining the hitch team. They went past pride. In some spots, using other animals as well, becoming a Budweiser team member was depicted as a lifelong ambition.

In "American Dream" a Clydesdale colt longingly looks at a photo of a Budweiser hitch team hanging on the barn wall. Then he walks over to the head halter and puts his small head through, trying with all his might to pull the wagon, with it hardly budging. When it begins to move, the camera reveals two large Clydesdales pushing from behind. As the little horse pulls the wagon out of the barn, a hitch team trainer turns to the Dalmatian and says, "I won't tell, if you won't." Again, human emotions are used, from the desire of the colt to join the team, to the empathy of the larger horses who assisted him, to the compassion of the trainer who didn't want the colt to know he'd been helped.

The 2008 Super Bowl "Team" spot featured a Clydesdale named Hank who didn't make the hitch team. After the horse was rejected, the Dalmatian encouraged him to try again.

As the spot plays the *Rocky* movie theme, the Dalmatian acts as Hank's coach, putting him through strength-training exercises. In the end, Hank makes the team and high-fives the Dalmatian (fig. 5.13).

Figure 5.13.   This TV ad was part of the ongoing Clydesdale and Dalmatian campaign to depict the honor of being selected as a member of the Budweiser hitch team.

Image courtesy of DDB and Anheuser-Busch Companies Inc., Budweiser [1]

Many other campaigns have used anthropomorphism. In the 2008 Westminster Dog Show, Petco aired two Saatchi & Saatchi, L.A. spots in the "Reflection" series. Each one showed a dog passing a mirror and stopping to admire itself. In one, the dog is wearing a red plaid sweater, showcasing the store's pet apparel. In the other, the dog is simply taken with its own coiffed good looks, referring to the chain's pet grooming service. The main message behind the campaign is that pets actually know when they are looking their best. The spot ends with the Petco logo on a swinging doggie door, reminding viewers of the famous, well-crafted slogan: "Petco. Where the pets go."

Other pet companies have also created commercials in which the animals have human emotions. Look at the long-running 9Lives campaign with Morris the finicky cat. Or the use of Garfield the cat, first introduced in 1984 in the Embassy Suites campaign, with slogans like "At Embassy Suites, you don't have to be a fat cat to enjoy the suite life."[4]

Tweaking a Brand's Strategy

After ten years of using a deprivation strategy for the "Got Milk?" campaign, the creative team at Goodby, Silverstein & Partners (GS&P) shifted directions and highlighted milk's health benefits. This shift occurred after the team realized that an entire generation of young people had only heard about the agony of missing one half of a perfectly paired food combination, like cookies without milk, or cereal without milk. This generation had not seen earlier campaigns that talked about milk's nutritional benefits with slogans like "Milk. It does a body good." Senior copywriter at GS&P on the "Got Milk?" campaign, Paul Charney, explains the strategy shift like this:

> We had to evolve the campaign from the "Deprivation" strategy. We had to figure out how to get across these benefits again—that it builds strong hair and strengthens muscles—because it had been almost 10 years. There had almost been a generation of kids growing up more understanding it as a deprivation idea and not necessarily as this healthy drink. So, we had to kind of go back and reintroduce that concept, but keep it in the same vein of the campaign with the playfulness and the fun, with all those brand attributes.

This campaign is further discussed in chapter 9, where we explore new strategies for old and new media.

Getting the Creative Idea in a Flash

Although many campaigns start with group strategy meetings, creative team interactions, and account planner insights, some ideas come out of a simple observation of an ordinary, everyday occurrence. All of a sudden, that observation gets connected to the product and the solution appears in a Eureka! moment.

Linda Kaplan Thaler, CEO and chief creative officer of The Kaplan Thaler Group, shared some "Big Bang" ideas that came in a flash of revelation. To access breakthrough thinking, Kaplan Thaler quickly dismisses every previously used creative direction that is commonly implemented for any product category. This approach enabled her agency to create the "Totally Organic" experience campaign for Herbal Essences shampoo. Before those spots aired, most shampoo advertising showed smooth, shiny hair, before-and-after shots of damaged-to-smooth results, or emphasized vitamin-based ingredients. Now, the focus was on the luxurious self-indulgence women experienced in the simple, almost sensual joy of shampooing their hair.

The Eureka! moment came when the creative teams were about to give up and half-heartedly suggested using a celebrity. The one that came to mind was Meg Ryan, which reminded everyone of the funny, unforgettable scene when she faked an orgasm in *When Harry Met Sally*. In a flash, the campaign came to life: create a shower scene hinting at a sensual experience paired with the line "Totally Organic Experience."[5]

PEDIGREE®: A Strategic Writing Case Study

Sometimes a brand doesn't have a brand position. In that case, the creative team needs to make one up. This is what art director Margaret Keene and copywriter Chris Adams from TBWA\Chiat\Day did for PEDIGREE®. They highlighted the plight of shelter dogs in the "DOGS RULE®" campaign and promised that a portion of the proceeds from every bag of PEDIGREE® dog food would go to support homeless dogs. To emphasize this, Keene said the creative writing part of the campaign needed to shift the brand from just being known for preparing food for dogs to truly caring about dogs. "I think they needed to connect 'we make dog food' with 'we own and love dogs.'"

The earlier TV commercials from 2005 depicted dogs in shelters and revealed the dilemma, showing the experience from the dogs' perspective. They communicated their message in one unforgettable phrase: "I know I'm a good dog." By humanizing the predicament of shelter dogs, the PEDIGREE® campaign engaged people emotionally and questioned the belief that most shelter dogs exhibit problematic behavior. Instead, the ads showed, many good dogs end up there because of circumstance, like their owners' moving. That one line of copy, "I know I'm a good dog," encapsulated the problem, resulting in various steps that consumers could take. They bought more PEDIGREE® dog food, sent donations, and adopted more dogs from shelters. Information Resources reported that sales of PEDIGREE® food rose in 2007 to $558 million, a 6.1 percent increase in a year that the dog food category only grew by 2 percent. In addition, the now four-year-old "DOGS RULE®" campaign, which launched in 2005, has raised more than $4 million for around 3,500 shelters nationwide.[6]

The PEDIGREE® commercials, which ran in the 2008 Westminster Dog Show, are equally emotionally charged. There were three distinct directions. The first one discussed the adoption drive with poignancy. The second one showed the commitment of PEDIGREE® to product quality as an homage to dogs' quality of life. The third approach focused on the nutritious ingredients and used a humorous tone of voice.

The adoption-drive approach, which included spots with dogs that were turned over to shelters when their owners moved, used tug-at-your-heartstrings copy intensified by the delivery of *The X Files* actor David Duchovny. The second approach, which showed the deep love of dogs demonstrated by PEDIGREE®, discussed all the things dog lovers love about dogs. The third direction, which highlighted the healthful ingredients in PEDIGREE® food, presented a more whimsical approach to the copy.

To demonstrate each of the strategic approaches, here is a script from each.

◻◻◻

Three Strategic Copy Approaches for PEDIGREE®

1. *The Adoption Drive*

In this series, each spot is more poignant than the next. They're each a perfect example of emotional blackmail,[7] that is, writing that reaches audiences' consciences and makes them feel guilty if they don't take action.

VIDEO	AUDIO
DOG ROLLING OVER ON LIVING ROOM FLOOR	Bailey's family got a new apartment.
DOG LOCKED UP IN KENNEL	But, they don't take dogs.

PRODUCT BEAUTY SHOT   The PEDIGREE® Adoption Drive.

SUPER: DOGSRULE®.com   Help us help dogs.

Another dog that was abandoned was Echo, who was surrendered after a divorce split up the family. Echo appeared in the TV campaign, online, and in print (fig. 5.14). He was so adorable that many people

Figure 5.14.   This newspaper ad is part of the PEDIGREE® Adoption Drive—an effort that has raised awareness for shelter dogs, raised over $4 million for the cause, and helped countless dogs find loving homes.

Image courtesy of Mars Petcare US and TBWA\Chiat\Day. Photographic image courtesy of Laura Crosta. PEDIGREE®, DOGS RULE®, and other insignia are trademarks of Mars, Incorporated and its affiliates. These trademarks are used with permission. © Mars, Incorporated 2008. ᵐ

wanted to adopt him. To let people know that he finally was adopted, a second TV spot, featuring Echo, was created to show him enjoying his new home.

2. *We Love Dogs*

Notice, in particular, the use of specific writing techniques like parallel construction (underlined),[8] and the change in rhythm from monosyllabic (all caps) to multisyllabic lines (bold). See how the monosyllabic words like "walks," "runs," and "romps" slow the reader down. Pay attention to the way certain word endings harmonize with others like "the guardians and the comedians." When you read the script aloud, you can hear how easily the message is delivered and how lyrical the writing style is.

> *We're for dogs. Some people are for the whales. Some are for the trees. We're for dogs. The big ones and the little ones. The guardians and the comedians. The pure breeds and the mutts. We're for WALKS, RUNS, AND ROMPS. Digging, scratching, sniffing, and fetching. We're for dog parks, dog doors, and dog days. And, if there were an international holiday for dogs, to celebrate their contribution to the quality of life on earth, we'd be for that, too. Because we're for dogs.*
> SUPER: DOGSRULE®.com
> BEAUTY SHOT, SUPER: PEDIGREE®

This campaign also had an educational component, reminding people that while dogs enrich their lives they also need to be cared for. The ads were informative, but were presented with humor. One ad mentioned the short attention span of puppies, and was interrupted with this funny line, "Hey, is that a cat?" (fig. 5.15).

3. *Healthy Ingredients*

Here the golden retriever is thinking out loud. The writing is short and crisp, and the actor's delivery on the word "stupid" emphasizes dogs' universally recognized contempt for cats. When the dog shifts from

Figure 5.15.   This ad was created to show the benefits of having a dog in your family, while also educating moms and kids about responsible dog ownership.

Image courtesy of Mars Petcare US and TBWA\Chiat\Day. Photographic image courtesy of Arthaus. PEDIGREE®, DOGS RULE®, and other insignia are trademarks of Mars, Incorporated and its affiliates. These trademarks are used with permission. © Mars, Incorporated 2008. [n]

the product's healthy ingredients to his disdain for cats, it's funny and unexpected.

> *Everyone knows that protein builds strong muscles. Except for cats. They're so stupid.*
> BEAUTY SHOT: *PEDIGREE*®. *Really good food for dogs.*
> SUPER: DOGSRULE®.com

Another spot in this series, "Rub My Belly," was also turned into a print ad. Again, the whimsical copy is from the dog's perspective, with the dachshund begging to have his tummy rubbed to prove how soft its coat is from eating PEDIGREE® dog food (fig. 5.16).

Figure 5.16. This ad was created to tout the quality ingredients found in PEDIGREE® food in a fun, dog-loving way.

Image courtesy of Mars Petcare US and TBWA\Chiat\Day. Photographic images courtesy of Peggy Sirota (for the dog) and Arthaus (for the ad). PEDIGREE®, DOGS RULE®, and other insignia are trademarks of Mars, Incorporated and its affiliates. These trademarks are used with permission. © Mars, Incorporated 2008. °

When strong writing is paired with a strong strategic approach, the campaign is persuasive and powerful. Each of the above scripts showcases the impact a succinctly written script can have on the viewer, especially the intended audience of dog lovers. Without a doubt, many people felt deep compassion for shelter dogs' predicament when they watched the PEDIGREE® Adoption Drive commercials.

Great Writing Tips

Over the decades, talented copywriters have shared their secrets. Many write zillions of headlines before they find the one they want to use. Others can get the big idea in seconds, as we have discussed. Some labor over their copy and rewrite it until they feel it's ready to be shared with others, like David Ogilvy. It's inspiring to read about the different writing techniques of those who actually write copy. You can hear their commitment to perfection when you read their words of advice. Copywriters the world over face similar challenges. These and other copywriters from Great Britain, Asia, Australia, and the United States shared an entire book of advice in *The Copywriter's Bible*, compiled by the Designers and Art Directors Association of the United Kingdom.

British copywriter Chris O'Shea, after years of writing at various agencies, helped open the Chiat\Day London office in 1989. Then, in 1991, he paired up with art director Ken Hoggins to create their own shop: Banks Hoggins O'Shea. In *The Copywriter's Bible*, O'Shea—and others—discusses visualizing the consumer in his mind. Not just the statistics about the target audience, but a real person, similar to someone he might even know. And someone he could speak to one-on-one in a regular conversation. Here's what he says:

> All the time I fixed in my mind a mental picture of who will read what I'm writing. I don't mean "AB males aged 35–44 with a promiscuous attitude to white spirits" [clear alcohol]. I mean I think of an actual person, be it a friend, neighbor or relation who is in the target audience. When I see that person in my mind, I know what will appeal to them. That way I can write copy the way I believe all copy should be written: as a conversation between two human beings rather than an announcement from manufacturer to consumer. As I'm writing I try to keep it simple. This dictates that I write in "spoken" rather than "written" English.[9]

American David Abbott, who wrote for some major agencies which are now known as Ogilvy & Mather, DDB Needham, and BBDO, shared five pieces of wisdom when he was asked to theorize about copywriting. Although he has a Mac, he prefers to work by hand, writing down his ideas on pads of paper. He explains that reading all of his copy out loud permits him to hear "the rhythm of the line and ultimately the flow of the whole piece." Every seasoned copywriter understands how critically important it is to read aloud. Novices soon learn that lesson and begin the practice as part of their everyday process. Here are five tips from Abbott, including incorporating your own experience into your writing as well as including all the copy points in an easy-to-read manner:

1. Put yourself into your work. Use your life to animate your copy. If something moves you, chances are, it will touch someone else.
2. Think visually. Ask someone to describe a spiral staircase and they'll use their hands as well as words. Sometimes the best copy is no copy.
3. If you believe that facts persuade (as I do) you'd better learn how to write a list so that it doesn't read like a list.
4. Confession is good for the soul and for copy, too. Bill Bernbach used to say "a small admission gains a large acceptance." I still think he was right.
5. Don't be boring.[10]

The last tip is one of the best ones. If you're tired halfway through your copy, your reader won't even get that far. Infuse your writing with energy, passion, and excitement. Breathe life into it.

British copywriter Steve Henry, who graduated first with an English literature degree from Oxford University and then created his own shop, Howell Henry Chaldecott Lury, in 1987, offers a handful of pointed tips. He explains the necessity of establishing a comfortable working relationship with other creative team members. He also stresses the importance of writing in a different voice for each client, so no one could pick out a specific writer's block of copy. It shouldn't sound like the writer. It should sound like the brand. Here are his tips:

Tip One is work closely with the art director, designer, typographer, Mac operator, etc.

Tip Two is do anything to make the body copy readable. If all else fails, keep your sentences so short that someone with the IQ of an orangutan can keep up. Right? Got that? Terrific.

Tip Three is one which a lot of top copywriters ignore. Every piece of body copy you write should be different. It should have your personal input but it shouldn't have your recognizable signature on it. Your clients are all different, and they deserve something unique.

Tip Four is do it differently. Don't try to emulate anybody else's style.
The most important thing about any ad is to do it differently. Write it
upside down, in Jamaican patois, or with every fifth letter missing.
Tip Five is read the other contributions [from other writers] in the book.
There are much better copywriters than me in this volume.[11]

Adrian Holmes, a British copywriter with extensive experience at numerous agencies, opened his firm, Lowe Howard-Spink, in 1989, and served as joint
creative director. He confesses that some of his best copy is some of the hardest
to perfect. He mentions starting at the end and writing toward that. In other
words, decide what you want your audience to walk away knowing and write
with that message in mind. He also shares that he implements the sonata format
of ABA, in which the last line of copy refers back to the headline to reinforce
the main idea. Holmes is also an advocate of editing down superfluous words to
fine-tune the copy and maximize the message. Here's what he advises:

I still find the going tough. And the bits of writing I'm most pleased with
always turn out to be the toughest to do. However, for what they're worth, here
are my Ten Tips for Copywriters—techniques I've either developed myself or
picked up along the way.[12]

Ten Tips for Copywriters

1. Make the most of your deadline (He waits until the last minute).
2. Before starting your copy, work out where it'll end.
3. Keep the reader rewarded.
4. Don't over-egg the mix. Beware of loading your prose with too many
   jokes and verbal conceits.
5. Read poetry.
6. Read your copy out loud to yourself.
7. Don't get too precious about your words.
8. Treat your copy as a visual object. Does it have balance? Do any of
   the paragraphs seem excessively long or heavy-looking? Does it look
   inviting to the eye?
9. Observe the sonata structure (ABA – Exposition, Development and
   Recapitulation) [This format was discussed in chapter two and will be
   discussed later in this chapter under Checklist of Copy Techniques.]
10. The good is the enemy of the great. You've completed you're 15th
    draft. You finally sit back and say to yourself: yup, that's good. Con-
    gratulations. Now tear it up and do it again. Only better. I told you
    this writing business was tough.—Adrian Holmes [13]

Checklist of Copy Techniques

Strong writing includes a wide range of different techniques to help the reader digest the information effortlessly. New writers forget that they're writing to people who are actually going to read their copy. They're not writing a college theme paper, or an article for a newspaper. They're writing copy designed to persuade someone to take action. Therefore it must be clear and easy to understand. If it's written, as in a print ad or an online website, rather than spoken, as in broadcast or online videos, it must be read without struggling. It should flow, with one line moving into the next.

Strong writing means you don't let go of the readers' "hands" as you take them along a journey. Imagine that you're guiding some friends through a forest, across a brook, or down a mountain trail. You're familiar with the path and you want to be sure to show them your favorite spots, while not losing them along the way. Likewise, you hold the readers' attention by making sure your writing invites them to continue. Just remember, someone will be reading your words, so make each one count. Make each sentence interesting. Make each benefit relevant.

Be sure you're writing in the correct tone of voice for your audience and for your product. For example, you wouldn't use text messaging or teenage, vernacular language for a sixty-plus market or for a medical center. Keeping your audience and product in mind every time you write will ensure that you use the appropriate message and the appropriate tone of voice.

Now let's look at a short checklist you can refer to as you create copy. Having a list of writing techniques strengthens all promotional writing because they make it easier to read. The entries in this short list will make the copy more readable and, ultimately, more digestible to the audience.

Eighteen Copy Techniques and Tips

1. *Alliteration*—You already are familiar with alliteration. You just might not know the name. If you've ever recited the tongue twister that starts "Peter Piper picked a peck of pickled peppers," you've used alliteration. This specific use of repetitive sounds makes writing more sonorous, like *Super Saturday Sale*. It's obvious how alliteration keeps the reader going.
2. *ABA*—This uses the 3-part sonata format that gives the reader a sense of completion. Part "A" is the headline. Part "B" is the body copy that clarifies the headline. The second "A" is the closing line, which refers back to the headline, reiterating the main idea. It doesn't have to be an exact restatement of the headline, but it refers back to the concept.
3. *Weave*—Weaving your copy creates writing that flows from the beginning to the end by using the main idea and carrying or "weaving" it through the copy.

4. *Connectors*—Like copy glue, these words create bonds that make writing seamless. Here are a few words that can be used to "sew up" copy gaps: *after all, because, just in case, and, but, well, so, actually, finally, on the other hand, the fact is, the best part is,* and *more importantly.*

5. *Parallel construction*—The use of parallel construction is an effective way to give the copy rhythmic cadence. Just repeat a word, a phrase, or a part of speech. Here are two examples: 1) *No salt, no sugar, no calories,* and 2) *walking, jogging, running.* Parallel construction makes the copy stickier.

6. *Contraction*—Listen to the way your friends speak. Everyone uses contractions in their daily conversations. They'll say, "*We're* going to dinner," not "*We are* going to dinner." It's more natural. Promotional writing mirrors the spoken word.

7. *Vernacular*—In your daily conversations, you normally use contractions, common language, and casual phrases like *shoulda, gotta, yeah right, oh sure, no way,* and *veg out.* Pay attention to conversations when you're out and about: in restaurants, the gym, malls, and movies. Listen to how people speak. You'll be a better copywriter.

8. *Break grammatical rules*—Breaking grammatical rules works because the writing sounds more conversational and more natural. You're writing to the ear, not the eye.

9. *One- or two-word sentences*—This is the way we naturally talk. We use short phrases, not verbose sentences.

10. *Start in the middle*—Readers usually only spend three seconds reading the copy, so you need to move quickly. Just jump into act two, if this were a play. Don't bother with act one. There's no time. This will pique their attention and spark their curiosity.

11. *Call to action*—This line, found near the end of the copy, directs the audience. It tells them what to do: visit a website, stop by a store, place a catalog order, clip a coupon, and so forth.

12. *Buttons*—Use closing lines that don't have to echo the headline. These clever lines reward the reader with a little twist at the end and provide closure. For the last line of a Mexican restaurant ad that stressed price, this line would work: *Margaritas, Mariachis, Mexican Pizza . . . for Beans!*

13. *Read aloud*—There's one more way to help you write in your natural voice: Read aloud. When you do this, you can instantly identify sections that sound awkward, wordy, or as bumpy as a rock-strewn road.

14. *Talk to the reader*—Have a dialogue, not a monologue. Don't preach; engage their attention. Most of all, create a conversation. This is why reading along really helps.

15. *Visualize the consumer*—Keep a clear picture of a particular individual who would be reading this message. How would you speak to this person if he or she were sitting beside you?

16. *Reward the reader*—Make sure people feel they got something out of the copy. It should be informative, yet entertaining. When they come to the last line, readers should feel as if their time investment was worth it.
17. *Don't be dull*—No one wants to be bored to sleep. Remember, you're writing to a real audience, so keep their interest. Make your copy intriguing and they'll read every word.[14]
18. *Rewrite. Rewrite. Rewrite*—Eliminate all unnecessary words. Conduct a "which" hunt, deleting as many words like "which" and "that" as possible. Your goal is to have readers fly through the copy, not stumble along.

◇◇◇

On some types of products, for example . . . experience is highly desirable—knowing what's worked and what hasn't worked, and knowing some of the scientific facts involved . . . But, that knowledge and experience aren't nearly as important as [a writer's] expressiveness, his ability to think and to marshal his thoughts into persuasive English.—Leo Burnett[15]

If you don't enjoy writing it, no-one will enjoy reading it.— John Bevins[16]

I therefore think and if it's true it's a juicy irony, that good copywriters don't really do it for the clients or for the agency or even for the reader . . . they do it for themselves.—John Bevins[17]

Notes

1. Denis Higgins, *The Art of Writing Advertising: Conversations with the Masters of the Craft* (Chicago: NTC Business Books, 1965), 94.

2. Higgins, *Art of Writing Advertising*, 43.

3. money.cnn.com/2007/02/09/news/companies/gm_robotad/, accessed March 1, 2008.

4. query.nytimes.com/gst/fullpage.html?res=9D0CE5D61338F932A15756C0A967958260, accessed March 2, 2008.

5. Linda Kaplan Thaler and Robin Koval, *Bang! Getting Your Message Heard in a Noisy World* (New York: Doubleday, 2003), 50–53.

6. Eleftheria Parpis, "Must Love Dogs," *AdWeek*, February 18, 2008, 34–35.

7. Margo Berman, *Street-Smart Advertising: How to Win the Battle of the Buzz* (Lanham, MD: Rowman & Littlefield Publishers, 2007), 89–90.

8. Berman, *Street-Smart Advertising*, 94.

9. Chris O'Shea, quoted in *The Copywriter's Bible*, by The Designers and Art Directors Association of the United Kingdom (Switzerland: RotoVision SA, 2000), 134.

10. David Abbott, quoted in *Copywriter's Bible*, 84–85.

11. Steve Henry, quoted in *Copywriter's Bible*, 74.

12. Adrian Holmes, quoted in *Copywriter's Bible*, 10–11.

13. Adrian Holmes, quoted in *Copywriter's Bible*, 10–11.

14. Adrian Holmes, quoted in *Copywriter's Bible*, 10–11.

15. Berman, *Street-Smart Advertising*, 92–96.

16. Higgins, *Art of Writing Advertising*, 41.

17. John Bevins, quoted in *Copywriter's Bible*, 15.

18. John Bevins, quoted in *Copywriter's Bible*, 15.

Image Credits

a. "Know Your Roots" ad for Stone Ridge Orchard. Created by Sharoz Makarechi and Harris Silver at Think Tank 3.

b. "This is a Tree" vehicle ad for Stone Ridge Orchard. Created by Sharoz Makarechi, Matthew Dugas and Harris Silver at Think Tank 3.

c. "Directional" billboards created by Young & Laramore (Writer Bryan Judkins; Art Director Trevor Williams; Creative Director Charlie Hopper; Strategy Shawn Wilkie, Melissa Odom) for Steak n Shake restaurants.

d. "Hence the "n Shake" print execution created by Young & Laramore (Writer David Nehamkin; Art Director Penny Dullaghan; Creative Director Charlie Hopper; Strategy Shawn Wilkie, Melissa Odom, Tom Denari) for Steak 'n Shake restaurants.

e. "Brackets" print executions created by Young & Laramore (Writer David Nehamkin; Art Director Jeff Morris; Creative Director Charlie Hopper; Strategy Shawn Wilkie, Melissa Odom, Tom Denari) for Steak 'n Shake restaurants.

f. "Little Black Dress" TV spot created by Young & Laramore (Writer David Nehamkin; Art Director Matt Ganser; Creative Director Carolyn Hadlock; Strategy Tom Denari, Ann Beriault, Kurt Ashburn) for Goodwill Industries of Central Indiana, Incorporated.

g. "Purse" truck wrap created by Young & Laramore (Writer David Nehamkin; Art Director Kevin Christie; Creative Director Carolyn Hadlock; Strategy Ann Beriault, Kurt Ashburn) for Goodwill Industries of Central Indiana, Incorporated.

h. "Guilty of Being Born To A Prostitute" ad for Safe Space. Created by Sharoz Makarechi and Matthew Dugas at Think Tank 3.

i. "Those Jews. Always fighting for money." ad for Jewish Boxers created by Sharoz Makarechi and Harris Silver at Think Tank 3.

j. "Hey You Want a Knuckle Sandwich on Rye With That?" ad for Jewish Boxers created by Sharoz Makarechi and Harris Silver at Think Tank 3.

k. "Robot" TV spot created by Eric Hirshberg, Eric Springer, and Mike Bryce of Deutsch LA for General Motors.

l. This TV spot was created by DDB for Anheuser-Busch Companies Inc., Budweiser.

m. This newspaper ad was created by TBWA\Chiat\Day.

n. This ad was created by BWA\Chiat\Day.

o. This ad was created by TBWA\Chiat\Day. Image courtesy of Mars Petcare US and TBWA\Chiat\Day.

Interviews

Paul Charney, personal communication, March 7, 2008.

Adam Glickman and Craig Feigen, personal communication, February 11, 2008.

Margaret Keene and Chris Adams, personal communication, January 4, 2008.

Sharoz Makarechi, personal communication, February 13, 2008.

Eric Springer, personal communication, May 2, 2007.

CHAPTER 6

How Designers Approach Strategy Visually

◇ ◇ ◇

Does this advertisement move an idea from the inside of my head to the inside of the public's head?—Rosser Reeves[1]

The Strategy behind a Good Idea

There is no document that outlines the creative concept or idea development stage. The document we have looked at—the creative brief—concentrates solely on marketing assessments and an overview of communication goals. Creative, its interpretation and its ultimate ability to produce a sale, is the driving force behind any single ad or campaign. Everything creative—copy and layout—begins and ends in the creative brief. Before any brainstorming takes place, any copy is written, or any concept laid out, the creative team needs to thoroughly study the creative brief.

The creative brief lays an informational foundation for the creative team to build upon. It outlines what creative efforts need to accomplish and is the rationale behind creative direction. The creative team will use the knowledge about the target to define the audience to whom they are talking. Objectives will determine what the creative efforts need to accomplish. To better grasp the picture in totality, here's a basic checklist for developing a solid strategic direction.

1. The strategy and positioning will determine the main creative direction.
2. The message is what is being said to the consumer or end user.
3. The tone of voice is how the message is written. Is the voice friendly, authoritative, or humorous?
4. The point of view is who's delivering the message. Is it an advertiser (self-serving), a consumer/spokesperson (testimonial), a person's conscience (emotional blackmail)? Here's an example of each:

Self-serving:	"Ford, where quality is job one."
Testimonial:	"L'Oréal, because I'm worth it."
Emotional blackmail:	"Michelin. There's a lot riding on your tires."

5. The tactics are how the message will be implemented: billboards, flyers, Web banners, e-zines, and so on.
6. The key consumer benefit is how the product or service helps the audience.
7. The support statement assures the target, explaining "why to buy."
8. Media placement is where the message is being delivered: on a website, in a print ad, in an out-of-home venue.
9. Product positioning can most easily be understood when considered as six separate types: 1) Positioning in the marketplace. Is the product global, national, or regional? 2) Positioning in sales. Is it first, second, or third? 3) Positioning in real estate. This is where the product is located in the stores: on end caps, on island displays, on higher or lower shelves? 4) Positioning in the media. In which media is it advertised: TV, online, out-of-home? 5) Positioning in the medium. Exactly where in a specific medium does it air or run? On drive time for radio, in TV programs as product integration, online as skyscrapers (vertical narrow ads on websites)? 6) Positioning in the mind of the consumer. What do consumers currently think about this product? Not what the advertiser wants them to think, but what do they actually think?
10. The unique selling proposition, which highlights a product trait or unclaimed characteristic by competitors, distinguishes the product in the marketplace and benefits the consumer.
11. The slogan, which succinctly encapsulates one main idea, acts as a sticky consumer takeaway.

These must all work in harmony to deliver a cohesive, targeted, and relevant message. Other aspects of briefs are not included here, as they were discussed earlier. These include examining your competitors' work and their strategies, determining what you want the audience to think, and defining your brand personality, which answers these two questions: 1) Who would the product be if it were a famous celebrity? 2) What relationship would you have if this person were a friend or relative? Obviously, there is a great deal to consider when developing an on-strategy, on-target campaign.

Now, let's turn our attention to examining the main message or big idea. A great idea can usually be stated in one sentence: the key consumer benefit. It is what you do with that sentence strategically that determines if the idea will come to life and become memorable.

All creative efforts must be written and designed specifically for your target audience, using language they can relate to, from sophisticated and formal to casual and vernacular (street talk). In addition, creative solutions must show that they understand consumers' problems, offer relatable scenarios, and appear in a medium they frequently see.

If the creative team misses the target (in tone or media placement) and is off-strategy, the ad or campaign will have no direction, no impact, no strong brand identity, and no chance of standing out amongst its competitors. This kind of advertising usually carries what we call a "seen it all before" creative label. This means the idea has been used before—sometimes many, many times. When you've seen something once, it's interesting; when you've seen it two or three times, it's boring. Once consumers are bored, they stop paying attention to the message.

Today's consumer is bombarded with an estimated 10,000 advertising messages each day. A good creative team recognizes this and looks for an innovative way to make its product stand out among the clutter. GEICO did it with the "Gecko" campaign, and Aflac did it with the "Duck" campaign.

The Idea of Teamwork

Once the creative team has decided on a creative direction, the next step is to determine a visual/verbal solution that will bring the idea to life. Coming up with that extraordinary idea is not as easy as most people think it is. It involves engaging both sides of the brain effectively. As the left side sorts out all the research you've collected and digests the creative brief, the right side begins the imagination process.

All great ads begin with a good idea. A good idea comes from an active imagination, observation, experience, or just plain luck. It is the thing that drives strategic solutions. All good designers need to be culturally diverse, open-minded, adventurous, and receptive to a multitude of influences. This realm of endless possibilities, this dream state, is the place to define and build ideas. Go beyond the YouTube culture and look at the world as it was and as it is. What was is very important in defining what is and what could be.

Go outside your own likes and dislikes. Start with music. Try experiencing new sounds like those from the archives of rock, jazz, blues, or country western. Music is a powerful communicator. Everyone relates to it in one way or another. Music makes listeners active participants, whether they're reminiscing or actively singing along.

Next, go to museums and art galleries to see how art, like advertising, marks history, expresses cultures, and defines attitudes. Attend independent film festivals, another cultural mirror. Note how your peers speak and represent culture both past and present. Go to the park or the mall and people-watch. Play with a child. Talk to the elderly. Don't define or label anything you see; just experience it. After all, if we want our advertising to touch readers', viewers', or listeners' response mechanisms, we need to understand their world.

Readers and viewers alike respond to stimulants—whether they remind them of something from their childhood or college days, or provoke them to imagine something they haven't yet experienced, but wish to. If you plant the thought, the consumer will decide whether or not to experience your idea.

Your imaginative thoughts will eventually lay the groundwork for an idea. That idea will need to be developed into a concept direction for your client's product or service.

Concept development begins with discussion. Then it evolves into producing and then eliminating hundreds of ideas that just don't measure up. Open your conservative mind, and your liberal imagination will follow.

Daydreaming and role-playing are a designer's first line of attack when struggling to solve a client's advertising problem, and they are actually an important part of the design process. Those carefree dreams acted out in the backyard—when you imagined yourself a pilot, astronaut, explorer, princess, clown, or juggler—are just waiting to be resurrected. Feel free to act up and act out. Jump aboard that broomstick horse; rebuild that impenetrable fort made of boxes, sticks, and whatever was left over from mom and dad's last home-improvement idea. Or better yet, run outside or look out the window and examine that passing cloud for a recognizable image. You'll find these are the kinds of thoughts and acts that inspire award-winning ads and memorable slogans.

Guaranteeing the success of an idea often requires collaboration. Once an idea bounces around in your head, and once you've got it under control, it needs to be bounced off a colleague before it can be molded into a good idea. As discussed in chapters 2 and 3, you need a partner to play the idea game; this is why creatives often work in teams.

Who Are the Creatives?

The creative team is made up of an art director—a visual right-brainer—and one or possibly more copywriters — the verbal left-brainers. This team is responsible for developing the idea, writing ad copy, and designing promotional messages that bring the key consumer benefit to life. The creative team takes these ideas and customizes them to each media vehicle's strengths and limitations. When left- and right-brained people work together, visual and verbal communication becomes a powerful problem-solving combination.

"Creative" as used in this text is a broad term for the conceptual process, as opposed to "creatives," a term commonly used to describe art directors and copywriters. The creative team is composed of some very eclectic personalities. Job titles, which are as diverse as the personalities that fill them, depend on where you are in the country and the size of the agency. We will talk here only about the most commonly accepted titles.

Creative Director. This title probably varies most across the country, but basically these people are team leaders. They handle administrative and management functions and are most often involved with television and other high-profile projects.

Art Director. The art directors are the visual idea people. Job titles range from junior through senior levels. Art directors are the workhorses of the advertising agency. They have their hands in everything. On any given day they could be working on newspaper, magazine, point-of-purchase (P.O.P.), direct mail, television, digital, or out-of-home messages for any number of products or clients. People in this position need to know all the details involved in the creative process, from conceptual development through photo shoots and production.

Copywriter. The copywriters are the verbal idea people. These very talented and creative team members focus on writing copy, and, like art directors, have a range of titles. Copywriters often find themselves brainstorming and writing copy for multiple media vehicles and even more diverse types of products.

Members of the creative team begin the creative process by staring off into space, clearing their minds of all prejudices or preconceived notions about the product or service. Somewhere between here (mind) and there (space), a good idea waits to be discovered and developed. The creative team needs to anticipate the product or service by asking itself all the important questions, or those the target might ask about the product or service, beginning with who, what, when, where, why, and how.

The biggest enemy to creativity is the lack of exploration. If you take shortcuts by failing to fully research both your client and the competition, your ideas will lack focus and be unimaginative.

Great ideas take a lot of work; once you think you've found a direction that will solve the client's problem, you'll do a lot of reworking to perfect it.

Once the creative team has analyzed the brief and come up with a few ideas that merit further development, the next step is to give the ideas a visual/verbal voice. Each idea will have a personality and image assigned to it through the use of type, overall layout, color, and visual images. Let's take a look at what it takes to bring an idea to print or production.

Understanding the Stages of Design

In this section, we'll look at four stages of the design process: concept, thumbnails, roughs, and super comprehensives.

Concept

The first stage in the design process is brainstorming or concept development. Concept sets the strategic tone and direction for a single message or a combination of advertising and promotional messages. This is where bad ideas come to die, and good ideas get a second look and perhaps an overhaul and facelift. It's also where daydreams begin to surface. Here, the creative team hammers out sometimes hundreds of ideas, only 10 percent of which will bear further development.

Thumbnails

Thumbnails, or "thumbs," are the second stage in the design process. Word lists or other brainstorming techniques, as previously discussed, play an important role in thumbnail development. Ideas generated there become a reality at this stage.

Thumbnails are small, proportionate drawings (usually measuring around the size of a business card) that are used to place your concept ideas down on paper. Each thumbnail idea should reflect your key consumer benefit and include directions for expressing the strategy and tone. Each should reflect a different headline, subhead, and visual; no two should sound or look alike.

The word "doodle" best describes what a thumbnail should look like. Diverse headlines, visuals, and layout styles should offer varied solutions to further develop your strategy.

You will rarely have a single thumb that ends up as the final design choice. It is more likely that two or more will be combined to create the overall look of the final ad. The point is to have multiple options for the creative team to discuss and compare with the parameters laid out in the creative brief.

Being able to work fast is critical in design. Developing a thought and then quickly sketching a thumbnail wipes out the pressure and anxiety associated with a blank page.

Roughs

Roughs, or "layouts," are the third stage in the design process, and they are chosen from your best thumbnail ideas. Roughs are often presented to the client, especially an established client. Roughs are done full-size, when possible, and are done in color, if relevant.

Depending on the media, each rough should include a different headline that highlights the key consumer benefit and strategic direction, a possible supporting subhead, and visuals and layout style if presenting multiple concepts. If you are creating a campaign series, each series should include at least three pieces, and the concept based off the strategy and the key consumer benefit should be evident in the headline, theme, character representative, repetitive layout style, and typeface.

Because clients see roughs and review all ideas, they should be tight, clean, and accurate. It is important they be checked against the creative brief to be sure the ads or promotional devices are both on-target and on-strategy before presentation to the client. Professional-looking layout and conceptual skills should shine here. The account executive will present the client with three to five design options at this stage. However, it is rare for any ad to make it past the client in its original form. Most likely, it will be sent back to creative for minor tweaks—or worse, a major overhaul.

Super Comprehensives

The fourth and final stage in the design process is known as super comprehensives, or "super comps." Although not technically a part of the design process, super comps are created from your final roughs. They are generated on the computer with all headlines, subheads, photographs and illustrations, a logo and—for the first time—completed body copy in place, simulating exactly how the finished design will look and read.

Ideally, the super comp will mimic the rough as closely as possible; however, this is where most minor changes made by the client will be addressed before going to press or into production.

Building a Product's Visual/Verbal Personality

There are no rules as to how an ad or promotion should look. The only guidelines are those set by the medium in which the ad or promotion will appear or any printing or promotional restrictions.

Begin by taking another look at your strategy, and then consider how that idea could be delivered and initially perceived. Readability and legibility issues will also play a key role in your choice of layout style, typeface, and visual. Readability is achieved when viewers can read an ad at a glance. Legibility refers to whether, in that short look, they understood the message. Many of the components appearing in the ad are of equal importance; it's the art director's job to organize the various components into a cohesive package.

For a retail account, components might include a screaming headline, sale dates, grand openings, new locations, and multiple products—each needing descriptive copy or price points. Usually several photographs or illustrations will be needed to show the products. You may also need to add detailed copy and a logo that will not get lost along the way. Each additional component will help you determine how the varied components will be displayed.

Organizing components is the key to success in any medium. Remember, even though an ad is cluttered, there must be one dominant image. It is the art director's job to decide what that one dominant element should be, based on information found in the creative brief. A large headline personalizes the message, showing the product alone, in use, or in a setting, allows the consumer to interact with the product. Alternative or electronic media are great opportunities to showcase a slogan or catch phrase.

Elements That Make Up an Ad. What Goes Where?

There is no right or wrong answer to the question of what goes where in a design. An ad or promotion can be nothing more than a visual, or it can be extremely copy-heavy. As long as it is informative, advances both the strategy and the product's image, and creates interest in the minds of the consumers, you're on the right track.

Any ad or promotion can be made up of the following five elements: 1) headline, 2) subhead(s), 3) visual(s), 4) body copy, and 5) logo. Not every element needs to be present in every ad; however, order is somewhat predetermined.

The order in which elements appear depends on the strategy being emphasized. If the headline has a great consumer benefit or is extremely important to the ad's direction, then it must go first; place it at the top of the design. If the visual says more than words can, place it at the top of the design. This thought process helps you to determine which element should be the dominant element on the page.

Controlling the order of what target members see and read aids them in understanding the advertised message.

Readability, Legibility, and Design

One of the greatest challenges to advertisers is convincing people that they need advertising. Very few people will admit to wanting to see advertising. So it's important to make sure, when readers are glancing at a newspaper, flipping through a magazine, scrolling through a webpage, or participating in a promotion, that the advertiser's message is clear enough to be quickly read and understood. A designer's goal is to get the reader or viewer to stop and spend time with an ad or promotion by reading it from start to finish.

The choice of type style and the printable surface, and the use of white space, dominant elements, and color, to name a few, can all affect the ease with which a message can be understood and acted upon. It's important that all advertising be legible at a glance.

White Space. Every well-designed ad or promotion should have white space. This refers to the white of the background surface, which is used in setting off and organizing elements contained in the design as well as bringing order to chaos. White space frames your design and creates an elegant, sophisticated look. The less white space an ad or promotion has, the more cluttered or disjointed it appears. The amount of white space you use will depend on your strategy and the overall look you are trying to achieve. Effective use of white space is the key to an organized design that enhances readability and legibility.

The strategic use of white space is our first line of attack in the battle for readership. White space creates a stopping place for the eye, making reading easier. White space also brings order to any surface.

The lack of white space in an ad can indicate the quality of the store and the products it sells. In the consumer's mind, clutter means low budget. It's important to remember that it's not always about what you say, but about how the viewer perceives it.

Dominant Elements. Visuals tell the story in pictures. Every ad or promotion needs to have a dominant element, one thing that really draws the viewer's eye. This element can be a headline, a visual, or a grouping of visuals. Not everything in an ad or a promotion is of equal importance, even though the client may think so. Only one visual or verbal element can advance your strategy, and your key consumer benefit, and it should be obvious.

A dominant visual can free up the whole page. Visual options include featuring the product with or without a background, in use, placed in a setting, or all alone on the page. A dominant visual can be created by taking multiple related visuals and grouping them, thus creating a presence with weight. Use visuals as the dominant design element when you have something important to show your viewers. Use a headline when what you have to say is more important to the target than what you have to show.

Whichever option you choose—headlines or visuals—the dominant design element must have a point. It should work to further promote the visual/verbal message.

Once all the elements are in place, there are a few additional ways to express the product or service's personality stylistically. Visual options include such things as photography, illustrations, color, layout style, and logo design. Verbal options include choice of typeface and type style, and any character representatives or spokespersons used. Let's take a look at each one.

The Visual Parts of Design

The visual chosen for any creative piece is important. It should take into consideration the medium (or media) to be used, as well as the product or service to be advertised. The visual the target eventually sees is a representation of the client's product or service, and it reflects the brand's personality or campaign strategy. Designers can decide how to present that image—perhaps through the realism of photography, or with the artistic expression of an illustration or graphic design. A more simplistic approach can be achieved with black-and-white line art, or budget constraints might call for clip or stock art. Whatever image becomes the visual voice of your client's product, it should support your strategy, headline, and key consumer benefit, and reflect both the target's and the product's image.

Photography. Believability is one reason to use photographs. Unfortunately, photography can be expensive, especially color photography. The decision to include a photograph instead of an illustration or line art depends on the strategy, the image of the product or service, and the medium.

The visual reality offered by photographs allows readers to see patterns, textures, quality, and color as if the product were sitting before them. The idea of visual variety offers designers the option to showcase the product alone or in use, placed in a relevant setting, or being compared to a similar product.

There is no better way to create a mood, project a product's attributes, or conjure up emotions than with photographs, especially those with people in them. Although photographs take time to set up and shoot, consumers may prefer them in ads promoting services such as banking and investing, or those featuring food products. Photographs can more easily show the product being used, allowing consumers to envision themselves using the product or service.

Using a photograph gives credibility to a product, as do the models featured in them. Don't use anyone who appears unlikely to use the product or service. Be sure models are suitably dressed and are the right age and sex.

Black-and-White Photographs. Why use black-and-white photos when you can use color? One reason is price. It is much less expensive to use a black-and-white photograph than a color photograph. Another reason is that a black-and-white photograph stands out against a lot of color. This independence in appearance attracts the reader's attention.

Black-and-white photographs are also excellent mood or attitude setters. Some topics, such as drinking and driving, or the horrific results from such behavior, are more painful to view in color. Sadness or isolation, even the passing of time, can be represented best in black and white—especially in contrast to all the bright colors on adjacent pages or in other locations.

Some organizations, especially charities, do not wish to look too affluent or wasteful when soliciting donations. They might prefer black-and-white photography to color. Fashion ads in black and white are certainly a contrast. They stop readers, making them spend just a minute longer on this anomaly.

Spot Color. An excellent alternative to full-color photographs is black-and-white photographs that feature a spot of color. The result is referred to as spot color. This is an excellent way to highlight the product by making it stand out in stark contrast to the rest of the photograph. Spot color can give a visual the illusion of three-dimensionality. By adding a spot of color to the photograph, the designer can control eye flow, drawing the viewer's eye directly to the product.

The choice to use photographs in any media, especially color photographs, requires a large budget. However, color photography at any level, such as spot color—is worth the price. It brings an ad alive and helps to create interest and involvement from the consumer.

Clip or Stock Art. Using either clip art or stock art is a great option when money is tight. Clip art is an existing line art drawing. Stock art is existing photographs of all varieties that can be purchased and then used. These terms are often used interchangeably. The only problem with using clip or stock art is the small chance that it may have been used in another ad. To make your clip or stock art unique, try combining one or more photos or cropping unwanted areas.

Illustrations. Illustrations, unlike line art, have tonal qualities. So they are more like a photograph. But unlike photographs, illustrations are created rather than reproduced. With illustrations, advertisers can take a more analytical approach—by presenting charts and graphs—or a lighter approach—by creating characters to represent the product.

The choice between using an illustration or a photograph is an interpretive one. Photographers capture reality, but if you want something more imaginative, an illustration can create reality. If you are looking for a nostalgic, homey look, you might choose an illustrator with a Norman Rockwell or Grandma Moses style. If your concept calls for a retro approach, you may look for someone who uses a Peter Max or Andy Warhol style.

Illustrations can create a mood or trend as easily as a photograph. Depending on the style and color, they can represent a laid-back or upbeat approach.

The choice between an illustration and a photograph also depends on the product or service. For anything that features customer service, an emotional appeal, or food products, consider photographs. To create personality, think illustrations. For ambiance, it's a toss-up. One thing is for sure: illustrations and graphics are less expensive design options than four-color photographs.

Line Art. Black-and-white line art consists of a line drawing that has no tonal qualities. A drawing is a great choice when your ad is spotlighting products with small details, such as lace tablecloths or delicate china patterns. Drawings simplify a design and create a strong black-and-white contrast on any surface.

Graphic Design. Graphic design uses a combination of visuals and type to colorfully, symbolically, and uniquely represent an idea or concept. Graphics have great potential when color is an option. If your client's product is youthful or modern, consider using a more expressive or energetic approach. Graphic design represents life and situations abstractly. Design styles and color usage can re-create time periods and suggest liberal or conservative views. Bold, colorful graphics suggest youth and energy, while subdued colors reflect relaxation and stability. Bright colors, often chosen for their symbolic meaning, can be combined with both geometric and organic shapes to create modern and bold designs. These shapes when presented together are often disjointed, and they are used to create an alternative view of life. When set off by a lot of white space, this design style screams new, bold, or eclectic, especially if the advertising surrounding it uses a more traditional approach.

If you need something simpler, a graphic can also be nothing more than a single divider line between columns of copy, a graphic box used to highlight copy points, or a logo design.

In the end, successful advertising efforts that attract attention are "memorable" and initiate action, accomplish the stated objectives, strategically advance the key consumer benefit, successfully answer the consumer's question, and show consumers why they should buy.

The Meaning of Color

Effective color choices can be used as design elements. Certain colors evoke specific emotions and can be used to set a mood or attract the eye. In the unfortunate event the target should forget the product name, often the unique color combinations on packaging can help with recall when determining which product to purchase.

Color can make us feel warm, cold, stressed, or lethargic. We know the sun should be yellow and the sky blue. The elegance, reassurance, or casualness of a color comes from our life experiences. We see life in color and use it to describe an event, an emotion, the passage of time, or life and death.

When using color, be sure it does not compete with other colors on the page, but instead complements the mood you are trying to create. Elegance is portrayed with more white than color. Red and yellow are hot. Blue is cool and green is natural. Be careful not to use too much color, or the ad or promotional device can become stressful or look gaudy to readers.

Placement on the Page

Layout style, or how elements are featured or placed in the design, determines what your concept will say about itself. Will you be using lots of white space, for an elegant feel? Will you insert a dominant photograph to draw the viewer's attention? Are you incorporating multiple small illustrations, scattered throughout the copy, to instruct the viewer how to use the product or service? Do you want to section off the ad to show the viewer multiple benefits?

Think of layout styles as the clothes for your concept. Does it shout sporty, sophisticated, or modern? Does it demand attention through words, or is a visual worth a thousand words? When you're designing, it's important to consider what you want the ad to project visually to the consumer, as well as what it says.

The Logo and Slogan as a Visual/Verbal Symbol

A discussion about visual/verbal relationships would be incomplete without a discussion of logos. A logo is the symbol—and ultimately the image—of a company or product, and should be prominently displayed on any creative piece. A logo can consist of nothing more than the company or product name represented typographically; it can also be a graphic symbol or a combination of type and graphic. A logo's graphic means nothing until positioning gives it meaning.

Sharoz Makarechi, founder and creative director of Think Tank 3, talks about the idea and image behind the logo design for Total Immersion (fig. 6.1):

> The logo is not exactly a shark, because it has no teeth. It's kind of a person with a cap on whose arms are becoming more like fins. It's suggestive. That's what logos are supposed to be. It's not a figurative logo. It's a shape that's reminiscent of a fin on a shark, possibly, something that's moving forward, clearly. The lines are also smooth as well as sharp. It's a difficult thing to manage. There's a bit of a feeling of flight and movement towards it. It's a lot of nuance of details to get to this one mark, so that it represents this whole company and all of these different products that they have.[2]

Slogans. Memorable slogans give voice to a company's philosophy or a product or service's overall image. The slogan must aid in positioning the product. It must say what the target needs to know about the company or product. Good slogans have longevity and add to a product's brand image, thus building brand equity.

One of the ways to make a product memorable is to tie the slogan to a product or service's image. It should make an association through visual/verbal cues. Consider how a product works or when the product is used: Some kind of word association, pun, or rhyming scheme may be memorable and representative. By using visual/verbal cues, the slogan represents a product's image and message.

Figure 6.1.   This abstract image subtly suggests the lengthening of a swimmer's arms to be more finlike as the stroke technique becomes more efficient.

thinktank ³ | A MODERN DAY THINK-SHOP   contact: harris@thinktank3.com   info: Logo for Total Immersion

Image courtesy of Think Tank 3ᵃ

Slogans are meant to last a long time, but there are few that have lasted longer than the Maxwell House coffee slogan "Good to the last drop." It was first used by the Coca-Cola Company in 1908, and its origin can be traced back to a statement made by Theodore Roosevelt to a party guest to describe the coffee he was drinking.

The Verbal Parts of a Design

Typeface. The typeface used in an ad, for example, is as important as the message itself. Understanding the visual message of type is critical to building or maintaining a brand's image.

The choice of typeface should reflect the personality of the product or service. Type is not a whimsical or temporary choice. Like layout style, once a typeface is chosen, it should appear in every ad—no matter what the media vehicle.

The typeface should become a representative device for that product or service. Type is an art form of shapes, curves, circles, and lines. Making these elements a part of your product's personality is an extension of the conceptual process. An ad's type should also reflect its target audience. Bigger type and less formal layouts work well when attracting younger consumers, whereas cleaner, more structured layouts work well in attracting older consumers.

Type Styles and Identifiers. There are two distinct varieties of type styles, serif and san serif. A serif typeface has feet or delicate appendages that protrude from the edges of the letters, as in the type you're now reading. These appendages can appear at the top or bottom of a letter. San serif type has no appendages.

Type is categorized by its typeface. Typeface refers to type of a specific uniform design. A typeface is part of a larger type family, which includes all the sizes and styles of that typeface. A font consists of a complete character set in one typeface and style: for example, all italic upper- and lowercase letters, numbers, and punctuation.

Almost every typeface comes in varying weights. Weight represents the thickness of the typeface's body. These weights include ultra light, light, book, medium, demi bold, bold, ultra bold, and ultra black, to name just a few.

The Language of Type. Different type designs reflect different images, moods, or even genders. Serif typefaces, because of their delicate lines, have a more feminine appeal. San serif typefaces boast straight, unadorned lines that give them a more masculine appearance. This masculine/feminine appeal can sometimes be achieved using differing weights of the same typeface. For example, Helvetica, a san serif typeface, comes in so many weights that Helvetica Light—a stately, tall, and thin typeface—bears little resemblance to the bulky, stout-looking Helvetica Ultra Bold. Serif typefaces such as Goudy—a round, elegant, yet squat typeface—can represent both masculine and feminine products. The best place to begin when determining which typeface and style to use is to match likely candidates to the creative strategy, the product's personality, or the tone of the ad, and experiment from there.

Type Design Rules of Thumb. When designing, the number of typefaces used in an ad should be controlled. The basic rule of thumb is two typefaces per design. The headline, subhead(s), announcement devices, and any prices are usually set in the same typeface. The body copy and descriptive copy are set in another. As a rule, smaller copy blocks such as body or descriptive copy are set in a serif face for ease of reading. There is no limit on the different weights that can be used within a design, but common sense should rule the day.

Although there are no hard-and-fast rules about mixing serif and san serif typefaces within an ad, it is best to use one style throughout. The number of point sizes in an ad should also be controlled. An ad with multiple faces in various styles and sizes takes on a circus feel and is perceived as inexpensive or low-end. However, any device, if used consistently and repetitively, avoids the need to play by the rules.

Logos are a graphic element and are not considered a typeface. They do not need to match the style of the advertised message.

Type as a Graphic Element. If you look at type—*really* look—you will see its beauty beyond content. Its form alone is a graphic device. Each typeface portrays a personality, an individualism that takes shape via content. The very randomness of the letterforms creates a uniform message with character and flair. Whether it's childish, traditional, expensive, or shabby chic, each typeface awaits the shape and expression given it by the designer.

A typeface's personality should strategically match the image projected by the product or service and the image of the target audience. However you decide to manipulate type—whether by condensing or expanding it, or by increasing or decreasing letter, word, or line spacing, type size, or line length—readability and legibility should take precedence over design.

Spokespeople and Character Representatives

When you have something you want to say visually, consider using a visual voice in the form of a spokesperson or animated character representative.

The spokesperson for any product is important. He or she must be likeable, with an appearance that fits the campaign's overall visual/verbal concept. To determine an appropriate spokesperson, ask yourself: Who does this product remind me of? Remember, it's your product's personality that sets it off from the competition, especially if there are no major differences between brands in the same category.

There are three basic types of spokespersons.

1. Celebrities
2. Specialists and CEOs
3. Common Man

Celebrities. A celebrity's popularity with younger target audiences can be transferred to a product, and this popularity can actually build a product's brand equity. It is important that the celebrity's professional image be tied to the product's strategic direction. This image translates to the product, so any character flaws that arise in a celebrity over time will reflect upon the product. Celebrity endorsements can be broken down into five different areas:

1. Unpaid Onscreen Spokesperson
2. Paid Onscreen Spokesperson
3. Celebrity Voiceover

4. Dead-Person Endorsement
5. Animated Character Representative

Unpaid Onscreen Spokesperson. Charities supported by the celebrity are the usual benefactors of an unpaid onscreen spokesperson.

Paid Onscreen Spokesperson. A paid onscreen spokesperson is one of the most common types of spokespersons. A celebrity is paid to tie his or her image to a product and physically represent it in all advertising efforts.

Celebrity Voiceover. This type of spokesperson is used for radio and television. Voiceovers are a less expensive use of spokespersons because they deliver the message offscreen and the celebrity is not identified or seen.

Dead-Person Endorsement. Dead people can't speak, but their images can. The use of old interviews or movie clips can associate personality traits, activism, and even nostalgia with a product. The use of this type of spokesperson is very controversial and often considered in bad taste.

Animated Character Representative. Believe it or not, the Keebler Elves and the Pillsbury Doughboy are celebrities. We like them, we trust them, and they have been around so long that we consider them friends. They might make us feel a little nostalgic, and we may even associate their images with specific events.

Specialists and CEOs. If something needs to be proven, use specialists in the field, like doctors, scientists, or engineers. If you want to develop a philosophy, create a friendship, or instill trust, use a CEO or owner of a small company or business.

Common Man. The common man can be an everyday person who uses the product and can talk about his or her experiences, or a paid actor representing the common man based on feedback from real consumers. One famous example, discussed in greater detail in chapter 8, is Jared Fogle, who lost 245 pounds eating at Subway. Why use an actor when you can use a real, common man? This type of advertisement has nothing to do with trying to deceive the public and everything to do with how the message is delivered. A trained actor will be able to deliver the message with less effort and with more believability. Any time a substitution is made, it must be stated in the ad. That said, common man endorsements are becoming more frequent. It is thought that celebrities, with all their power and faults, have saturated the market and are becoming less believable. They also limit the length of time a campaign can run: star power rarely lasts as long as a product's does.

Personality Traits for an Effective Spokesperson

In order to reach out and touch the target, the character or spokesperson must resonate with the target. If consumers don't like or respect the image or person delivering the message, they will tune out. We all search for people like ourselves, so personality traits should reflect the target's self-image and life-style. When developing a character or hiring a spokesperson, consider the following traits:

1. Appearance
2. Likeability
3. Trustworthiness
4. Expertise
5. Credibility

Character representatives begin in an art director's imagination, much like a live spokesperson does. The choice to use a live person or to create a character spokesman has more to do with strategy and less to do with budget.

There are times when you can't find an actor who fits the client's direction or the art director's conceived personality for the product. When you can't find it, you create it. Budget can also affect whether a spokesperson will be local talent or a celebrity. But at any level, live talent is more expensive to maintain than a character on a page.

Character representatives or "icons" may come from word association, folk-lore, historical characters or events, or even people from an art director's past experiences. Character reps are easy to work with; they have no demands, are never late, and never grow old. Their images can and often do last longer than those of live spokespeople. Here are a few character representatives you may recognize:

1. Aunt Jemima
2. The GEICO Gecko
3. The Energizer Bunny
4. The Jolly Green Giant
5. The Keebler Elves
6. Charlie the Tuna
7. Mr. Clean
8. The Pillsbury Doughboy
9. Tony the Tiger
10. Snuggle
11. The Charmin Bear

It is important to remember that you want the campaign to run for a long period of time, perhaps decades. If you keep in mind how the concept can grow and mature over time, you can almost guarantee the campaign will have staying power. This is one of the reasons to stay away from current trends and celebrities and create your own trends and your own celebrities through spokespersons or character representatives.

Are You On-Target and On-Strategy?

In the end, an effective creative series must be on-target and on-strategy, both visually and verbally, throughout the varied types of ads and media. The creative team must ask itself, throughout the creative development stages, if the creative is still on target with the stated objectives. Is the creative strategy effectively reflecting those objectives? Has the creative brief successfully dissected the product or service in order to understand its features and benefits? Is the visual/verbal message screaming out the key consumer benefit and strategy? If the answer to all of the above questions is yes, the creative efforts are on-target and on-strategy.

Ineffective creative has diverted from the strategy, key benefit, or stated objectives. If the visual look and the verbal message are inconsistent, and if the key consumer benefit is not apparent on all pieces, the creative is off-target and off-strategy.

Great concepts and successful creative must be on-target. Advertising that is off-target can be very entertaining, oftentimes even brilliant, but if it doesn't create sales and raise awareness, it's useless.

Notes

1. Denis Higgins, *The Art of Writing Advertising: Conversations with the Masters of the Craft* (Chicago: NTC Business Books, 1965), 64.
2. Sharoz Makarechi, personal communication, February 13, 2008.

Image Credit

a. "T.I. Guy" logo for Total Immersion created by Sharoz Makarechi and Matthew Dugas at Think Tank 3.

CHAPTER 7

Where Campaigns and Brands Go off Course

◇ ◇ ◇

You can't bore people into buying. —David Ogilvy[1]

Why Some Campaigns Wander Off-Strategy

Some campaign messages fail for a variety of reasons. They may underestimate the loyalty of the brand's audience. The may create a vague, innocuous message. They may create a campaign that creates panic. They develop controversial, offensive, vulgar, overtly sexual, or racially charged campaigns. They may be unclear or inaccurate in other languages. They may be perceived as unethical, or too simple, or too easy to mock. There are other reasons as well. Below is a short list of some of the most easily recognizable campaign problems.

◇ ◇ ◇

Reasons for Strategic Dilemmas

1. Disregards brand loyalty ("New Coke")
2. Lack of clarity (Burger King—"Where's Herb?")
3. Causes panic (Cartoon Network—"Aqua Teen Hunger Force")
4. Offensive or controversial material ("United Colors of Benetton")

5. Ethnic derision (www.SalesGenie.com)
6. Overtly sexual reference (Carl's Jr. "Paris car wash")
7. Oversimplification of problem ("Just Say No" to drugs)
8. Questionable ethics (Wal-Mart "flog")
9. Cultural confusion (Nova car name)
10. Easy-to-create parody ("Make 7-Up Yours")

1. Disregards Brand Loyalty

In April of 1985, when marketing executives at Coca-Cola introduced New Coke, they broke the cardinal rule: Never forget brand loyalty. They were giving loyal Coke drinkers an updated variation of their beloved drink. What happened to Coke, the real thing? Loyal Coke fans love the taste. That's why they choose it over Pepsi. Their reaction to the change to New Coke was a resounding thumbs down.[2] They felt betrayed. They felt insulted. They practically felt abused. Touching the coveted Coke formula was an irreverent, almost heretical act. Before you take something away and replace it, the key question is: Does your audience want a change?

Coca-Cola wasn't the only cola that wandered off course. Around five years later, during a movement for clear products that projected purity, including the 1993 introduction of Miller Brewing Company's Clear Beer, Pepsi promoters fell into the same trap as Coke. They developed an all-new Pepsi, promising the same great taste, but in an all-clear version: Crystal Pepsi. What did the Pepsi loyalists say? "Nay, no thanks!" When they buy cola, they expect it to be the color of cola, not the color of a lemon-lime drink. Between the early 1990s and the first years of 2000, other clear beverages and products emerged. Many companies unsuccessfully launched new products, like Coors's clear malt Zima and Amoco's clear fuels, the Crystal Clear Ultimate line, which was presented under the "Your car knows" slogan. However, clear dishwashing products like Ivory's clear dishwashing liquid and competitor Colgate's Sensitive Skin dishwashing liquid fared better.

2. Lack of Clarity

Sometimes an idea that seems very clear to the creative team doesn't make sense to the consumer. If all advertising or marketing campaigns had one objective in common, it would be to deliver understandable messages. However, as a creative talent, when you're working on creative ideas, you have volumes of background information in your mind. The problem is that the audience is never privy to any of that. They only receive the final communication. So if that message is vague or too obtuse, the audience simply doesn't "get it."

In the 1980s, a brand wandered off course. This time it was the advertising message itself. Vague, confusing, and basically unclear, Burger King's "Where's Herb?" campaign (1985 through 1986) left the audience bewildered. When the commercials asked, "Where's Herb?" no one knew who Herb was, what he looked like, why they would want to find him, or even what the point was. It was dubbed the "most elaborate advertising flop of the decade ['80s]," by *Advertising Age* magazine. If someone were to find Herb, the discoverer would receive $5,000. Even more vague were the clues to find Herb: "I'm not Herb because I eat at Burger King."

The campaign wasn't relevant or clear, but the reaction was unmistakable: pure disdain. After a negative backlash, Burger King finally disclosed that Herb was a nerd with tape on his glasses in a tightly fitted suit. At that point no one really cared. It was so confusing that people thought that only geeky guys ate at Burger King.[3]

3. Causes Panic

Some campaigns inadvertently create mass panic. When a campaign introduces guerrilla tactics—those catch-the-consumer-wherever-they-are messages, including sidewalks, staircase backs, escalator sides, and even urinals—sometimes placing unidentifiable objects with cryptic, specifically targeted messages in unexpected places can cause public alarm.

On January 31, 2007, a guerrilla marketing campaign went awry when Turner Broadcasting's Cartoon Network attempted to promote its late-night cartoon program, "Aqua Teen Hunger Force," featuring two pals: Frylock, a box of French fries, and Master Shake, a milkshake. The marketers expected fans to recognize the cartoon characters, which appeared on electronic devices that looked like circuit boards with external wires that were placed along bridge overhangs and in subways in Boston and nine other cities. Unfortunately, these devices, with their alien-type icons—later identified as Mooninites from the TV show—looked like bombs. An all-city alert was launched, calling in local bomb squads, shutting roads, and creating fear. Although the campaign, which was planned for a ten-city run, garnered a tremendous amount of attention, it also caused an unnecessary panic and sense of emergency in a highly sensitized post-9/11 era.[4]

This panic was not unlike the one Orson Welles inadvertently created in his electrifying delivery on the 1938 CBS radio show in which he dramatized an H. G. Wells science fiction novel, *The War of the Worlds*, about an imminent

Martian invasion. What made it even scarier was that the show aired the day before Halloween.[5]

4. Offensive or Controversial Material

Campaigns can also unintentionally offend an audience with inappropriate or insensitive messages. One Sony campaign was even accused of racist tones for a 2006 billboard in Holland that introduced the new PlayStation Portable (PSP) white model using what many felt were racial overtones. The image showed a white female avatar aggressively holding the face of a black female avatar, portraying a violent interaction between the two. It was supposed to contrast the difference between the new white ceramic model and the existing black PSP model. Although it may have tried to depict the white PSP model wrestling for market dominance over the black PSP model, unfortunately it wasn't perceived that way. People saw people, not gadgets, in a physically hostile exchange. Although this was only one of more than a hundred images included in this campaign, this one particular image created a strong negative backlash. Sony eventually admitted this billboard was a blunder.[6]

Starting in the mid-1980s, Benetton generated seemingly endless negative press over its ongoing "United Colors of Benetton" campaigns, with striking images by celebrated photographer Oliviero Toscani. Some people found some of these ad images so distasteful, they felt compelled to protest outside the stores in Europe. What Benetton wanted to do was draw attention, through seemingly shocking images, to social issues. In 2005, another ad, which showed a homosexual couple moving into kiss, ran in Italy much to the vociferous outrage of local parents and the irritation of the Vatican.[7] As recently as 2007, a Benetton ad showed an image of an emaciated, anorexic woman.

Benetton's highly publicized images from various campaigns fall into several categories, as discussed on Benetton's website. These images include a black woman breastfeeding a white baby; a black horse mounting a white one; a newly born baby, still unwashed with the umbilical cord still intact, to name a few. These ads depict the idea that anything natural cannot be considered vulgar. Deemed equally offensive was an ad that portrayed a naked buttock branded with an "HIV Positive" stamp.

One Benetton ad showed a young Jewish boy and a young Arab boy with their arms on each other's shoulders. Another ad showed a priest and nun kissing. These images were part of the "cycle of difference" series and depicted polar opposites, including good and evil, as well as young people of totally different and often conflicting cultures. In the "cycle of reality" series one ad depicted a man, David Kirby, dying from AIDS, on his deathbed and surrounded by his grieving family.[8]

Although each of these and other ad campaign images created controversy, they also drew attention to social taboos, various forms of prejudice, global health challenges like AIDS, and other societal issues. What many people never realized was that Benetton has sponsored many social, artistic, educational, and cultural activities and has supported global organizations that deal with poverty, hunger, and social injustice, including the World Food Program, United Nations Volunteers, *SOS Racisme*, and the International Federation of the Red Cross.[9]

5. Ethnic Derision

Another way campaigns can be offensive is if they mock groups of people because of their ethnicity or nationality. Using cartoon animation with stereotypes for ethnic groups, especially mimicking their accents, was a problem for the 2008 Super Bowl SalesGenie.com ads. One spot showed a salesman, Ramesh, being ordered by his boss to double his sales or he would be fired. Pleading to his boss in a thick Indian accent, Ramesh begged not to be fired because he had seven children. Another spot emphasized workers' Chinese accents and featured two pandas: Ching Ching and Ling Ling. They were worried that their store, Ling Ling's Bamboo Furniture Shack, would go out of business without more sales.

Although the spots focused on the dilemma workers face with low sales and how SalesGenie.com could solve the problem by providing one hundred sales leads, the message was lost because people were affronted by the fake foreign accents and the worker stereotypes. Again, what may seem funny to some people is often found offensive to the group being mocked.[10] Special care must be taken to empathize with people from all cultural backgrounds and to learn to appreciate their particular viewpoints, even if they are not openly shared.

6. Overtly Sexual Reference

Okay, everyone knows sex sells, but how far can a campaign go before it's crossed the line? One particular TV commercial, the 2005 Carl's Jr. spot "Paris Car Wash" with Paris Hilton washing a car in a tiny swimsuit dripping in soap suds, caught the media off guard. The closing superimposed lines on a black screen were "The spicy BBQ burger," followed by "That's hot," Hilton's signature phrase. There's no denying that the ad created a great deal of attention and put Carl's Jr. on the map for more than its burgers.

Another campaign, which aired from 2006 through 2008, used a strongly rhythmic jingle, "Ride It Like a Ford," paired with sexy girls smiling with their dates. The music and the visuals were strongly suggestive and could be criticized for being too sexually overt. Apparently some viewers want more subtlety from advertisers. Parodies of the "Ride It Like a Ford" campaign were created and uploaded to YouTube, as were those of other campaigns discussed in this section.

7. Oversimplification of Problem

Public service announcements (PSAs) that try to change consumer behavior can be very effective, as in the Mothers against Drunk Driving (MADD) commercials of adorable home videos of children having fun before they lost their lives as a result of being hit by drunk drivers. However, some PSAs, like former first lady Nancy Reagan's "Just Say No" campaign, which ran from the mid-1980s through the early 1990s, oversimplify the problem for addicts, casual users, and curious bystanders. People addicted to drugs can't just say no. Just as many can't instantly quit smoking. A physical addiction is an undeniable craving. People using drugs recreationally don't think they have a reason to say no. They think they have their drug use under control. Finally, people of all ages who are told not to do something, especially young adults, invariably find that particular taboo the most intriguing. These are a few of the reasons the "Just Say No" campaign didn't change behavior in the way it was intended.

8. Questionable Ethics

Another place campaigns can go off course is in the misuse of a medium. Take, for example, the furtive corporate use of a personal medium, like blogs. One thing most people can assume about blogs is that they're one person's honest opinion. You can agree or disagree with the comments, but you at least are reasonably sure they're an individual's statements. That all changed in 2006, when Wal-Mart was exposed for using bloggers affiliated with Edelman, the PR firm. Wal-Mart's fake blog was called a "flog" and overnight a new word was born.

The two blogs appeared separately. One was on the home page of Working Families for Wal-Mart (WFWM), an organization designed by Edelman to showcase Wal-Mart's commitment to families through an open forum. The second was on Paid Critics, a WFWM subsidiary site, which exposed Wal-Mart's many harsh critics. The travel blog Wal-Marting through America, which chronicled two bloggers' positive experiences with Wal-Mart as they traveled across the country, was eventually shut down. The hidden truth that the two bloggers were writers paid by WFWM hurt Wal-Mart's already damaged reputation.[11] It's very difficult to reestablish a company's credibility once trust is compromised.

9. Cultural Confusion

Other problems can drive campaigns off course when multiple languages are involved, such as slogan translations. Whether the message is changed because of a careless translator or an oversight by a distracted employee, the result is the same: embarrassment. Here are a few cultural bloopers which should serve as a strong reminder to anyone working on a global account.

1. The "Got Milk?" campaign was taken to Mexico and to the California Milk Processor Board's surprise was translated into another kind of milk with the line "Are You Lactating?"
2. The famous General Motors Chevrolet model "Nova" went to Central and South America. The words "no" and "va" together mean "doesn't go" in Spanish. However, there are conflicting reports as to the veracity of this translation because most people say *no funciona*, rather than *no va*, when a car or mechanical device doesn't work.[12]
3. Another famous slogan mishap was the introduction of Clairol's curling iron, the "Mist Stick," into Germany, where the word "mist" meant manure in the vernacular, so the name was turned into the "Manure Stick."[13]
4. When Gerber sent baby food to Africa, they kept the packaging consistent with what they used in America, a cherubic baby's face, only to find out that in many African countries, the picture on the label reflects what's inside the can or jar to facilitate shopping for the many who are illiterate.[14]
5. Electrolux vacuums made one unfortunate faux pas when its Scandinavian company introduced the product into the United States with this unforgettable line: "Nothing sucks like an Electrolux."
6. Finally we come to the campaign in which the Italian translation of Schweppes Tonic Water turned it into this unappetizing name: Schweppes Toilet Water.

10. Easy-to-Create Parody

Creative talents can accidentally create campaigns that can easily fall victim to ridicule. Although it seems obvious now, the "Make 7-Up Yours" creators probably never knew that this line would ultimately be divided into "Make 7" and "Up Yours." It appeared in homemade videos, known now as consumer-created content, and even on T-shirts with "Make 7" on the front and "Up Yours" on the back. A quick search on YouTube will reveal some slick and very humorous parodies of the original "Make 7-Up Yours" commercials. In the process of creating catchy campaigns, even the most seasoned professionals can make an easy-to-poke-fun-at blunder.

Campaigns Can Be Offensive, But On-Strategy

Even though it may be difficult to explain why some people are offended by certain commercials and others aren't, some commercials cross the line of what's generally accepted as tasteful or appropriate behavior.

Cartoon characters, which historically have been associated with brands and used as beloved icons, like Tony the Tiger and the Pillsbury Doughboy, aren't always created to be adorable or endearing. One character, launched in the spring of 2003, was Lamisil's "Digger the Dermatophyte," which some people found disgusting. He was the cartoon monster created to depict a toenail fungus in a way that would remind viewers to take this condition seriously.

Unfortunately, if you're having a snack, seeing this creature and hearing how he can attack toenails could really turn your stomach.[15] Bloggers and their readers called this a stomach-turning ad, labeling Digger "creepy," especially when the monster lifts up the nail accompanied by a creaky door sound effect.[16] Creepy or not, Digger was unforgettable and viewers became more familiar with nail fungus.

In 1998, Pepsi aired two TV spots that, in an attempt to be cool, ended up turning people off. The first one, "Gnat," featured a cartoon bug that began gyrating and singing to the Rolling Stones' hit "Brown Sugar" after drinking just one tiny droplet of Pepsi on top of a bar. The second spot, "Pierced," showed a young guy with soda spurting out of his piercings while he was drinking a Pepsi at a concert. Although both of these spots tried to appeal to a narrow, teenage market, the Generation Next group, they fell short of the mark and looked anything but cool, while alienating Pepsi's wider market.[17]

Even when humor is used, commercials can still be called offensive. Here's an example. The 2006 Haggar slacks "Making Things Right" campaign used an exaggerated response to everyday societal annoyances to show the pant's flexible waistline. To talk to the 30- to 45-year-old regular guy who doesn't know fashion labels, but does know the name of each golf club, friends Pete and Red show how to deal with life's irritations.[18] They demonstrate the pants' flexibility while addressing a few pet peeves: 1) their daughter's deadbeat boyfriends, 2) sexual harassment from female coworkers, 3) their negligent neighbor's overgrown yard, and 4) the always-late cable guy.

Intended to be funny little lessons from Pete and Red, stories that included physically throwing teenage boys out the living room window could be considered as promoting violence. The sexual harassment spot included a role reversal in which female coworkers were making lewd comments to Pete and Red because the men looked so hot in their Haggar slacks, and even included a condescending pat on the behind by one of the women. When dealing with a lazy neighbor's overgrown lawn, Pete and Red shipped in goats to "mow" the lawn. To get even with the perennially late cable guy, they removed the ladder once he was on the roof, demonstrating the slacks' ease of movement. These spots showed a dry sense of humor that some found offensive. It's possible that the target audience, the non-GQ-reading everyday guy, found them funny, and perhaps discovered or rediscovered the comfort of Haggar slacks.

◇ ◇ ◇

Well, sometimes when a group of people work on a creative project together, it becomes a little inbred. Everybody sort of begins thinking alike. That's fine except that you sometimes lose your objectivity and you lose your focus.—Phil Dusenberry[19]

Holding the Strategy to One Specific Orientation

Campaigns can also go off course during the developmental stage. The creative teams might move in a direction that addresses another important consumer benefit, but doesn't answer the main objective. Or they might use an inappropriate tone of voice for that brand. Or they might come up with a direction that will attract media attention, but not address a benefit. These and other quandaries that sometimes steer creative teams off course will also be discussed later in this chapter.

When creative teams look to develop solutions, sometimes there are multiple facets to one strategy, with each one focusing on another aspect of the brand. These different points can inadvertently misdirect the creative teams and cause them to develop an off-strategy message. Scott Linnen, vice president/creative director/copywriter at Crispin Porter + Bogusky, explains the importance of having one accurate assertion to act as a reference point in order to stay on-strategy.

> If you have this one clear statement or clear vision that might have different facets, you can go back to it and test the work and ask questions based on the strategy to make sure you're staying within the zone that you want to be in to create the ads and communication.

To safeguard against going too far forward with an off-strategy idea, copywriter Chris Adams at TBWA\Chiat\Day always looks for campaign ideas that validate the strategy and bring it to life. Here's how he explains how he avoids going off course creatively:

> I don't think it happens that often, because I think once you buy into a strategy as a creative, you understand where you're going with it. Being more of a rational person, I start rationalizing why an idea is working as we're building it. You get more excited about an idea because you see more and more ways that the strategy is coming to life in cool ways.
>
> It's not like it's a self-fulfilling prophesy, but the process of understanding the strategy and building it and baking it into the work I think helps to protect you from getting too far down the path that's not on strategy.

The real question is what happens when there are so many ideas that the team isn't sure if it's headed in the right direction, or if somehow it has wandered away from expressing the main strategic idea. Adams admits that they probably get lost in an off-strategy idea from time to time, but that his team has so many ideas that "you forget about all the little failures you have along the way." Often someone on the account or client side will show them where they wandered off strategy, but "to be successful, you have to quickly move past that."

The ability to let go of an idea that one of the creative talents originally thought was viable allows them to more readily free themselves and press forward for a new solution.

Being Hypnotized by a Great Idea

Some ideas are so exciting that they're almost intoxicating. They can lure a team into a creative stupor because of their power to entice. They seem to hypnotize the team into following a new direction with their creative allure. Eric Springer, executive vice president/group creative director at Deutsch L.A., commented that super ideas can take the creative team off course and change the direction:

> You get off-strategy all the time. You start thinking about what's funny, or what's going to be emotional, or what's going to be exciting to see. It might be very funny, like a monkey hitting someone over the head with a tire iron, but it has nothing to do with why I would want to sign up with DIRECTV because they have high-definition television.

Nowadays, agencies include account and media planners in idea generation or creative strategy validation. The account planners, who act as liaisons between the agency and the client, supervise the account on multiple levels, from defining client objectives and preparing creative briefs to ensuring campaigns meet strategic goals. Media planners, who are in charge of researching, evaluating, and selecting appropriate media vehicles, may even suggest ideas for new media.

Matt Jarvis, who works with Springer as the director of account planning for GM, feels that the account planners need to have flexibility and should not be hard-nosed about sticking to the strategy if it means killing a great idea:

> You'll have situations where you have a great strategy and everyone's on board with it, and excited about it. And then, through the creative process, someone comes up with something that is off strategy. But when you look at it, you say, "That would really work." Creativity is messy. As a strategist, you have to embrace that. In my opinion, there's nothing

more detrimental to the creative process than an overly rigid account planner who judges work based on its integrity to the brief versus commitment to the greater objective.

Flexibility Aids Creativity

Although most agencies begin with the creative brief, the ability to be flexible allows creative teams to give ideas the freedom and power to redirect the overall strategic direction. At Crispin Porter + Bogusky, the account planners—"cultural anthropologists," or cogs for short—work closely with the creative teams in the development of a strategy. In an industry where big ideas rule, it can be beneficial to let them lead, by constantly questioning if the original direction was the best one to choose. CP+B creative Tiffany Kosel and Scott Linnen agree. Kosel confesses, "Sometimes you realize the strategy isn't working." She explains:

> If everyone starts to attack it with the same strategy, and everyone veers off in the same direction to a different strategy, we have to sometimes go back and rethink it. "Is this the right strategy? Is it true to the brand? Is it honest? Is there a reason why we're not *coming up* with ideas?" When you do hit on a great strategy, it's easy to come up with work that pays off.

When the strategy isn't right, they have to go back and "rethink it and tackle it a different way." Linnen said at CP+B, "It's organic. It's constantly changing. It's okay for the strategy to bend and be evolving as you're working on it." Kosel shares how the brief guides the creative solution: "It's just a starting point. It's a way to get to the real, true strategy and a bigger idea. I don't know if that's the same way with every agency." She explains that the strategy is allowed to be flexible. By allowing this flexibility, the strategy becomes lifelike and can almost breathe. At CP+B, she adds:

> It's nice here that it's allowed to be organic because it's really about finding the right place, and the right idea, and the right positioning. If it takes a process of changing it to get to that—working through it—then I think in the end, it becomes stronger.

It's Okay If Another Teams Solves It

Sometimes one team just doesn't find the answer. The team solution wandered off strategy and somehow never found its way back. When this happens to one creative team at Goodby, Silverstein & Partners, senior copywriter Sara Rose and senior art director Lea Ladera have learned to release the campaign and move on. They say it's not difficult to go off course, and usually even better ideas come to mind. Ultimately, because several teams may be working on the same project, they realize they occasionally need to allow another team to move forward in a new direction. Ladera says,

> So, sometimes you can fix [the campaign ideas] if they're still kind of close to the insight. But sometimes, you just have to start over and another team may solve it.

Rose concurs, stating that redirecting yourself is part of the idea-generation phase. "You can wander a little bit." Then they go create lists of ideas and put them into a story format. After that, she says, "you can tell pretty quickly what is working and what's on-strategy and what's not." She goes on to say, "Whoever cracks it, and whoever creates something that the client wants to do, ultimately produces it."

When the Tone of Voice Doesn't Fit the Brand

Sometimes it's not the strategy that's wrong, but the tone of voice that isn't consistent with the brand's. A team can somehow develop a message that the brand wouldn't deliver. Creative directors Carolyn Hadlock and Charlie Hopper from Young & Laramore say they needed to really be careful about the tone of voice for Steak n Shake. Hadlock says that sometimes with clients, but especially with Steak n Shake, "It's not that it's off-strategy in a big way, but it's a nuance in the voice that isn't right. [It's] the voice of the brand. Sometimes I'll hear [Hopper] talk about the nuance of it, which I think is even harder. You're kind of splitting hairs."

This can happen with talents who haven't been working with the client for a long time. They're not fully fluent in the brand's particular voice. So what they're creating is not what would be natural to the brand's everyday speech. Hadlock says they are responsible for maintaining a consistent voice. "We're the keepers of that." Hopper shares these insights:

> Steak n Shake talks in a very nonconformist way. We don't use the typical language of a restaurant or a food kind of service. And you can know that, but you end up, if you haven't been living it, saying things in a boring way, or a formal way, that we would typically undo. There's a definite voice that people have to eventually pick up on.

Each brand has its own individual voice, or the way it would convey a message. Certain brands would or wouldn't say something. Hadlock adds, "The extreme examples would be, nothing is ever 'piping hot' or 'golden brown.' And, nothing is ever 'succulent,' or 'delicious,' or 'tasty.' We just don't say that. We try to stick to the facts, and let you figure out that it would taste good if it were made of real milk, or whatever."

Other agency creative talents also talk about being true to the voice of the brand. Each message must sound natural to the brand's personality. For example, in the Mac versus PC commercials, the Mac actor always sounds relaxed, laid back, and cool, not stiff like the PC actor. So Mac as a brand personality is perceived as the "cool guy" and PC is seen as the "suit."

Eric Springer at Deutsch says messages go off course when they are not aligned with the intrinsic character or basic nature of the brand.

Some of the best spots I've ever seen, and the most award-winning spots, were complete failures, because they didn't take the time up front to pair the perfect creative message with the personality of the client.

An example of this would be if the creative team were developing a campaign for a cardiac unit at a hospital and the message were humorous or whimsical. The facility would be portrayed as taking too casual an approach to something as serious as the life-threatening conditions facing its patients.

◇ ◇ ◇

The art of advertising is getting a message into the heads of most people at the lowest possible cost.—Rosser Reeves[20]

Finding a New Solution to Showcase Other Benefits

Paul Charney, senior copywriter at Goodby, Silverstein & Partners, says he often finds himself going off strategy and discovering a great new idea that strongly represents a new benefit or product attribute. He mentions the possibility of bending the idea to fit the strategy, but acknowledges it can't be forced to fit if it's ultimately addressing another issue or attribute. Charney says, "If you come up with a great idea and everyone's really excited on your team, I think in that scenario, that should not be the only thing you show."

The question then is if you've gone off strategy, should you present that creative work to the client? Or instead show solutions that clearly reflect the strategy? If your work has digressed from the client's objectives, will the client think you haven't fully digested the directives set out by the agency brief?

Charney explains that whenever you show off-strategy work, you need to demonstrate how it will benefit the client's overall goals and showcase another product benefit. It would also be a good idea—if your work ventured off course—to go in armed with research that substantiates the creative digression. He emphasizes that it is important to be candid and open about the work, adding:

> I think it wouldn't be smart to do that [only show the off strategy concept], unless you feel so good about it. If you show something else, you're going to give the client an out, which sometimes you don't want to do.

He says that it might be a good idea to "keep it in your back pocket." This is especially true if you really believe in the idea. He says sometimes helping the brand "could be as simple as getting them a lot of attention." It could be an exceptional PR opportunity that would generate extensive news coverage.

However, when the idea screams to be heard or seen because it is so powerful, so right for the brand, Charney adds, "I think you should show it. If everyone's really excited about it, let's say on the agency's side, you should share it, and recognize it, and be upfront about it."

Ultimately, no matter how wonderful the campaign idea might seem at the time, it is always wise to allow time for it to simmer in its creative juices. This way the creative, account, and media teams can reflect on whether this direction could be offensive to a particular audience; completely off strategy, but still offer a new consumer benefit or garner media attention; confusing to the audience; addressing too narrow a market; or be off course in some other way. Sometimes a transgression very obvious to others may be invisible to the team creating the solutions. It's wise to run ideas past people not involved in the account, and even wiser to show the work to any group being depicted in the campaign.

Notes

1. David Ogilvy, *Confessions of an Advertising Man* (New York: Atheneum, 1981), 97.

2. Michael E. Ross, "It Seemed Like a Good Idea at the Time," MSNBC, April 22, 2005, www.msnbc.msn.com/id/7209828, accessed February 24, 2008.

3. whoworemyclothes.blogspot.com/2007/04/im-not-herb.html, accessed February 24, 2008.

4. Michael Powell, "Marketing Gimmick Goes Bad in Boston. Light Devices Cause Bomb Scare," *Washington Post*, February 1, 2007, A03, www.washingtonpost.com/wp-dyn/content/article/2007/01/31/AR2007013101958.html, accessed March 7, 2008.

5. Stefan Lovgen, "'War of the Worlds': Behind the 1938 Radio Show Panic," *National Geographic News*, June 17, 2005, news.nationalgeographic.com/news/2005/06/0617_050617_warworlds .html, accessed March 10, 2008.

6. Ryan Block, "Sony under Fire for 'Racist' Advertising," Engadget, posted July 6, 2006, www.engadget.com/2006/07/06/sony-under-fire-for-racist-advertising/, accessed March 7, 2008.

7. Barbara McMahon, "Italy Snaps over Gay Poster Excess," *Observer* (Rome), September 18, 2005, www.guardian.co.uk/world/2005/sep/18/gayrights.italy, accessed March 10, 2008.

8. About Benetton campaigns: press.benettongroup.com/ben_en/about/campaigns/history/, accessed March 10, 2008.

9. "About Benetton—Cultural and Social Activities," press.benettongroup.com/ben_en/about/cultural/, accessed March 10, 2008.

10. Lisa Takeuchi Cullen, "SalesGenie's Super Bowl Ads Are Super Offensive to Indian and Chinese Workers," Work in Progress, Worklife, Workplace, *TIME*, February 4, 2008, time-blog.com/work_in_progress/2008/02/salesgenies_super_bowl_ads_are.html, accessed March 4, 2008.

11. Tom Siebert, "Pro-Wal-Mart Travel Blog Screeches to a Halt," *Media Post Publications*, October 12, 2006, publications.mediapost.com/index.cfm?fuseaction=Articles.showArticle&art_aid=49698, accessed March 5, 2008.

12. Gerald Erichsen, "The Chevy Nova That Didn't Go. Commonly Told Tale Is Just an Urban Legend," About.com, spanish.about.com/cs/culture/a/chevy_nova_2.htm, accessed March 5, 2008.

13. www.4to40.com/fastforward/index.asp?id=468, accessed March 5, 2008.

14. moronland.net/moronia/moron/1064/, accessed March 5, 2008.

15. Rob Walker, "The Beast under Your Toenail. Lamisil's Stomach-Turning Ad," *Slate Magazine*, July 14, 2003, www.slate.com/id/2085432/, accessed March 7, 2008.

16. Gael Fashingbauer Cooper, "Readers Crown Best, Worst Commercials. Hate the Toenail Monster; Love the Identity-Theft Ads," MSNBC, August 4, 2004, www.msnbc.msn.com/id/5591893/, accessed March 5, 2008.

17. Bob Garfield, *And Now a Few Words from Me* (New York: McGraw-Hill, 2003), 179–180.

18. Suzanne Vranica, "In Haggar's Bold Ad Blitz, Middle-Aged Is the New Young," *Wall Street Journal*, November 6, 2006, B1–B2.

19. Garfield, *And Now a Few Words From Me*, 181.

20. Denis Higgins, *The Art of Writing Advertising: Conversations with the Masters of the Craft* (Chicago: NTC Business Books, 1965), 64.

Interviews

Chris Adams, personal communication, January 4, 2008.
Paul Charney, personal communication, March 7, 2008.
Carolyn Hadlock and Charlie Hopper, personal communication, May 25, 2007.
Matt Jarvis, personal communication, May 22, 2007.
Tiffany Kosel and Scott Linnen, personal communication, August 31, 2007.
Sara Rose and Lea Ladera, personal communication, June 10, 2008.
Eric Springer, personal communication, May 2, 2007.

CHAPTER 8

On-Strategy Campaigns That Spin Out

What Does Spin Out Mean?

Advertisers of all sizes want their target audience to instantly recognize their campaign. The way to do this, as we discussed in chapter 4, is to establish a distinguishable, on-strategy visual and verbal message. People should know who's advertising as soon they see the campaign. This is true for the "Energizer Bunny," the "Milk Mustache," and the "Absolut Bottle" campaigns.

The big idea is one that works equally well in various media, with each medium supporting the other. Even small corporations can accomplish this if they find one huge idea that can "spin out" and be repeated in relatable variations. The one rule to remember is to stick to the basics: be consistent. Use the same message, same tone of voice, same typographical treatment, same kind of visuals, same colors, and the same slogan. Every promotional message should be related to the next and be immediately identifiable as part of the same campaign.

Long-Running Campaigns

Campaigns that have longevity are said to spin out, and the brand itself ultimately becomes an icon in many different ways. First, it can become closely associated with an animated character, like the Energizer Bunny, Tony the Tiger, or the Keebler Elves. Second, the product itself can be idolized, as in the long-running "Absolut Bottle" campaign that made the actual bottle the visual star. Third, the effect of the product in use can be featured, as the milk mustache in the celebrated campaign of the same name. Fourth, the brand can create a mobile campaign, like the Oscar Mayer Wienermobile, that travels around the country spreading the word. Five, the name can become the icon through the slogan: "With a name like Smucker's, it's got to be good." Six, the logo can become the identifiable icon, like the Nike Swoosh.

Some campaigns have long-running histories, and some are still going on today. Here are a few examples. The Energizer Bunny was created in 1989, with the slogan "The Energizer Bunny Keeps Going." The Absolut bottle-as-the-star campaign was started in 1980 by TBWA, with "Absolut Perfection" as the headline in the first ad. The "Milk Mustache," with the instantly recognizable white mustache, was created in 1994 by Bozell Worldwide. The Oscar Mayer Wienermobile was first introduced by the company itself in 1936.

Milk and Nike: Instantly Recognizable Images and Slogans

These two campaigns, Milk and Nike, have two elements in common. They both have an immediately identifiable icon and an equally famous slogan. Everyone is familiar with the Nike Swoosh and the milk mustache. They are also equally familiar with the slogans "Just Do It" and "Got Milk?"

Amazing as it may seem, the Nike Swoosh, created in 1971 by Carolyn Davidson, a graphic design student, only cost the company $35, the student's fee. Later, in 1983, Phil Knight, cofounder and chairman of Nike, showed Davidson his appreciation with a gold Swoosh ring and Nike stock. Today, it is one of the most readily identifiable icons in the world, and it has appeared frequently without the Nike name.

Nike's slogan, created in 1998 by Wieden+Kennedy, is now more than twenty years old, just five years younger than the "Got Milk?" slogan, created by Goodby Silverstein & Partners in 1993. Celebrated by both the press and advertising industry professionals, these slogans have been seen in all media, on promotional items, and on everyday apparel. In fact, since 1995 the "Got Milk?" slogan has been licensed to dairy boards across the United States and to countless products, from cereals, Barbie dolls, and Hot Wheels to teen and infant clothing.

The long-running "Milk Mustache" campaign first launched on November 7, 1994, with supermodel Naomi Campbell wearing a white mustache. Year after year, it continues to feature other famous personalities wearing that instantly recognizable white mustache. It has included chocolate mustaches sported by celebrities like *Late Show with David Letterman* musical director Paul Shaffer in 1997 and *Fear Factor* host Joe Rogan in 2002, as well as icons like Uncle Sam on July 2 and 3, 2002, in *USA Today*.

In 1997 the California Milk Processor Board, the group that represents milk processors across the country, introduced the "Milk Mustache" Mobile Tour, which travels around the country honoring moms as the chief health officers of their families. The mobile includes computer kiosks where families can nominate their moms as their official chief health officer, photo areas where everyone can don a milk mustache and take home a photo as a memento, learn some exercise tips from Curves representatives, and get to sample milk.[2] The "Milk Mustache" campaign is today still one of the most recognized.

Campaigns like these exemplify the strength of a single idea that can continue in multiple cross-promotions and all media. Strong campaigns like "Just Do It," "Got Milk?" and the "Milk Mustache" keep going and going, just like the Energizer Bunny.

How to Find an Idea That Spins Out

These campaigns make it look easy to create a campaign concept that spins out. Well, spinning out a strong idea isn't the difficult part. Creating a concept that lends itself to all kinds of applications is the challenge. That's what takes the brainpower. So, how do you know if your idea has legs? First, ask these questions.

◇ ◇ ◇

Fifteen Questions: Will the Concept Spin Out?

1. Is it catchy (easy to remember)?
2. Is it flexible? (Can it adapt to new promotional vehicles?)
3. Is it a BIG (REALLY BIG) idea?
4. Does it engage the consumer's imagination?
5. Can it become part of current culture and vernacular?
6. Does it have "talk" value?
7. Can it go viral? (Does it beg to be shared with others?)
8. Does it create buzz?
9. Does it cause a paradigm shift?
10. Does it reposition the brand in a fresh, new way?

11. Does it engage the audience?
12. Does it surprise or shock the audience?
13. Does it distinguish the brand by competitor comparison?
14. Does it have an unforgettable icon?
15. Does it have a celebrity spokesperson?

Now, let's examine these questions more closely, one at a time.

1. Is it catchy (easy to remember)?

Once you hear some campaign ideas, you can't seem to get them out of your mind. Look at the Meow Mix jingle. All it is is the product name, sung over and over again, "Meow, Meow, Meow," yet even after just reading it, I bet you'll be humming or even singing the entire jingle out loud. The simplest ideas are the ones that resonate and stick.

Although most companies are moving away from jingles, Oscar Mayer has revived and promoted its two jingles, "Bologna Song" and "Oh I Wish I Were an Oscar Mayer Weiner," through Wienermobile auditions across the country. As soon as most people hear the first line—"My bologna has a first name it's O-S-C-A-R"—they can finish the entire jingle. The same goes for "Oh I Wish I Were an Oscar Mayer Wiener."

2. Is it flexible? (Can it adapt to new promotional vehicles?)

Who hasn't seen the Oscar Mayer Wienermobile, if not in person, at least on television? And who hasn't heard about the Budweiser hitch team with the famous Clydesdales? Here the brands have gone on the road, as have the Hershey's Kisses Kissmobile, the Truly Nolan car with the mouse ears and tail, the giant Pepperidge Farm Goldfish, Planter's Mr. Peanut, and "Milk Mustache" Mobiles. But the idea doesn't have to be delivered as an actual giant mobile. It could be a hot air balloon and fly in the Macy's Day Parade, or make appearances at events, or be integrated into TV late night talk shows. It just needs to be able to work in any promotional manner, from products and apparel to toys.

3. Is it a BIG (REALLY BIG) idea?

The Energizer Bunny had legs from the start. The slogan promised what others couldn't deliver: that the batteries really did keep going and going. But it was more than the batteries that were tireless. The entire campaign still hasn't run out of steam, decades after the introduction of the "spokes hare" in 1989 by Chiat\Day, which continued the drumming pink bunnies used in a TV spot developed by DDB Needham Worldwide. The Energizer Bunny has appeared in more than 115 commercials, on numerous TV shows, the *Emmy Awards*, ABC's *Wide World of Sports*, *The Late Show with David Letterman*, and seemingly countless other broadcasts.

4. Does it engage the consumer's imagination?

When Clara Peller barked, "Where's the beef?" in the endearing 1984 Wendy's commercial, created by Dancer-Fitzgerald-Sample, she asked the previously unspoken question. By doing so, she challenged consumers to demand a bigger burger, while humorously highlighting that the answer was at Wendy's.

5. Can it become part of current culture and vernacular?

When DDB introduced Budweiser's "Whassup" in 1999, I don't know if Vinny Warren, the campaign's creator, and his team expected the phrase to catch on the way it did. It was instantly scooped up and heard everywhere from TV late night shows to water cooler conversations.

6. Does it have "talk" value?

Some products are launched with campaigns that generate extensive press coverage. The iPod stimulated the public's interest when Omnicom Group's TBW\Chiat\Day created the "Silhouette" campaign in 2003 that featured the iPod's unmistakable white earbud cords set against silhouetted people dancing to their favorite tunes across solid, neon-colored backgrounds. The campaign integrated a range of famous artists and musical genres, from Bob Dylan and U2 to Wynton Marsalis and Eminem. It also utilized the same distinctive visuals in every medium, including print ads, billboards, giant wallscapes (ads on buildings), and high-energy TV spots.

7. Can it go viral? (Does it beg to be shared with others?)

When Crispin Porter + Bogusky first created the Burger King website www.SubservientChicken.com on April 8, 2004, it was just sent to a few friends, who sent it to a few friends, and so on. What started as a fun idea of a guy dressed in a chicken costume who executed typed-in commands, inadvertently ended up being one of the most successful viral campaigns, with more than 385 million hits and 12,142,314 unique visitors within one year of its launch.[3]

8. Does it create buzz?

The "Aflac Duck" campaign, created by The Kaplan Thaler Group in 2004 for the American Family Life Assurance Company, was such a breakthrough idea that it catapulted name recognition from a mere 12 percent awareness rate to more than 90 percent in just three years. When asked to say the company's name, more than one third of the people quack it like the quirky and lovable duck in the commercials.

9. Does it cause a paradigm shift?

Thanks to Jared Fogle, the everyday guy who lost more than 245 pounds eating at Subway and then kept the weight off for more than ten years, people started to rethink their lunch options. Positioned as the fast-food restaurant with all-fresh ingredients, Subway convinced dieters who had never considered eating at Subway to try it. The "Eat Fresh" campaign, created by Euro RSCG and launched on May 7, 2006, drove the point home. It showed sandwiches being made fresh, right in front of customers, not hidden in the back and kept warm under heat lamps as in most other fast-food restaurants that primarily served burgers and fries.

10. Does it reposition the brand in a fresh, new way?

One campaign instantly comes to mind as being responsible for totally transforming a brand's image from boring to cool: raisins. Once the California Raisin Board introduced the "Claymation Raisins" campaign, the way people saw raisins would never be the same. These funky, sneaker-wearing, instrument-playing raisins were singing and dancing to Marvin Gaye's hit song, "I Heard It Through the Grapevine," making the spot an instant success. It was created in 1986 by Seth Werner and Dextor Fedor, two copywriters at the Foote, Cone and Belding agency in San Francisco. The raisins were so popular that soon spin-off products were sold everywhere, including rubber figurines, T-shirts, and toys.

11. Does it engage the audience?

The Budweiser "Frog" campaign, created by DDB in 1995 and launched during the Super Bowl, forced the audience to "connect the syllables" when three frogs each croaked one syllable of the Bud-weis-er name. When they finished, the viewers had to put it together and enjoy that Eureka! moment when they figured out the frogs were saying Budweiser. Everyone who saw the spot enjoyed the moment of discovery and was completely entertained. The campaign continued with more frog spots, followed by a pair of Budweiser lizards, Louie and Frank, who were jealous of the frogs and sought their destruction, only to be rebuffed by a frog "tongue-lashing."

12. Does it surprise or shock the audience?

As we saw in chapter 7, the "United Colors of Benetton" campaign showed shocking images like a nun kissing a priest, a man on his deathbed, and an unwashed newborn baby, among others. The 1980s campaign stirred a range of emotions from outrage and protest to reverence.

13. Does it distinguish the brand by competitor comparison?

Over the years, various campaigns have created a their-versus-ours approach, but few have received as much attention as the Mac versus PC campaign. Both brands are depicted through the personality of actors, with the PC being the geek and the Mac being cool. We will discuss this campaign in more detail a little later on.

14. Does it have an unforgettable icon?

Brand icons or mascots have been around for decades. Whether they're cartoon characters like the Keebler Elves or real live animals like Morris the Cat, they're instant brand identifiers that create an emotional bond with the audience. Who doesn't smile when they think of Tony the Tiger or the Clydesdale horses? Some of the icons have been around for decades, like the Jolly Green Giant, which was created in 1928 by the Minnesota Valley Canning Company. Others have existed for more than a century, like the Michelin Man, which was created in 1898 by Edouard Michelin.

15. Does it have a celebrity spokesperson?

When Nike teamed up with Michael Jordan in 1985 to create the Air Jordan Line, both the company and the athlete began an exciting partnership that would last for decades. The pairing worked perfectly because Nike was the shoe created by athletes for athletes. So when basketball superstar Jordan joined Nike not just in name, but in actual product development, the result was a shoe they created together. Although its primary purpose was performance, it was also matched with cool designs. The product, which delivered what it promised, catapulted Nike into shoe star status.

Using the above fifteen questions as a guide will help determine whether the campaign concept has legs. When you're looking for a big idea, consider all the campaigns that have continued for years and try to analyze what elements factored into making these ideas such long-running successes.

Spinning Out the Strategy

Ultimately, advertisers are looking to create unforgettable visual and verbal messages that stay in consumers' minds for long periods of time. Tiffany Kosel, associate creative director/art director at Crispin Porter + Bogusky, explains that when she and partner Scott Linnen, vice president/creative director/copywriter, are searching for the idea that is most relevant to the brand, they look for what they call "the tension." She says they ask this question: "What's the cultural, psychological, and social thing that makes this potentially sticky?" Linnen adds, "It just helps to focus you on the single-minded question that the advertising wants to answer."

When the idea is culturally relevant, reflecting everyday life, it resonates even deeper with the consumer. When that happens, as in Nike's ubiquitous "Just Do It" campaign, the idea goes beyond shoes and athletics. It addresses lifestyle, the consumer's individual lifestyle, in a personal and culturally relevant way. It changes culture. Linnen shares that this was something they strive to do: "We're forever trying to change culture. It's what we live for."

Another example, their agency's MINI Cooper slogan, "Let's Motor," does exactly that. Kosel explains, "It can be applied to just cars or how you are in your everyday life and how you approach life. It's just thinking on a bigger scale."

Some campaign strategies focus on the shared core values between the consumer and the brand. Take, for example, the innovative Mac versus PC campaign: the actor depicting the Mac, Justin Long, was the cool guy, while the PC actor, John Hodgman, was the nerd. This helps the consumer say, "Oh, that brand's just like me: cool." As Jeffrey Wolf, partner/director of account planning at Deutsch N.Y., explains, "Basically when you think about values, they are what underlie our attitudes and drive our behavior."[4]

This strategy is, as we've mentioned, married to the brief. So when TBWA\Chiat\Day creative team Margaret Keene and Chris Adams talked about the PEDIGREE® "Must Love Dogs" campaign, it was clear that the direction, a declaration of how people love dogs, came directly from the brief. This campaign, in particular, demonstrated how a brief that perfectly captures a shared core value between the brand and the consumer can be the vehicle that fuels the creative direction. Adams explains: "We want to be a company where everything we do is for the love of dogs. And so, Margaret and I sat down to try and begin articulating that in *consumer speak*." He says that as they were working away, Keene was toying with visuals of dogs and he was playing with words. After he had created a copy line he liked, he noticed Keene had an image of a sleeping puppy on a billboard on her screen. Suddenly, the entire campaign strategy came down to two words: the famous "DOGS RULE®" tagline. "All it needed was a simple little line. It's almost like the whole campaign came out of just attaching her visual image to the "DOGS RULE®" tagline I had just been working on." They took that one idea of the slogan and the visual of a puppy and spun the concept out into a series of three-dimensional billboards with candid, lifelike photographs. Notice how each of the billboards draws your eye up and demands your attention.

Those two words, "DOGS RULE®," are so well chosen, they work in all media. It's that big idea that not only resonates with the audience, but easily

Figure 8.1. The following billboards were part of the original launch of the "DOGS RULE®" campaign to celebrate the demonstrable love for dogs shown by PEDIGREE®.

Image courtesy of Mars Petcare US, TBWA\Chiat\Day. Photographic image courtesy of Arthaus. PEDIGREE®, DOGS RULE®, and other insignia are trademarks of Mars, Incorporated and its affiliates. These trademarks are used with permission. © Mars, Incorporated 2008.[a]

Figure 8.2.

Image courtesy of Mars Petcare US and TBWA\Chiat\Day. Photographic image courtesy of Sharon Montrose (for the dog) and Arthaus (for the billboard). PEDIGREE®, DOGS RULE®, and other insignia are trademarks of Mars, Incorporated and its affiliates. These trademarks are used with permission. © Mars, Incorporated 2008. [b]

Figure 8.3.

Image courtesy of Mars Petcare US and TBWA\Chiat\Day. Photographic image courtesy of Sharon Montrose (for the dog) and Arthaus (for the billboard). PEDIGREE®, DOGS RULE®, and other insignia are trademarks of Mars, Incorporated and its affiliates. These trademarks are used with permission. © Mars, Incorporated 2008. [c]

spins out and can be used on billboards, print ads, T-shirts, and even a pop-up "store" (fig. 9.10) at the 2008 Westminster Dog Show to enable adoptions and support dogs in shelters through product sales and on-site donation collections. Adams explains how the main idea, or the heart of the campaign, needs to work everywhere:

> I think there's something when you talk about the seeds of the campaign, or know you've got a line or a visual that works; outdoors is a really great place to start because if you can do something that's big, and endemic, and meaningful there, you can extrapolate it out into all the different media where you can get more involved and more intricate. But I think something we always try to do too is [ask]: Would you wear the T-shirt? If you've got a campaign idea, and an articulation, and a visual language that's cool enough that you'd want to wear the T-shirt in public, you're probably on to something.

Spinning Out an Icon

For years, people have identified Budweiser with the iconic Clydesdale hitch teams. Continuing the idea of using the Clydesdales, but changing them by giving them human emotions, as discussed in chapter 5, was how DDB's creative team of art director Adam Glickman and copywriter Craig Feigen kept the campaign exciting. They created little stories with the Clydesdales to drive home the earlier-discussed strategy—the prestige of joining the Budweiser hitch team. Three spots in particular come to mind: "Donkey," "Commercial Zoo," and "American Dream." In the former, a little donkey dreamed of being a Clydesdale. The commercial shows him practicing the Clydesdale walk and hitch pull. But the funniest moment was his wearing hair extensions to look more the part. He goes for an interview, and when asked why he wanted to be a Budweiser Clydesdale, he bayed his answer. He says, "I musta said something right," and ends up joining the team.

Continuing with the interviewing-to-be-on-the-hitch-team idea, Feigen and Glickman created "Commercial Zoo," in which several zoo animals showed up at the Budweiser farm with hopes of being added to the hitch team like the donkey. One clever line is spoken as a driver says to the donkey, "Now look what you started." The spot closes with a pig with hair extensions on his legs running and saying, "Gosh, I hope I'm not too late." It's very funny, and another example of a great "button," or clever closing line.

In "American Dream" a young Clydesdale enters the bar and nuzzles up to a photo of the hitch team, as if he's picturing himself in the photo. He turns around and places his small head into the full-sized harness, pulling forward.

He is not yet strong enough to move the attached Budweiser wagon, but hidden from his sight are two Clydesdale hitch team horses that push the wagon along from behind, inching it forward. One of the hitch team drivers watches the young horse pull the wagon out of the barn, assisted by the two back horses. He leans over to the Dalmatian sitting beside him and says, "I won't tell if you won't," leaving the young horse to imagine he managed to move it by himself. Of course, these are only a few examples in a long line of beloved Clydesdale Super Bowl spots.

How to Spin Out an Online, Interactive Campaign

Many agencies are creating exciting interactive online websites, like www.Coke.com and www.Dove.com, and fun and informational games, like Starbuck's www.PlanetGreenGame.com. The real question becomes how to create an interactive online idea that has multiple related components to it, as in a series of print ads. We will look even deeper into interactive campaigns in chapter 9.

How Small Businesses Can Spin Out Ideas

Once you've developed your on-target, on-strategy campaign, where do you go from there? How does a small business owner, entrepreneur, or solo-preneur apply these principles on a limited budget? There are many ways that smaller companies can speak directly to their audience. The Internet has opened up a worldwide communication vehicle that puts companies on equal footing, enabling even tiny companies to create a global presence.

Business owners who are strong writers can create regular blogs to discuss new products or continue an open dialogue with their audience. People can exchange ideas, share suggestions, ask questions, and interact in an open forum tied back to the business owners' blog site. Entrepreneurs who used to create paper newsletters and pay for postage to reach their audience can now create and distribute online newsletters, or "e-zines," without the cost of a design team or mailing company. They can subscribe to an e-zine service like www.ConstantContact.com, www.PinstripeMail.com, or www.EnFlyer.com, all of which offer predesigned graphic templates, so they can just insert copy.

Think Tank 3 created a blog for Stone Ridge Orchard—a campaign discussed earlier in chapter 5—under the capricious name www.organicschmorganic.com, even though there's nothing humorous about the site. The whole idea of the name was to poke fun at the often misunderstood and misused word "organic." Because it was a fun idea, though, the agency put the words on stickers and placed them on apples and bags of food to drive people to the website, which is actually a blog. Sharoz Makarechi, founder and creative director of

Think Tank 3, says the site offers information and clarification about organic foods because the head agriculturalist is a wonderful writer. She explains that it works as a marketing tool through social networking, "because the farmer is so intelligent about how he talks about the food" (fig. 8.4). She adds:

It is a live blog, and it's updated all the time. We consider that social media. Where people can go, and they're linked in. Then from there, they would

Figure 8.4.   This well-written blog was created to be the Social Media aspect of Stone Ridge Orchard's advertising plan. It takes advantage of the client's pre-existing knowledge of and advocacy for sustainable agriculture to dispel common myths and offer accurate information about organic foods.

Image courtesy of Think Tank 3 [d]

be linked to our website, where they can see the campaign. But, there are also links to other farmers, people of like mind, and grocery stores—the better grocery stores like the Whole Foods and the Balducci's.

On the site, the agriculturalist explains that organic doesn't mean that the food hasn't been sprayed. As Makarechi explained on page 88, "It means that it's sprayed with sprays that are considered organic by the USDA." It is this kind of specific information that health-conscious people are looking to learn. Blogs that answer questions people are hungry to ask create places that like-minded people congregate.

Savvy entrepreneurs can also create detailed databases that can be organized in any variety of ways, for example, by geography, buying frequency, and interests. One way to enhance their databases is to join an online social networking group with a professional contact focus like www.LinkedIn.com or social networking groups with a business-to-business focus like www.MerchantCircle.com and www.SelfGrowth.com, where people could be interested in their products or services. Business owners can also create a series of articles that relate to each other, creating a public relations type of campaign. Many online sites encourage article submissions, like www.SubmitArticles.com, www.SubmitArticlesForFree.com, and www.SubmitYourArticle.com. Some social networking sites, like www.Work.com, offer highly professional expertise and readers would instantly catch any careless typographical errors. They also refer each other to insightful articles and websites.

Promotional Items Can Still Spin Out Campaigns

Marketers today are still using promotional items to spin out campaigns. When Makarechi wanted to extend the Stone Ridge Orchard campaign discussed in chapter 5, she used the logo, a group of multisized dots resembling grapes, and the "Know Your Roots" slogan in multiple media such as trucks (fig. 5.3). Old-fashioned promotional items never lose their appeal, especially when they reinforce, or spin out, the main message. Every consumer touch point serves as another communication vehicle.

In addition to T-shirts, small business owners use Post-it notes, flashlights, and other promotional items, as well as more technology-related giveaways such as jump drives, mouse pads, and computer cases. The point is, if the promotional item drives home the overall campaign in a traditional medium, but with an innovative message, it can still work hard to support the marketing efforts. Trade shows are still viable vehicles to attract prospective clients, introduce new products, and launch new campaign messages. Business owners could hand out mini-business card CDs, three-dimensional flyers, and digitally trackable

DVDs that drive attendees to their website, a must-have for any entrepreneur. Although the options are practically limitless, whatever is incorporated as part of the marketing campaign—from national trade shows to local community sponsorships—helps to extend and strengthen a corporate image.

Notes

1. Linda Kaplan Thaler and Robin Koval, *BANG! Getting Your Message Heard in a Noisy World* (New York: Doubleday, 2003), 146.

2. www.milkpep.org/promotions/grassroots/milk-mustache-mobile/, accessed May 10, 2008.

3. Margo Berman, *Street-Smart Advertising: How to Win the Battle of the Buzz* (Lanham, MD: Rowman & Littlefield Publishers, 2007), 3.

4. Berman, *Street-Smart Advertising*, 170.

Image Credits

a. This billboard was created by TBWA\Chiat\Day for Mars, Incorporated.

b. This billboard was created by TBWA\Chiat\Day for Mars, Incorporated.

c. This billboard was created by TBWA\Chiat\Day for Mars, Incorporated.

d. "Organic Schmorganic" blog created for Stone Ridge Orchard as part of the Know Your Roots™ campaign by Think Tank 3.

Interviews

Scott Linnen and Tiffany Kosel, personal communication, August 31, 2007.
Margaret Keene and Chris Adams, personal communication, January 4, 2008.
Sharoz Makarechi, personal communication, February 13, 2008.

CHAPTER 9

New Strategies for
Old and New Media

◊ ◊ ◊

What you must do, by the most economical and creative means possible, is attract people and sell them.—William Bernbach[1]

Traditional Media Takes a New Twist

Only a few decades ago, people were less mobile and had fewer media options. Mostly they received the news in newspapers and twice a day on network news: during dinner or before midnight. They read magazines, saw billboards along the roadways, used store coupons, received catalogs and other direct mail pieces, listened to the radio, and basically had all their media touch points.

Reaching a large number of people was much easier because advertisers knew where and when to find them. Now, the few places guaranteed to reach a mass market at the same time are limited to a handful of TV events: namely the Super Bowl, the Oscars, and other award shows. Media fragmentation has made reaching a wide audience a relic of the past.

A few brilliant spots became instantaneous classics, like Apple's one-time Super Bowl "1984" spot. Other famous campaigns might have taken more repetitions, but were still embraced by the masses and became part of the vernacular, like Wendy's unforgettable "Where's the Beef" slogan, also created in 1984.

Timeless campaigns were launched in various media, and were not restricted to just television, even if the main thrust began there, like Chrysler's challenging line presented by Lee Iacocca in the 1980s, "If you can find a better car, buy it." Or Volkswagen's famous 1962 print ad for the Beetle by Doyle Dane Bernbach (DDB) with the shocking headline "Lemon."

Messages today can still make an indelible impression, but often in a new way. Now a campaign can get launched without even being a campaign, but rather a fun idea that's shared on the Internet. When creatives at Crispin Porter + Bogusky were playing around with ways to promote Burger King's chicken sandwiches and wanted to show each other an offbeat idea, they e-mailed it to one another. What they developed was a website with a guy in a chicken suit whose movements were programmed to physically respond to commands you typed in.

Www.SubservientChicken.com became an immediate hit and a viral marketing campaign was inadvertently launched as one person e-mailed another, who in turn e-mailed another. What has happened is that word of mouth has been transformed into word of Web; this rapid transmission of ideas via the Internet is described as viral. When agencies create fun, interactive online messages in a new way, people want to share them with their friends.

Even though online banners ads are common today, when they incorporate interactivity, they offer an instant connection with the audience. Just as online games and interactive websites both entertain and engage the viewer, interactive banner ads can create a fun way to enhance the emotional bond with the brand.

One example is the Volkswagen "_____ like a Rabbit" banner ad campaign, created by Crispin Porter + Bogusky. Here Web surfers are invited to fill in the blank. Once they type in a word, a series of animations execute the command. So for "Hop like a Rabbit" the Volkswagen Rabbit hops over speed bumps. For "Multiply like a Rabbit," a black VW Rabbit follows a white VW Rabbit into the "tunnel of love." After a few sound effects, the garage door opens and a series of multi-patterned VW Rabbits exit. For "Drink like a Rabbit" the VW Rabbit pulls up to a gas pump and gets fuel. An example of the sequence of animated banner ads is the "Wash like a Rabbit" command, where viewers can watch the Rabbit get scrubbed with rotating brushes as it goes through an automatic car wash (fig. 9.1).

Notice how the same principles that apply to ad campaigns apply to online ads as well. Each ad uses the same style of type, the same visual treatment (cartoon), the same placement of all the components: the headline, graphic, and slogan. The one difference, of course, is that consumers can now "play" with the ad and see an immediate response.

Figure 9.1.   To re-launch the Volkswagen Rabbit in North America, we created Interactive web banners inviting people to fill in the blank. Type in "Run" like a Rabbit, and the quick and nimble Volkswagen takes off down a stretch of road. Type in "Eat" like a Rabbit, and it stops at a gas station for a quick gas-sipping fill-up.

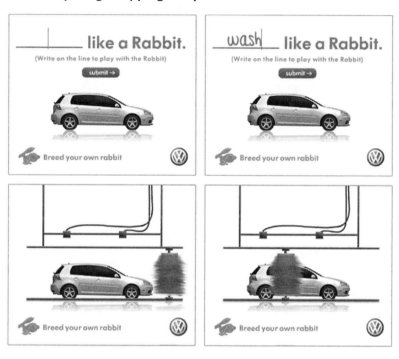

Image courtesy of Crispin Porter + Bogusky and Volkswagen [a]

To target a specific geographic region, CP+B also created ads that spoke directly to the audience in certain cities. Each ad showed three images of animals indigenous to the region, stacked vertically one over the other, with the headline at the bottom. For Miami, the images were an alligator, a mosquito, and a rabbit. For New York, the visuals were a rat, a pigeon, and a rabbit. The headlines were respectively "Hey, Miami, the Rabbit is back" (fig. 9.2) and "Hey, NYC, the Rabbit is back" (fig. 9.3). Just three images and a one-line headline reminded members of that community that Volkswagen was reintroducing the Rabbit to their area. Although targeting a certain audience is not new, using both a visual and verbal approach that singled them out regionally was a fun way to arouse the locals' interest.

Figure 9.2.   To re-launch the Volkswagen Rabbit in North America, Crispin Porter + Bogusky created various print ads (as seen here and on page 179) that spoke directly to the target audience using vernacular language and images of animals indigenous to the region.

Image courtesy of Crispin Porter + Bogusky and Volkswagen [b]

In addition, they created a "Transit" ad that ran as outdoor boards, bus shelters in transit, and as wildpostings (ads in unexpected places) in fifteen specifically targeted markets, as well as on buildings (wallscapes) in major cities on both the east and west coasts, including New York, Los Angeles, and San

Figure 9.3.

Image courtesy of Crispin Porter + Bogusky and Volkswagen [c]

Francisco. It was even used as street furniture in four separate markets. Both the visual and verbal message spoke directly to the everyday commuters by presenting Rabbit information in the form of a subway map route (fig. 9.4).

The Rabbit campaign showcased the use of online interactivity combined with geographic targeting through print. In the next two campaigns, we'll look at how the Internet was used to market insurance and the New Zealand Army.

Figure 9.4. To re-launch the Volkswagen Rabbit in North America, Crispin Porter + Bogusky created this ad, which was used on outdoor boards, bus shelters, in transit, as well as in wildpostings in 15 key markets, urban walls-capes in N.Y., L.A., San Francisco, and as street furniture in 4 markets.

Image courtesy of Crispin Porter + Bogusky and Volkswagen [d]

Innovative and Interactive Online Advertising

When the Answer Seguro Online Insurance Company in Argentina wanted to remind Internet surfers to insure their homes, it turned to Del Campo Nazca Saatchi & Saatchi to create a series of animated banner ads in a teaser campaign called "Burning Home." A teaser campaign is a series of ads that withholds the advertiser's name and then finally reveals it in the last ad. The banner recreated the toolbar of an Internet browser, right over the user's actual toolbar (fig. 9.5).

The first ad showed the "home" button on fire on the toolbar menu, with smoke billowing up. The second banner ad showed a larger fire and more smoke. The third ad showed bigger clouds of smoke with the headline "Insure Your Home" followed by the Answer Seguro Online logo and phone number. When viewers clicked the banner, they were connected to the Answer Seguro Online "Home Insurance" information page. The campaign targeted a market that was over twenty-five and decision makers regarding insurance and other home-related services. What made the campaign particularly intriguing were

Figure 9.5.   The banner recreates the toolbar of an Internet browser, over the user's real toolbar. The "home" button catches fire. At that point the message "Insure your house" appears, and later the Answer Seguro Online logo. If clicked, the banner links the user to the Home Insurance information page.

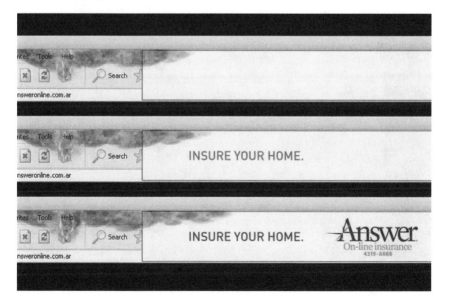

Image courtesy of Saatchi & Saatchi [e]

the ever-increasing flames that continued to flare up and draw attention to the "help" button, acting as a not-so-subtle reminder that you may want to reach out for help to insure one of your most valuable possessions: your home.[2]

Another animated banner ad for Answer Seguro Online Insurance Company, created in 2005 by the same agency, was the "Man" banner ad. It was designed to remind people to buy car insurance. As described by the Saatchi & Saatchi team, it showed a man whistling and walking around a blank space with only a cursor. He grabbed the cursor and ran off. Then a headline appeared with a surprising message: "When you least expect it, you can be robbed." Who would have expected anyone to steal the cursor? That's exactly what made the campaign so imaginative (fig. 9.6).

This banner ad was designed by the creative team of Chavo D'Emilio, executive creative director; Mariano Serkin, creative director; Guadalupe Pereyra, copywriter; and Javier Lourenco, art director. The website, called "Thief," which featured the banner ad, was launched January 2, 2005 by Web developer Denken in Buenos Aires. It was created in English and Spanish with two different URLs: http://www.dnkn.com/answer/default.htm (English) and http://www.dnkn.com/answer/answer_esp.htm (Spanish). The entire campaign was under the direction of a mini-army of supervisors, who are often unrecognized

Figure 9.6.   This banner appeared in Answer´s Web page and was designed to encourage people to hire a car insurance company.

Image courtesy of Saatchi & Saatchi [f]

and behind the scenes, including two production managers, Adrián Aspani and Cosme Argerich, and the three-person account executive team of Pablo Ordoñez, Esteban Tarling, and Vicky Patron Costas.

In 2004, the New Zealand office of Saatchi & Saatchi created another campaign, "Force9," for the New Zealand Army. It used the Internet in a fun and interactive way. This online game enabled players to choose missions, engage in virtual combat, and "experience" Army assignments. The first screen was a main menu where visitors could select their mission from a list of these and other exciting challenges: a rescue, an escape, a hurricane disaster, and a dangerously icy catastrophe. Once they clicked on their chosen assignment, they were linked to a briefing screen that explained exactly what the mission was. To add to the pressure of completing the assignment, participants were reminded to move quickly. This game was designed as a recruitment tool that encouraged young people to go online and find out more about the New Zealand Army (fig. 9.7).

A related banner ad called "Detonator," which was posted on New Zealand websites that targeted youth, listed jobs, and recapped the news, allowed visitors to learn what life would be like in the army (fig. 9.8).

One constant in advertising is the need to integrate effective verbal and visual information in every medium. Technology is just another format in which

Figure 9.7.   This "Force9" challenge requires the player to camouflage his face before engaging in his next game mission.

Image courtesy of Saatchi & Saatchi [8]

Figure 9.8.   To promote the "Force9" game site, challenges were embedded into web banners. These examples asked users to assemble a rifle correctly & camouflage a tank in desert conditions.

Image courtesy of Saatchi & Saatchi [h]

the message is delivered. Agencies today must find a way to implement the creative strategy as they integrate new media.

Multimedia Becomes Integrated in Novel Ways

For years, advertisers have used multimedia campaigns that included TV, radio, print, direct mail, outdoor (now renamed out-of-home or ambient media), and other media to create an integrated message. Today, advertisers are still using one medium to support another, but in an even more integrated way. Instead of having a TV spot along with a related billboard in Times Square, now the billboard, as in Absolut's 2006 campaign, could tell passersby to text message or call in on a Web-enabled phone and download a free, four-minute mp3 Lenny Kravitz track on the spot.

Another campaign that used a Times Square board in an interactive way was the Lexus IS model launch. In the spring of 2005, Team One, a Saatchi & Saatchi division, created an interactive mosaic designed to coincide with the fall launch of the 2006 Lexus IS model. The plan was to generate interactivity and pique interest in the model while capturing vital consumer information. People would register online for a chance to win a new Lexus IS and to be part of a giant photomosaic on the huge electronic Reuters billboard in Times Square. An image can be found at nelsdrums.com/portfolio/?p=25.

People were invited to upload their photographs so their image could be integrated into the collage. Winning images were selected and the participants were notified of the website address to view the photomosaic, the exact location of their image in the mosaic, and the time of the live webcasts from Times Square. People could log onto the site and search for their own images as well.

This campaign integrated new technology that enabled a seamless transference and integration of visual files.[3]

In 2003, its San Francisco agency, Goodby Silverstein & Partners (GS&P), also developed a highly interactive website that integrated consumer's photographs while showcasing the ease of digital photography with Hewlett-Packard (HP). GS&P created the "You +hp" campaign, which invited consumers to upload their photographs and photo essays, "YOUStories." These became part of an online photo gallery or visual blog. Examples of ads from the 2003 "You +hp" campaign can be found at www.hp.com/hpinfo/newsroom/hpads/you/photography/index.html.

Another company, New Era Cap Company, the largest headwear firm in America, also used the Reuters megaboard in Times Square in the "Are You Part of the New Era?" campaign.

Each of these campaigns is a perfect example of the way agencies are creating integrated and interactive messages by blending old or traditional media with new technology.

Why is this happening? Because society has totally changed the way we receive and exchange messages. People are more mobile, more connected, more distracted, more overwhelmed with information, and more inundated with multitasking. No wonder they're practically impervious to advertising messages and their attention spans are so short. If that's not enough, they're bombarded with zillions of almost-alike products and have the Herculean task of quickly determining the differences to decide which one to consider purchasing. It not only has to fit their lifestyle, but also solve a problem, show a benefit, and speak directly to them in their tone of voice. That's why traditional advertising can no longer do the job alone.

The Need for Long-Term, Strategic Thinking

Sometimes in the haste to integrate new media into a campaign, new advertisers or small business marketers may forget the importance of long-term thinking. You can't just take a print ad and turn it into a website just because you need Web presence. You need to back up and ask: What does my advertising need to accomplish? What's the consumer's "takeaway message"? How can my product or service help solve a problem or fill a need? New media is not the salve to soothe a marketing itch and it cannot be expected to solve undiagnosed advertising problems.

So, what needs to be considered when marketers want to expand their use of media? How do they convert the message from one medium to another? This is a challenge for even the most seasoned advertising professionals. What must not be lost in the fray is the marriage of the visual and verbal message, which must be expressed in an appropriate way to single out a specific audience. Most importantly, it still must deliver the strategy outlined in the brief.

Problems occur when people try to use a message designed specifically for one medium, like television, and put it in another, such as the Internet. In the same way you can't just translate a campaign message from one language to another, you can't just translate media. You need to recreate the message for a different medium as you would for another language.

How do you keep the strategy alive when you move from print to out-of-home advertisements or from TV to the Internet? Although writing a TV spot is completely different from creating Web copy, it still isn't a totally new creative process. Why? Because the same basic principles of message development apply. Each medium must have an instantly understandable message and a compelling visual that drives the point (key consumer benefit) home, while supporting the overall strategy.

What keeps the strategy consistent is the repeated use of the brand's identifiable and established image in each medium. It is critical to have an instantly recognizable campaign regardless of where it appears. What unifies the campaign is the deliberate repetition of the visual and verbal components: placement and selection of type, choice and combination of colors, stylistic treatment of images, target-specific tone of voice, and the main message. Being consistent in the overall layout drives home any promotional message.

Twists and Turns of New Media

As marketers look to develop innovative, consumer-relevant media, they now even create new places to spread the word. Messages on airport luggage carousels, telephone poles, building walls, sidewalks (called floor talkers), power line cords, shopping cart handles, paper cups, drinking straws, pedestrian crossing stripes, subway straps, and street sewer grates are becoming less unexpected as media meet audiences wherever they are.

Advertisers have even created promotional stunts to get people's attention. One ad by TBWA\Japan for Adidas shoes stopped traffic by having live people, tethered on three-foot ropes, play soccer on a regular billboard. Saatchi & Saatchi caused pedestrians to take a double look by showing a lifelike image of a giant cup of coffee on top of manholes in the streets of Manhattan. The steam coming up from the manhole made the coffee appear to be piping hot and steaming. The headline surrounding the outside of the cup read, "Hey, City That Never Sleeps. Wake Up. Folger's." (This ingenious out-of-home message can be seen at www.businessweek.com/the_thread/brandnewday/archives/2006/05/folgers_manhole.html.)

OfficeMax's Chicago introduction of its multicolored rubber-band ball logo used both a global positioning satellite and a mobile projection system. It projected its bouncing ball logo off the sidewalks and buildings in downtown Chicago. The projection system was placed inside a vehicle that traveled up and down Michigan Avenue; the ball's bounce and location was determined by the speed with which the vehicle was traveling. Not only did this guerrilla tactic help promote a new logo design, but it kept in character with OfficeMax's new campaign position to have "fun, passion and innovation."[4]

Digital taxi cab-top advertisements, called VIDs, or Vert Intelligent Display videos, could also target specific audiences using satellite signals that could be programmed to send a message according to street address, time of day, or zip code. Thus stock message reports could be projected near Wall Street and McDonald's breakfast specials could be sent during the morning hours near specific restaurant locations.[5]

Opting in to receive advertising messages helps companies establish an even deeper relationship with their audience. For example, pharmaceutical companies are even sending cell phone messages to remind consumers when to take their medications. Other marketers are offering coupons through cellular text messages.

Retailers are using audio spotlighting to send advertising messages that target a specific consumer in certain sections, for instance, a motion-activated recording that projects a narrow sound beam that would speak to a singular shopper. New York City bookstores and other businesses like supermarkets or electronics stores could produce messages triggered by a passerby and have the invaluable opportunity to highlight a sale on a specific product as that one shopper walks past.

Agencies are also introducing multisensory approaches in their campaigns. In 2006, Pepsi used scent, as well as sound chips like the musical Hallmark cards, in one of its print campaigns, showing a novel use of a traditional medium. This multimedia approach, created by Omnicom's OMD, was called "the new sound of cola." The sound chip was placed in an insert inside the October 16 issue of *People* magazine. The sound chip played jazz music from a then-running TV spot to reinforce the message. The scent strips offered whiffs of Pepsi's black cherry and French vanilla flavors.[6] This allowed Pepsi to engage three of the reader's five senses: sight, sound, and smell.

According to Harold Vogt at the Scent Marketing Institute, the scent marketing industry will surpass the $500 million mark by the year 2016.[7] Scent strips demonstrating perfume scents have been inside magazines for years, even to the dismay of allergic readers, who were often overwhelmed with a perfume's heavy aroma as soon as they opened a page. Well, new technology has been developed that holds the scent in a special kind of paper until the consumer releases it with touch. Although it is much more costly than traditional scratch and sniff paper, Avon has embraced this technology because it is a nonoffensive way to showcase its products.

Scent was added to a "Got Milk?" campaign by the creative team at Goodby, Silverstein & Partners. They added an automatic sprayer that released the aroma of chocolate chip cookies at bus shelters carrying the "Got Milk?" message. Some people protested that this caused people to get hungry while they were waiting for their buses. Of course, it did. However, the innovative use of scent in an old medium, bus shelters, created a lot of media attention.

PEDIGREE® dog food has even used store floor talkers (messages on floors) with images of dog bowls filled with food set with scent strips. When dogs try to lick the food, they send the message to their owners of just how irresistibly appetizing the food is.

This and other innovative ads posted at Gush Magazine can be seen at www.gushmagazine.com/category/Edgy-and-Innovative-Ads/P0/. One imaginative ad, created by QG Propaganda to promote the roller coasters at the Hopi Hari amusement park in São Paulo, Brazil, showed images of people with arms raised as if they were on the ride, standing on the backs of escalator steps. Even shopping cart handles and conveyor belts in supermarkets are now vehicles for ads. Conveyor belt messages are created by a patented, photo-quality printing system developed by EnVision Marketing Group, from Little Rock, Arkansas. Seatback tray tables in airplanes, once an unexpected place for a message, are now used more commonly, like the Verizon messages on US Airways planes.

It seems as if someone always comes up with another unexpected place to deliver a message. TBWA\London used cocktail umbrellas to increase drug-rape awareness. Messages were set on beautifully decorated cocktail umbrellas, which were inserted into women's drinks when they left them unattended at bars. The startling message, which served as a powerful wake-up call, was "This is how easy it is to spike your drink." These are all examples of ambient advertising.

Although the list is practically endless because media is being created every day, here are a few examples of alternative, but no longer new, media vehicles:

- Satellite Radio
- Blogging
- Instant Messaging

- Podcasts
- Online Advertising
- E-mail Marketing
- Mobile Marketing
- Viral Marketing
- Viral Videos
- Social Networking Sites (www.LinkedIn.com, www.Squidoo.com, www. Self-Growth.com, www.Work.com, www.Digg.com, www.MySpace.com, www.YouTube.com, www.Facebook.com)
- Games
- Supermarket Video Displays ("shelf talkers")

With new media emerging every day, researchers are having a hard time defining and naming what's new anymore. Perhaps the best way to describe these new vehicles is to call them emerging media. Many are so unusual, they may never become mainstream media. Others are just so expensive, they would be virtually impossible for small businesses to implement.

Innovative Thinking for Tired-Out Media

Having a big budget doesn't necessarily guarantee unusual marketing solutions. More and more agencies are intrigued by the seemingly limitless media possibilities today. Crispin Porter + Bogusky is famous for creating new media. Its teams develop clever and unexpected places to deliver messages, like putting the MINI Cooper on top of an SUV, or placing a full-size MINI on a billboard, or even putting one inside a giant toy car model box in a shopping mall. Scott Linnen explains how his agency reenergized the billboard and other worn-out media:

> We did a fun campaign for MINI that also worked like mad. Just look at mediums that people would think, "Oh, I don't want to do that. That's a direct mail letter, or that's a matchbook cover." And it turns out to be something that changes culture.

The creative team of art director Tiffany Kosel and copywriter Linnen shares how they think up these new media ideas. Linnen discusses how ad placement has changed over the years, explaining how years ago, everyone would have voted for a Super Bowl commercial above all other media, but they now find that "with Burger King cups, there are millions of impressions a day. That's more impressions on consumers than seeing a Super Bowl commercial."

Of course coffee cup lids have been around forever, but few companies have thought of using them to hold more than liquids. Now they can speak to the audience in the middle of their everyday activities. Being able to target an audience right where they are is called media intersection. This has become an effective way to reach today's fragmented audience.

Case Study: Campaign Blends
Traditional Media in Innovative Ways

Agencies aren't abandoning traditional media. They're rethinking its application. The Martin Agency wanted to drive home a clear, simple message for UPS, using traditional media in an untraditional way. Led by creative director Andy Azula, the creative team introduced the "Whiteboard" campaign in January 2007. The brilliance behind the idea was evident in an instantly identifiable visual that worked in all media. The agency accomplished this by showing an image of a warehouse. By adding wheels, it became a UPS truck. The idea was jotted down as if it were handwritten with a brown marker on a whiteboard. This ordinary-looking whiteboard and marker were just like the ones found in most meeting rooms. So people in their target audience—from shipping managers and others who arrange package deliveries to employees of small businesses and CEOs of sizable corporations—could easily relate to the messages simply because they appeared on the same kind of whiteboards they used in their offices. This instant familiarity enabled UPS to speak directly to its multiple audiences.

To fully integrate the message, the creative team didn't just use a brown marker, the color of UPS. They also put the slogan "What can Brown do for you? ®" on the side of the marker and rested it on the base of the whiteboard, where it would normally be placed. Everything about the campaign seemed like "business as usual." Azula explains the thinking behind the campaign like this: "We could add equity to the color associated with the brand. Maybe we could add meaning to the color brown by incorporating innovation, creativity, and logistics."

Although the use of a whiteboard and brown marker was very clever, what really separated this campaign was the unexpected way it was presented: Innovative planners on the account and media teams developed imaginative placement and unique usage of traditional media. Of course, you've seen sponsors' names at sporting events and on commercials during sportscasts. But what The Martin Agency did was integrate the "Whiteboard" into various sports programs by sportscasters themselves, who would write the scores using a "Whiteboard" with the UPS logo and image. The art department at the sports channels, not the agency, created these sports program "Whiteboards." Azula asked the TV channels to show the agency what they could do with whiteboards. An amazing fact is that the agency didn't produce or pay for any of the added brand placements. Azula explains it like this:

The sports channels were very creative. Each station developed its own application with whiteboards, including The History Channel, the Travel Channel, sports shows, and ESPN. UPS actually even asked to have the logo made smaller on some applications. We had approval over executions, and we approved them, or made changes, and passed them on to the client. We ended up with eighty different executions. Some of the cable stations used the whiteboards themselves to promote their shows.

The Martin Agency also used traditional media in a novel manner when it placed ads in magazines. For example, instead of creating the standard full-page ad, the team worked closely with *Entrepreneur* magazine's content editors and designed a "Whiteboard" ad that showcased innovation, which appeared at the end of a feature section that discussed innovation.

It repeated this strategic approach with other business-related publications. With *Inc.* magazine, they targeted a global market and designed strip ads that ran at the bottom of the page with the headline, "Opportunity Knocks." For *Forbes* and other business publications, they used vertical strip ads on the outside panels of facing pages. The "Distribution" ads ran in *Fortune, Forbes, BusinessWeek, Harvard Business Review, Wall Street Journal, Chief Executive, CFO Magazine, Supply Chain Management Review, World Trade,* and *Global Logistics & Supply Chain Strategies* Magazine (fig. 9.9 and fig. 9.10).

Some traditional single-page ads like the one below ran as well. Notice the interactive component to this ad (fig. 9.11). The empty boxes await a check mark, inviting consumer participation, much like the questions asked on the website, where visitors are prompted to explain what their shipping needs are, as in the Solution Finder page.

Instead of using the customary billboard space in Times Square, they went below ground, where the commuters were. Here's how Azula describes this approach:

At Times Square, so many messages are above ground, but your audience is below ground (riding the subway). The more surprising the information, the more impact it will have. For example, the UPS billboard sign in the subway said, "Delivering earlier to more places." The idea is about globalization. Every wall had a whiteboard with just the website: http://ups.com/whiteboard. The columns in the subway platforms became giant markers.

So even the everyday subway traveler was reminded to use UPS with the same "Whiteboard" visual, this time driving them to an interactive website, "Whiteboard Headquarters," where they could answer questions posed by Azula. The visitors' answers allowed UPS to specifically respond to each visitor.

Figure 9.9. This pair (figures 9.9 and 9.10) of print ads appeared in facing pages of business publications to emphasize the global reach of UPS deliveries.

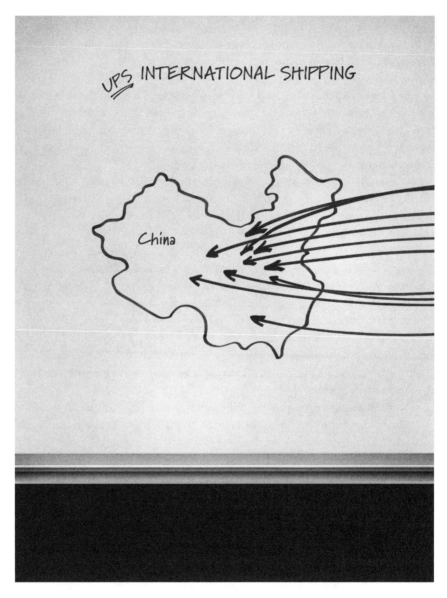

Image courtesy of The Martin Agency and UPS [i]

Figure 9.10.

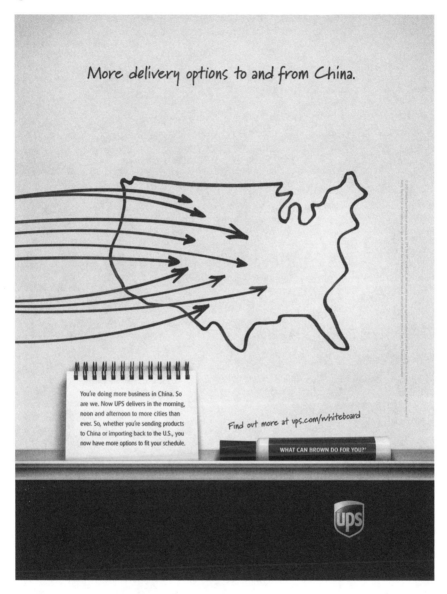

Image courtesy of The Martin Agency and UPS [j]

Figure 9.11. This print ad highlights the ability of UPS to handle specific international shipping requests.

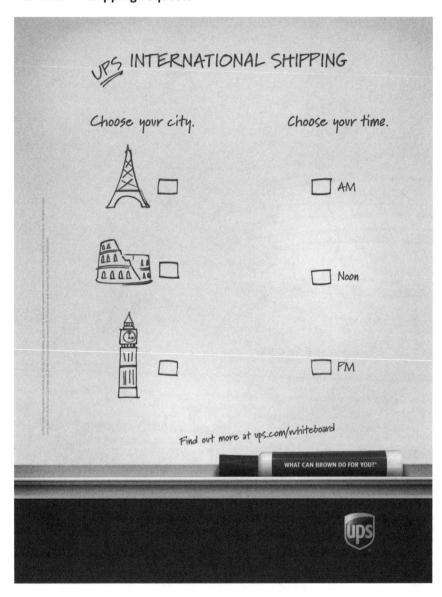

Image courtesy of The Martin Agency and UPS [k]

For the TV spots, Azula himself actually delivered the UPS message, using a whiteboard, and talking to the camera in a friendly, relaxed manner. When they were deciding on the talent, focus groups preferred him to other actors. In the commercial, he explained how easy it was to use UPS, while writing on a whiteboard with a brown marker, like a classroom teacher, not like an actor. The frame grab below is from the 30-second "Paperless" spot (fig. 9.12).

Another 30-second TV spot, "Conveyer Belt," demonstrates the same laid-back, business-as-usual tone of voice (fig. 9.13). In the script below, you can almost hear Azula's voice as he speaks to the camera, as if he's speaking to his staff in an office meeting. The capitalized letters show the video and the bold upper- and lowercase letters represent the audio portion of the spot.

The billboards in the campaign looked like giant whiteboards and included the little shelf holding a brown marker with the slogan, "What can Brown do for you? ®" All of the headlines were creative and catchy, yet clear in their consumer benefits. There is no question what UPS was offering, even when it included a little humor with a play on words. Instead of "Rise and shine," the billboard stated "Rise and sign," with the underlying message of earlier deliveries to more places (fig. 9.14). With a Chinese restaurant take-out carton as the visual, another billboard used the words "For really good Chinese delivery" Here UPS was touting its deliveries from China (fig. 9.15). As

Figure 9.12.   This :30 TV spot depicts how using online with UPS eliminates stacks of paper.

Image courtesy of The Martin Agency and UPS [i]

Figure 9.13.   This :30 TV spot shows how UPS can help make a global supply chain more efficient.

Image courtesy of The Martin Agency and UPS ᵐ

:30 UPS "Conveyer Belt" Script

ANDY WALKS UP TO WHITEBOARD. WE SEE "YOUR BUSINESS" WRITTEN AT THE TOP. A BUILDING IS DRAWN INSIDE A MAP OF THE UNITED STATES. A SYSTEM OF CONVEYOR BELTS PUSHES BOXES OUT TO DIFFERENT CORNERS OF THE COUNTRY.

ANDY: All right, your business. Well it looks like it's humming right along. Which is great. But you've got bigger plans— you wanna go global.

ANDY USES HIS FINGERS TO REDUCE THE SIZE OF THE U.S. AND MOVES IT OFF TO ONE SIDE. THE REST OF THE WORLD MAP APPEARS TO THE RIGHT.

ANDY DRAWS A UPS LOGO BUTTON ON THE LOWER LEFT. HE PUSHES IT.

ANDY: Well, with UPS, you'll get expert help with express shipping, air freight, even customs clearance. And international returns? It's easy.

SEVERAL ARCED LINES EMANATE FROM THE COMPANY, COVERING THE GLOBE. BOXES TRAVEL QUICKLY ALONG THE LINES. A COUPLE OF ARCS ARE DRAWN BACK FROM THE FOREIGN COUNTRIES WITH A FEW BOXES RETURNING TO THE COMPANY.

ANDY: It's not just your business. It's your global business with UPS.
Let's turn this up a little.

SUPER: What can Brown do for you?®

SUPER: Find out more at ups.com/whiteboard
UPS® (LOGO)

(Script courtesy of The Martin Agency and UPS.)

in the subway messages, the billboards invite the viewers to "find out more at ups.com/whiteboard," in a handwritten message on the whiteboard, in brown ink, the signature color for UPS.

Every aspect of the campaign referred back to the same message and the same visual, regardless of the medium, which also included direct mail, print ads, and 3-D outdoor boards. Each application used media in both traditional and novel ways.

Multimedia examples of the campaign can be viewed online with links from pressroom.ups.com/mediakits/factsheet/0,2305,1371,00.html. Most impressive, however, are the results of this campaign. According to a DRI Tracking Study conducted at the end of the first quarter of 2007, the "Whiteboard" campaign has:

- Given UPS its highest levels of unaided advertising awareness ever recorded: 67.6 percent.
- Helped UPS lead the category in unaided ad awareness, with UPS at 63.3 percent, FedEx at 43.9 percent, DHL at 13.6 percent, and USPS at 7.6 percent.
- Led the category in unaided brand awareness, with UPS at 90.9 percent, FedEx at 62.1 percent, DHL at 25.8 percent, and USPS at 22.7 percent.

Figure 9.14. This billboard demonstrates UPS morning delivery in a humorous way.

Image courtesy of The Martin Agency and UPS [n]

Figure 9.15. This billboard uses a whimsical approach to emphasize that UPS delivers to and from China.

Image courtesy of The Martin Agency and UPS [o]

Data from another DRI Tracking Study showed that revenue was up 10.3 percent for international shipping at the end of the second quarter of 2007, and up 14 percent for freight services in April 2007, as compared to April 2006.

In addition, Webtrends data showed enhanced online brand interaction, with more than 1.3 million visits to ups.com/whiteboard and 2,700 product demo views. UPS registered

- 26,019,485 online advertising interactions
- more than 3 billion ad impressions
- more than 75,000 create-your-own-Whiteboard e-mails sent
- more than 17,000 views of the television commercials online

This campaign proves that marketers looking to develop exciting and effective campaigns don't necessarily have to find new media; they just need to find a new way to use all media.

How Creative Teams Start to Integrate New Media

With all the new media being created every day by everyone in agencies, from media and account planners to creative talents, the question becomes: Do they change the way teams approach the solution? Kosel explains, "It allows [the process] to be more open, which can sometimes be more challenging because you're not just focused on one thing." Instead of worrying about how to write for a specific medium, it now can go the other way around. Kosel says, "For me, it's about having an idea, and finding the right home for it."

Other creatives agree. Matt Jarvis, director of account planning for the GM account at Deutsch L.A., says the one thing that has changed is that you "have a larger, more diverse stage," where you can not only connect with people, but also have them interact with the brand. He sounds enthusiastic as he explains:

Oh, it's making it more fun. You've got a much bigger toy chest to play with now. The fundamentals of communicating and marketing are still the same. You want to conceive of big ideas that move people in some way.

As discussed in chapter 5, the multimedia PEDIGREE® campaign had a measurable impact on the audience, increasing awareness and pet adoptions, as well as raising more than $4 million for animal shelters. The campaign didn't just include heart-tugging TV spots, billboards, and print ads, it included innovative, out-of-home messaging as well.

The campaign also introduced a Times Square "DOGSTORE" (fig. 9.16) where people could adopt dogs, be taped discussing their pet adoption story for the website www.DOGSRULE.com, upload images of their pets to be part of

Figure 9.16.   This pop-up store was created to raise money and awareness for shelter dogs and the PEDIGREE® Adoption Drive. All profits were donated to the cause.

Image courtesy of Mars Petcare US, TBWA\Chiat\Day. Photographic images courtesy of Peggy Sirota (for the dog) and Arthaus (for the pop-up dog store). PEDIGREE®, DOGS RULE®, and other insignia are trademarks of Mars, Incorporated and its affiliates. These trademarks are used with permission. © Mars, Incorporated 2008. ᴾ

an online mosaic of a million dogs, let their kids play on a giant doggie bed, or watch people interacting with puppies in the window.

To drive people to the pop-up store, life-size cutouts of dogs in the signature golden yellow of PEDIGREE® packaging were placed in Central Park with the message inside the cutout, "Wish I were here." The dog's message went on to say that the dog could be visited at the PEDIGREE® store at 46th Street and Broadway. What an ingenious way to create attention, stimulate curiosity, and drive people over to take a look at the shelter dogs available for adoption.

This campaign brilliantly used the technique of media intersection. This is used to reach unsuspecting audience members in the middle of their everyday life, interrupting them with an unexpected message. Campaigns that use media intersection effectively position well-targeted messages precisely where the audience is. A perfect example is the "Are You a Mitchum Man" campaign by Deutsch that wrote strategic messages on coasters and matchbooks in bars, specifically speaking to the intended audience: thirty- to forty-nine-year-old educated professional males. One on-target coaster message said, "If you let your buddy have the hot one, you're a Mitchum Man."[8]

Reaching a Hard-to-Reach Audience

Teenage audiences could be considered some of the most elusive. That could be why teenage artist Ashley Quails had an instant, loyal audience when she created colorful, energetic designs for MyFace pages for her friends. Rather than charging for her MyFace templates, she gave them away with a link to her website: www.WhateverLife.com. A prolific illustrator and fluent webpage designer, Quails created more than 2,500 designs before she was approached by her first sponsor: ValueClick Media. With approximately $70,000 coming in each month from one sponsor, she suddenly realized she had created an online business that was reaching more than a few hundred thousand young girls a day.[9] Today the site has numerous sponsors, more templates, website design tips, and mini-tutorials reaching a vast audience of those hard-to-target tween and teenage kids.

Even major marketers know they need to develop an innovative way to talk to a teenage market. OfficeMax turned to Vinny Warren, developer of the DDB Budweiser "Whasssup?" campaign and creative director at The Escape Pod, for help on a back-to-school promotion. Warren explains what Quails knew, "The obvious thing is, in the online world, you have to earn your own audience," just as the free templates and tutorials gave Quails's audience what it wanted. He continues, "If somebody's going to your whatever site, they want useful information or to be entertained or something."

When creating the back-to-school campaign for OfficeMax, Warren knew he had to reach the teen audience. So his team created a show that would appeal to kids. Since kids usually enjoy pranks, he arranged for students of New Milford High School in New Jersey to be "schooled" by OfficeMax (fig. 9.17). It aired three times in August on CW network and went on to be a Google video, with four times as many people seeing it on Google as on TV. It was also presented in several other forms, including a DVD.

The ultimate prank took place on June 23, when the students were told they would lose funding for the music program if they couldn't answer a series of ridiculous questions presented as a major oral quiz and present a stellar performance of a quickly rehearsed composition. After many nerve-wracking hours, these students were told they had been "schooled" and it was a prank. With that, they were treated to a wonderful surprise: a live concert by the All-American Rejects right in their school, sponsored by OfficeMax. After the August 2006 showing of "Schooled," students could go to OfficeMax and pick up a limited edition DVD of the show, along with a $50 coupon good toward school

Figure 9.17.   This show was created as an innovative way to reach high school students and persuade them to go to OfficeMax for their back-to-school needs.

Image courtesy of The Escape Pod [q]

supplies. Did it work? According to Warren it did, "because it was on Google, everything's measured on Google."

Almost everyone looking for anything today "googles it," meaning they go to Google first to find whatever they're looking for, just as people wanting to see the latest Super Bowl commercials go to YouTube as their first place to search. Or as young people go to YouTube to see who has posted the most interesting self-created video. In advertising this kind of homemade material, first called user-generated content, is now referred to as consumer-created content.

Having consumers create product-related content is a goal of many brands. Dove asked its audience to create their own TV spots that extended the "Real Beauty" campaign. Actual commercials shot by "real women" were aired on the Oscars, rather than the Super Bowl, because of its primarily female audience.

Using Websites in New Ways

Usually websites are designed to promote a product or service, to create a social networking community, or to act as a new broadcast medium through podcasts and Blog Talk Radio programs. However, now websites are also being used as sounding boards for happy and disgruntled consumers.

When Bob Garfield, author of *Advertising Age*'s popular column "Ad Review," was unhappy with the service he received from his cable company, Com-

cast, his frustration drove him to create the website www.ComcastMustDie
.com.[10] The main purpose of this site was to allow other disgruntled Comcast
customers, now "consumer vigilantes," to vent their anger in a general forum
of postings.[11] People from all over logged on to share their negative experiences,
much to the chagrin of Comcast.

Other consumer vigilantes have done the same thing. On June 21, 2005,
blogger Jeff Jarvis was so furious when his new Dell computer didn't work
that he blasted it on his popular site, www.BuzzMachine.com. But, he didn't
stop there. Infuriated by Dell's indifference to his complaints, Jarvis created
a post with this title: "Dell Lies, Dell Sucks." So, whenever people typed the
word Dell in Google, Yahoo, or any other search engine, his posting came up.
Talk about getting even and finding a brilliant way to harness the power of
search engines. (Maximizing search results is called search engine optimiza-
tion). Irritated consumers today don't sit back and take it. They sit up and
type back!

It is just this kind of annoyance over bad customer service that drove one
company to create a subscription-based online service, Angie's List. This website, www.AngiesList.com, allows people to post their personal reviews about
the service they received from various home improvement companies. With
most home repairs costing several hundred dollars, people are happy to pay a
small subscription fee to read unbiased, unsolicited comments from regular consumers like themselves. And people don't just complain about poor work, they
also rave about exceptional service.

The team of creative directors from Young & Laramore, Carolyn Hadlock
and Charlie Hopper, created a campaign that highlighted exactly what Angie's
List offered: the truth. That was something people were willing to pay fifty-four
dollars or more a year for—depending on the market—an in-depth honest as-
sessment of service. After all, that's a lot cheaper than having to redo unaccept-
able work.

As Hopper explains, "What we found was, people wanted to know the
good things as much as the bad things." They wanted to know that the painter
tracked red paint on the carpet and didn't bother to clean it up. Or that the
plumber not only did great work, but actually walked the dog when it needed
to go out. Hopper adds, "Everything in the campaign is either a positive experience, or what we would call a good-to-know experience. For instance, it's good
to know that the electrician hates cats."

The campaign, which drove readers to the website, included TV spots,
print ads, and billboards. One billboard headline read, "He put up the roof. We
put up with his music." One print ad used this alliterative and clever headline,
"Ratings, Reviews, and Sometimes Revenge" (fig. 9.18). The TV buy included
targeting news shows, because, Hadlock adds, "what we found was this [service]
is for the person who was in information-gathering mode. So, we ended up

Figure 9.18. Angie's List is a national company that helps new users learn from other's actual experience which service companies near them do good work, and which don't. One of a series, this ad quoted actual homeowner reviews to demonstrate Angie's List's ability to offer its users ratings, reviews—and revenge.

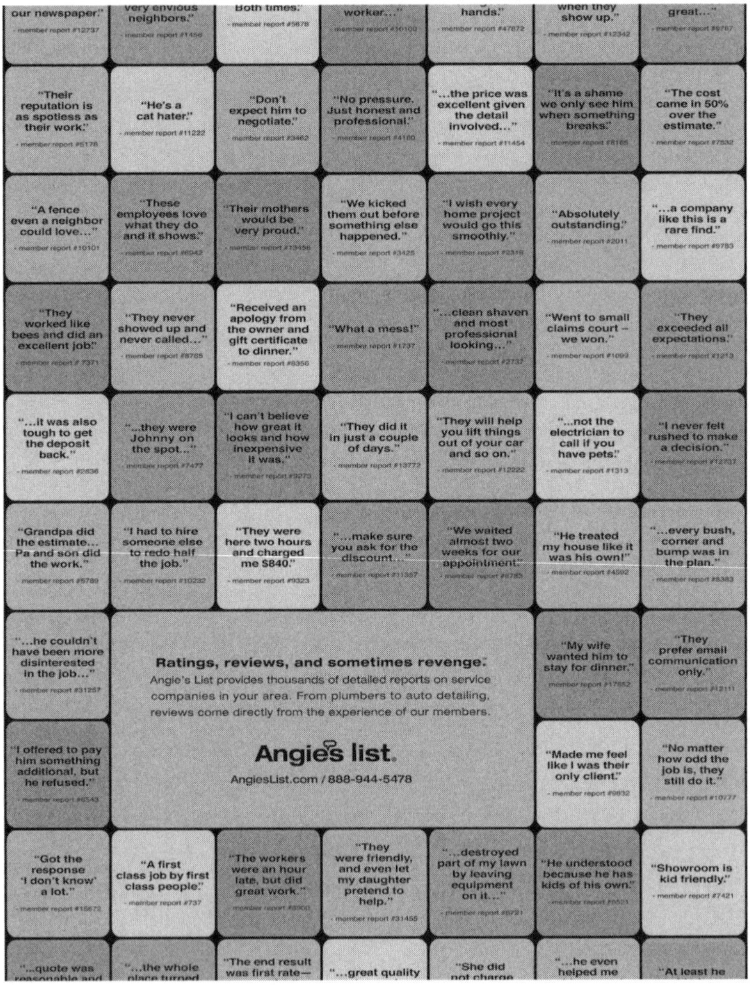

Image courtesy of Young & Laramore

having a broadcast strategy that was very news-based: FOX, MSNBC, and now even Imus, or what used to be Imus on MSNBC."

Alternative ways to use media are practically limitless, as new approaches are born every day.

A Quick Look at Online Video Marketing

Jessica Kizorek, managing director of Two Parrot Productions and author of *Show Me: Marketing with Video on the Internet*, discusses how the Internet allows people to choose if and when they see a message. They can opt in and accept messages or click away and reject them. Kizorek explains, "When marketing messages occur as a pesky intrusion, the viewer is likely to close them out as quickly as possible."

This gives consumers the power to choose what they allow past their filters. It gives them some control over messages that used to be intrusive. With DVRs becoming part of more people's everyday behavior, television viewing and the receipt of messages have been forever changed. Viewers can speed past messages intended for their consideration. In addition, people are spending more time online finding common areas of interest, creating communities of like-minded individuals who will more readily accept industry information and product suggestions. Kizorek comments on the power of the consumer to be selective in viewing and receiving messages:

> They get to say what they are going to pay attention to, what information they ask for next. If they get bored, they are gone. It's not a passive medium.

Kizorek explains how online video communication has yet to grow into what it could ultimately become once the technology is commonplace. Being in its infancy, who knows how this will affect brand-and-consumer interactivity and engagement? With the Internet's capability to allow for a specific interaction with a specific audience, today's marketers must present a clear explanation of how their product will improve the consumers' lives and why they need to buy it.

As with all media, advertisers have to know what they want the end user to know about their product or service. According to Kizorek, the question when deciding whether to include video as part of the marketing mix is: "What is it that video would accomplish for you that sending out a brochure would not accomplish?" This question is relevant when determining any medium, whether it's an online interactive game or an out-of-home message.

The Fun Factor of Interactive Media

The reason many agencies want to create online, interactive material is not just because it's fun for them and for the audience, but also because interactivity keeps the audience more fully engaged. One online game, www.GetTheGlass.com, for "Got Milk?" was created by Paul Charney, senior copywriter at Goodby, Silverstein & Partners. This interactive game not only educated the players about milk, but challenged them to find the last glass of milk by "driving" a vehicle around a winding road. Around 2,000 to 3,000 glasses were sent out to players who managed to successfully maneuver around the course. Although it was fun, the game still had enough educational content to intrigue educators about including it in the classroom. According to Charney, "there are a couple of teachers in California who are starting to have their students play it." This site was so well received that creative talents at other agencies were telling each other about it.

A second site, www.CowAbduction.com, was created using a totally different strategy than the famous milk deprivation campaign. Here the creatives came up with a way to showcase the benefits of milk by having an alien discover its elixir-like qualities. To get milk on the alien's planet, it was abducting cows from earth and taking them away in space ships. This "Brittlelactic" campaign led to the cow abduction site where the cow abductions were shown from the farmers' side. To prevent the abductions, farmers dressed their cows up in disguises to fool the aliens. The entire site is made up of fake stories of cow abductions. To demonstrate the abductions, a cow flies off the page as soon as a visitor's mouse clicks on it.

How did the agency get the word out about the site to generate buzz? Here's what Charney says:

> Well, what happens is it starts getting blogged about. We definitely seeded it. You know, we put up fake postings on other blogs, and other sites, and tried to get a little buzz going. And then, it sort of just happened. It just sort of moved.

That's usually how it happens. Word of Web now is even faster than word of mouth. The final question is, how does the integration of new media factor into the creative process? According to Lea Ladera, senior art director at Goodby, Silverstein & Partners, it just becomes "one more thing you should think about."

Another special feature of online media is that unlike print ads, or radio and TV spots, if you missed it, the message will not disappear. Online games and other Web messages last so they can be shared and passed on, giving them a little longer "shelf life."

Agencies today are looking to create interactive, entertaining, yet relevant messages in a refreshing new way, both with traditional and new media. Consumers with busy, hectic schedules are hungry for fun. This is why reaching them in interesting ways and in novel places can cause an "Oh, wow!" reaction. Seeing a piping hot "cup of coffee" on the ground shocks, then amuses, the pedestrian. The sudden appearance of the PEDIGREE® pop-up store in Times Square, discussed and shown earlier in this chapter, captured the attention of the media as well as that of pedestrians (see fig. 9.16). Even three-dimensional billboards can take on a larger-than-life feel when the images appear to jump off the board (see chapter 8, figs. 8.1, 8.2, and 8.3). Eye-catching images in unexpected places are why ambient campaigns like the earlier-mentioned Folger's manhole cover ad have received so much press. Creative teams today are looking to develop interruptive messages that gain attention from both consumers and the press.

Notes

1. Denis Higgins, *The Art of Writing Advertising: Conversations with the Masters of the Craft* (Chicago: NTC Business Books, 1965), 18.

2. The "Burning Home" campaign was created by the following team: Chavo D'Emilio, creative director; Hernán Rebaldería, Daniel Fierro, and Pablo Tajer, art directors and designers; Damián Lubenfeld, programmer; and Adrían Aspani and Cosme Argerich, production managers.

3. www.veniceconsulting.com/cases.aspx?id=98, accessed April 11, 2008.

4. Robyn Blakeman, *The Bare Bones Introduction to Integrated Marketing Communication* (Lanham, MD: Rowman & Littlefield Publishers, 2009), 278–279.

5. Margo Berman, *Street-Smart Advertising: How to Win the Battle of the Buzz* (Lanham, MD: Rowman & Littlefield Publishers, 2007), 16–17.

6. Laura Blum, "Pepsi Brings Smell, Sound to Print," *Adweek*, October 9, 2006, 10.

7. www.gushmagazine.com/article/something-smellslike-a-sale/, accessed May 8, 2008.

8. Berman, *Street-Smart Advertising*, 169–174.

9. Chuck Salter, "Girl Power," *Fast Company*, September 2007, www.fastcompany.com/magazine/118/girl-power.html, accessed May 7, 2008.

10. Bob Garfield, "Comcast Must Die," *Advertising Age*, November 19, 2007, adage.com/article?article_id=122094&search_phrase=Comcast+Bob+Garfield, accessed May 21, 2008.

11. Jena McGregor, "Consumer Vigilantes: Memo to Corporate America: Hell Now Hath No Fury like a Customer Scorned," *Business Week*, February 21, 2008, www.businessweek.com/magazine/content/08_09/b4073038437662.htm, accessed May 21, 2008.

Image Credits

a. This "Rabbit" online interactive banner ad was created by Crispin Porter + Bogusky for Volkswagen.

b. This "Miami Rabbit" print ad was created by Crispin Porter + Bogusky for Volkswagen.

c. This "NYC Rabbit" print ad was created by Crispin Porter + Bogusky for Volkswagen.

d. This "NYC Rabbit Transit" print ad was created by Crispin Porter + Bogusky for Volkswagen.

e. The "Burning Home" Internet banner created by Del Campo Nazca Saatchi & Saatchi for their client Answer Seguro On Line.

f. Answer's "Man" banner created by Chavo D´Emilio (Executive Creative Director), Mariano Serkin (Creative Director), and Guadalupe Pereyra (Copywriter) from Saatchi & Saatchi for the Argentine Insurance Company.

g. This is an image taken from "Force9," an online game, created by Saatchi & Saatchi for the New Zealand Army.

h. This image features 2 web banners used to promote "Force9," an online game, created by Saatchi & Saatchi for the New Zealand Army.

i. This image, from the "China Arrows" facing-pages print ads, was created by The Martin Agency for UPS.

j. This image, from the "China Arrows" facing-pages print ads, was created by The Martin Agency for UPS.

k. This image, from the "International Shipping" print ad, was created by The Martin Agency for UPS.

l. This frame grab, from the "Paperless" TV spot, was created by The Martin Agency for UPS.

m. This frame grab, from the "Conveyer Belt" TV spot, was created by The Martin Agency for UPS.

n. This image, from the "Rise and Sign" 3-D billboard, was created by The Martin Agency for UPS.

o. This image, from the "Chinese Delivery" 3-D billboard, was created by The Martin Agency for UPS.

p. This store was created by TBWA\Chiat\Day.

q. "Schooled," a branded content TV show, created by Vinny Warren (Creative Director) and Norm Bilow (Managing Director) of The Escape Pod for OfficeMax.

r. "Revenge" print ad created by Young & Laramore (Writer Jeff Nieberding; Art Director Pam Kelliher; Creative Director Carolyn Hadlock; Strategy Tom Denari) for Angie's List.

Interviews

Paul Charney, personal communication, March 6, 2008.
Jessica Kizorek, personal communication, May 18, 2007.
Tiffany Kosel and Scott Linnen, personal communication, August 31, 2008.
Matt Jarvis, personal communication, May 22, 2007.
Lea Ladera, personal communication, June 10, 2008.
Vinny Warren, personal communication, March 21, 2007.
Carolyn Hadlock and Charlie Hopper, personal communication, May 25, 2007.
Del Campo Nazca Saatchi & Saatchi, personal correspondence, May 15, 2007 and June 9, 2008.
New Zealand Saatchi & Saatchi, personal correspondence, June 9, 2008.

CHAPTER 10

Nuts and Bolts of Great Presentations

Few people have the time to stop and try to figure out what you're trying to say—Linda Kaplan Thaler and Robin Koval[1]

Pitching the Solution to an Advertising Problem

Preparing an advertising pitch or any type of presentation requires organization, teamwork, continuity, and creativity. The ultimate goal is to solve the client's advertising problem by defining the agency's direction for a product or service in a unique way.

Very competitive, the pitch process is more than a single presentation. It's the synthesis of months of research and business, media, and creative development which can pay off with the winning of a multimillion dollar account.

Overall, the difference between a presentation and an advertising pitch is minimal. A presentation is the formal or informal delivery of information to any size group. An advertising pitch on the other hand, can be defined as the formal, competitive delivery of sales, media, and creative ideas meant to solve a client's advertising problem. Beyond problem solving, a pitch must: 1) clearly and imaginatively outline your agency's qualifications and experience with this brand and overall product category, and 2) build credibility and instill trust in your agency's capabilities.

Once agencies decide to pitch, they will have anywhere from a week to over a month to prepare. The agency must move fast, but efficiently, to define the product category and brand, the competition, and the target. Equally critical is knowing what the client wants and needs. As a rule, the more cutting-edge your ideas, or the farther they are from the client's current advertising efforts, the more important it is for these ideas to be backed up with a sound business strategy.

Eric Springer from Deutsch describes their presentation approach when pitching a new and unique idea:

> Disruption is a powerful concept which we're proud to embrace. When we go in to pitch a piece of business, we're trying to establish a relationship on the basis of our intellectual talents, not just our creativity.
>
> At the same time, we're also selling the notion that if you don't push the envelope, that if you don't do something that's strategically disruptive, the brand is going to remain in the same place. What we try to bring to the table is an idea that lets you leap over what the competition is, and so we put our brave thinking in the context of a business strategy before we ever show ads that might be a little scary or different than what a client thinks they should be.
>
> In new business, you are trying to create trust, but still hopefully on the terms [that will make the client conclude that] these guys are so smart and have such an interesting way of thinking about my business problem, [we should be] having them do [our] advertising. They could be an asset to my company.

Depending on the parameters surrounding the product and client needs, the average presentation can last anywhere from ninety minutes to three hours. Most advertising professionals would agree the more time allotted the better. However, they would also agree that it's not how much time you have, it's what you do with it. The overall purpose is to both educate and entertain, while using as many interactive, attention-getting devices as possible to involve the audience in the presentation, creating interest.

The preparatory stage of a presentation, like the creative process, is the brainstorming and strategic development phase. The agency will begin the process by developing a presentation brief. Here the client and intended target (the end user) are defined, presentation objectives set, competition dissected (for both the account and the product or service), and the strategic solution outlined (business direction, media plan, and creative), all of which are necessary to solve the client's advertising problem.

Presentation development must:

1. Set presentation objectives
2. Educate and entertain
3. Create attention-getting techniques
4. Know the audience and its goals
5. Have a realistic, believable plan
6. Conceive a solid strategy to solve the client's problem
7. Be convincing and personable
8. Be on-target and on-strategy
9. Create something original
10. Present long-term options

Agencies enter every pitch knowing they are the best agency for the account, but that doesn't guarantee they will get it. Only about 20 percent of all pitches made are won. Participation is a time-intensive, emotionally draining experience that often costs agencies thousands and thousands of dollars. On one level, an unsuccessful pitch can reflect the team's lack of preparation or inability to connect with the client. On another, losing doesn't always mean your agency's ideas were not the best. Sometimes chemistry loses the account. Sometimes the client just likes the other guys better.

Lee Clow, creative director worldwide at TBWA\Chiat\Day, counsels being true to your agency's belief system, saying, "We go in and try to understand the client in terms of his needs and his wants and who is his audience. We try to show them how we think about the business and how we think about the advertising they should do. So if we get hired, we're hired for the right reasons. And if we don't get hired, it's because they didn't want what we sell."[2]

Who Talks the Pitch's Talk?

Before the presentation can be developed, delivered, and sold to the client, it's important the right people are in place to prepare and present.

Presentations can be led by one or two power hitters or by a series of senior-level department leaders. But most often, a presentation team includes an account executive to direct the pitch, an account planner to help develop strategic direction, a media director to illustrate media choice and direction, a creative director to oversee and present creative, and quite possibly, the specific account executive slated to handle the account, if landed. Depending upon need, additional experts in such areas as public relations, direct marketing, interactive design, or broadcast, to name just a few, will be included on the presentation team.

Preparation begins with the members of the team working together to come up with ideas for the presentation. Here is where good ideas are solidified and bad ideas are discarded. Each idea must relentlessly seek to define direction, relieve qualification concerns, and encourage acceptance.

When writing and delivering a presentation, it's important to have consistency in both delivery and voice. It's imperative that each team member not only knows his or her own part, but also those of the others on the team. Working together to develop the presentation, rather than segregating the teams and their sections of the pitch, creates a cohesive message from section to section. Interactivity between speakers is not only more interesting, but more educational to the prospective client. Knowing what each team member will say creates a more comfortable transition between presenters, eliminates uncomfortable pauses, and allows for tag-team question-and-answer sessions.

PHASE ONE:
Developing and Conducting the Presentation

The average advertising pitch will have five sections or phases: Phase one includes the preparation of a presentation brief, brainstorming, and the scripting and timing of the presentation. The second phase will introduce your agency members and their qualifications as well as inform, create interest, and build curiosity about your ideas. This is also where you will lay the foundation and set the tone for the overall presentation, build credibility, and build a rapport with the client. The third phase should educate and entertain by visually/verbally telling how your main idea(s) will solve the client's advertising problem, based on research and your expertise in the area. Here's where you must know what presentation materials you'll be using and how they'll be used. Phase four sums up your important points and ties them to your qualifications, while phase five addresses any questions the client may have.

Mastering each of these phases will guarantee a successful presentation. Landing the account will be based on how well the team successfully solves the client's advertising problem compared to competing agencies.

Let's begin by taking a look at preparation. Phase one includes: pitch or brief preparation, brainstorming, script writing, and timelining the presentation.

The Role of the Presentation Brief

A presentation brief, like a creative brief, is a small document that will outline what the presentation needs to accomplish and how it will be done. Developed by members of the presentation team, each brief needs to focus on how to solve the client's advertising problem by showing how your agency and your ideas reflect the client's goals. Additionally, the brief must focus on target needs and wants, accomplish a set of communication objectives, highlight how your ideas differentiate the client's brand from the competition, outline the overall tone of the presentation, project the major point to be focused on, and reflect the outcome of your strategy. The purpose of the brief is to help the presentation team brainstorm ideas and develop the overall visual/verbal voice for the presentation.

Brainstorming Ideas for the Pitch

Every good brainstorming session begins with a little research or gathering of background information. Research, whether gathered independently or supplied by the client, is the foundation for educating the team on the client's brand, overall product category, and strategic direction. It's important that a thorough understanding of the client, its past and current advertising efforts, its current problem, and your agency's immediate and future solution(s) back up the idea pitched. This information will eventually be used to support both the presentation and the advertising direction.

Presentation teams will typically incorporate two types of research into their presentation: general and specific. General research focuses on the target audiences' social, economic, and cultural interaction with the product or service and sets the product on a new direction. Specific research dissects both the product and product category, as well as the relevant competitors, making sure the information hits the intended target.

Once this factual foundation is laid, the team can use this information in brainstorming sessions to develop ideas that will help achieve the strategic goals laid out in the brief.

Once complete, the results of the brainstorming session will need to be ruthlessly edited down, leaving only those ideas that simply and directly solve the client's advertising problem. Each of these ideas will be further worked and reworked before all but one is eliminated and the visual/verbal route for the presentation is solidified.

In the end, proper preparation is the first step to building both credibility and trust, and it will help keep the presentation on target and on strategy as laid out in the presentation brief. Additionally, this attention to detail will help the team not only present from the client's point of view, but also lay the foundation for how your agency will handle the account in the future.

Outlining, Scripting, and Timing the Presentation: What Will Be Said and Shown

Begin with an Outline

Once you've completed the brainstorming sessions, the next step is to develop a point-by-point visual/verbal outline of what will be shown and said throughout the presentation. Outlines should be topical and brief, not descriptive and overly detailed—that is the script's job.

Like an ad, your presentation can be broken down into two simple categories: visual and verbal solutions. Both will help to tell your agency's version of the product's advertising story, by informing (verbally), and entertaining or explaining (visually).

Begin the outlining process by vertically dividing a sheet of paper in half. On the left side are the bulleted verbal points the presentation must cover. On the right is where you can either doodle or write out the possible visual solutions. This visual/verbal process will not only help the team imagine how the presentation will both look and sound to their audience, but will also provide a preliminary timeline.

The verbal portion of the presentation, covered in more detail later in the chapter, basically consists of: 1) What you will open with (the beginning), 2) What you're offering (the middle), and 3) The most important points you want the potential client to take away from the presentation (conclusion).

Visuals can replace or support the written or spoken word. Unlike text or dialogue, visuals and props are tangible. They can be experienced. Imagery can stimulate the viewer's imagination, demonstrate a use, or simplify a concept.

Visual experiences such as demonstrations have action. Visual aids such as props, ad mock-ups, or package designs that can be held, touched, and experienced can create effective, memorable metaphors.

Multisensory presentations involve the listener in an activity. Interactivity is important in any discussion, not only for engagement, but also for retention. Robert W. Pike in his book *Creative Training Techniques Handbook* offers the following statistics on retention:

We remember:

- 10 percent of what we read
- 20 percent of what we hear
- 30 percent of what we see
- 50 percent of what we hear and see
- 70 percent of what we say
- 90 percent of what we say and do

So the more interactive or participatory you can make the material presented to the client, the more relevant, memorable, and interesting it will be to them.

Some other good interactive tools or memory enhancers include:

- Slice-of-life story lines
- Statistics
- Questions
- Animatics
- Body language
- Analogies
- Quotations
- Tactile demonstrations
- Props
- Examples

Scripting the Tone or Story Line

Scripting the presentation is a lot like writing a novel or developing a movie or play. The characters must be interesting and engaging, and the plot needs to move your ideas forward as well as develop unique ways to overcome marketplace obstacles and competitive villains. The tone of the presentation's voice must reflect your agency and its direction for the client's advertising.

Using your outline as a guide, it is important before sitting down to write that you determine what kind of presentation you want. Will you use humor, quotes, analogies, or statistics to tell your version of the product's story? Will you present alone or in teams? Will you demonstrate something? If so, will your demonstration be tactile or projected onto a screen? Will you use props of any kind, such as mock layouts, flip charts, websites, packaging, animatics, or fully produced television or radio spots? Will you use a computer, easel, LCD projector, or layout pad?

A well-thought-out presentation must create enough interest and drama to both surprise the audience and hold their attention while the plot or presentation unfolds. To do this, the presentation must do more than just tell the product or service's advertising story, it must create opportunities for the client to interact with the message in much the same way as the intended targeted audience might experience the message.

When determining the presentation's visual/verbal route, it is important to remember that your audience will include both left- and right-brain learners. Some will be more interested in your verbal presentation, others will be more involved in the visuals that define the message, and still others will be stimulated by tactile demonstrations. Intersperse a little of each ingredient and it will be more memorable to all.

Writing the Presentation Script

- Be sure you begin your presentation with an introduction of who you are and who your agency is.
- Outline your knowledge of the client's product or service and let them know how you plan to differentiate it from the competition.
- Appeal to the client's rational and emotional sides. In other words, present the information factually and tie the facts to how the product or service will make consumers feel, change their lives, or solve a problem.
- Use visuals only to support a point or idea.
- A presentation should flow like a casual conversation between two people; keep your presentation from sounding like you're giving a speech or preaching.
- Keep it simple and concentrate on your main point(s). Even the best-prepared presentation will not succeed if it is off-target or off-strategy.
- Be sure to use transitions to tie the different sections together.
- Use action verbs to help the listener visualize what is being said. Good action verbs include: imagine, visualize, remember, or recall.
- To keep a list from appearing to ramble on, consider inserting words such as "furthermore" or "in addition."
- To prove a point, consider using the phrase "for example."
- To summarize several points, consider using "in conclusion" or "as a result."
- For more complicated issues, use multiple short paragraphs interspersed with longer ones. By breaking the message up into multiple short paragraphs, you can alter your pacing, making it easier to both present and understand.
- When preparing your presentation, avoid using long paragraphs or lists when possible. For one, it's easier to remember and two, it will keep detailed sections from appearing to drone on.
- Exact numbers can be difficult to follow in a presentation; round them off when possible.
- If it's difficult to say, it's probably difficult to understand as well, so slow down, vary your sentence length and pace, and repeat or summarize as needed.
- Keep terms and verbiage consistent throughout the campaign.
- Conclude the presentation by summing up the important points.

- It is never too early when preparing the written material for your presentation to proof for spelling, grammar, text formatting, layout, accuracy, and consistency.

Time Trials

Once the client has informed the agency how long you will have to present, it's critical the team create a timeline that synchronizes the presentation's various visual/verbal elements to fit within that time frame. A good timeline should dedicate 15 percent of the allotted time to the introduction, 75 percent to the middle or body of the presentation, and 10 percent to the conclusion. If allowing for questions at the end of the presentation, an additional 10 percent will need to be deducted from the middle of your pitch.

How you decide to present the information you have collected will determine length. It makes a difference whether you plan to memorize the presentation in its entirety, memorize just the beginning and ending, or rely on notes or PowerPoint slides. A memorized presentation is the easiest to time out. It often eliminates the temptation to go over the time limit and can make you look more prepared than using notes or reading off a PowerPoint slide. On the other hand, a presentation that has been memorized from beginning to end can be stoic, allowing for little or no spontaneity. It can often create awkward pauses if presenters should lose their place. Because of this, many professionals recommend memorizing just the opening and closing portions.

It's not against the law to have notes nearby, but they should not be used as a crutch. Notes and reliance on computer-generated slides often slow a presentation down, introduce a lecture-type feel, create inequity between sections, and encourage repetition. If you have to have notes, use them only as a safety net or as an at-a-glance timetable. This is especially helpful if your presentation is longer than ninety minutes.

Rehearsing the Presentation

The success or failure of months of research and preparation depends on delivering a polished presentation. Because of this, you cannot practice or rehearse enough. Like your projected images, you're a very important visual aid. It's important that the same care is taken to sell yourself as it is to sell the team's ideas. Begin by taking a good hard look at first your mannerisms and then your dress.

Our mannerisms, or body language, need to be seen and heard to be believed. A good way to see, as well as hear, the message you send to others is to practice your part of the presentation in front of a mirror or by using a video camera. All of these devices allow you to see your body language and facial expressions and listen to your voice, your pace, and your pitch. Be brutal, ask yourself: Is your delivery too dry, too authoritative, or too dull? Are you relaxed, with your hands naturally at your sides, or stiff like a propped-up mannequin? Do you rock from side to side, frown, make funny faces, blink too often, or swallow loudly? Do you look your audience in the eye, or glance away? Do you stand up straight, or lean on a podium? Do you know where you are in comparison to the projected images, or is your slightly oversized head blocking out the information? Do you fidget or use fillers like "ah," "err," or "ya know" during pauses, causing you to sound illiterate and nervous? Do you put your hands in your pockets? Do you play with your hair, jewelry, or clothing? Feel free to walk around if it relaxes you, but don't pace. Use your hands only for emphasis; do not look as if you're directing traffic.

Often our mannerisms are exacerbated by our fears. So no matter how much rehearsing will polish the presentation, it may not necessarily alleviate your fears about speaking in front of an audience. Surveys consistently show that speaking in front of an audience tops the list of personal fears. The old adage that "most people would prefer to be lying in the casket than give the eulogy" holds true for a lot of people. But remember, preparation is the key to greater confidence.

Stress can also manifest itself in the form of hyperactivity, so watch the coffee intake before any presentation.

One of the best ways to relieve tension is to arrive at the presentation early. Depending on the venue, arriving forty-five minutes to an hour before the meeting will allow you to catch your breath and arrange your thoughts. If this simple technique does nothing to reduce your fears, you might consider a more radical step—become an actor and enroll in an acting class.

Role-playing is a great way to manage, if not overcome, your fear of public speaking. Thinking of yourself as an actor playing a role often makes it easier to "perform" in front of others and helps develop the dramatic techniques and the voice control needed to deliver the words, entertain, and hold the audience's attention. Another option includes joining a local Toastmasters chapter, a national association that focuses on presentation skills.

If role-playing or group meetings are not your thing, and practicing in front of a video camera hasn't eliminated your stiff, robotic posture and fear of presenting, the only other option besides quitting is to just jump in with both feet. Remember the old adage "What doesn't kill you makes you stronger."

Finally, it's important to remember that the audience members are on your side. They have asked you here and want to hear your opinions. If you're prepared, no matter the adrenaline rush, you will appear relaxed and confident. Eleanor Roosevelt was right on when she said, "No one can intimidate me without my permission."

Here are some additional pointers to ensure you are in control of the presentation:

- Look at your audience. Begin by finding one friendly face in the crowd, making brief eye contact (three to five seconds), and then switching to someone else. Another option is to have your eye follow the shape of a "Z" around the room.
- Smile. Be sure to smile, not the whole time, but where appropriate, like after some important point or anecdote.
- Face forward. Never turn your back on your audience; you can't look them in the eye if you do.
- Move. If you have to move, do so. If you are uncomfortable and stiff, it will affect the presentation. Movement also helps hold the audience's attention.
- Voice pitch. Know your voice. Is it too high or too low? Do you talk too fast? Do you like to draw your words out, or worse yet, do you mumble? Be sure to practice speaking from the diaphragm and project. If your voice is overly loud, use a normal conversational tone. If using a microphone, take a few steps back or hold it further from your mouth. It's helpful to alter your pitch to attract attention and make a point. Just don't overdo it.
- Body language. Body language reflects attitude. Be sure yours has a presence and projects your agency's confidence, enthusiasm, and strength.
- Dress professionally. If you wouldn't wear it to a professional interview, it's inappropriate for a presentation.
- Pauses. Do not fill pauses. Use them to make a point.
- Silence is golden. If your audience is talking when you're ready to begin, don't raise your voice and ask for quiet. It's rude. Instead, just stand in front of the room and say nothing, this will establish your authority and the room will quickly quiet down.

Dressing for Success

Once all the visual/verbal preparation has been ironed out, what about you? How do you visually and verbally present? All eyes are on you, the orator, during the presentation. If you don't look polished and professional, even the best ideas could be rejected. You reflect your interest in the client's business by what you say and how you show and present yourself.

You are what you wear. *You* should be the center of attention, not your clothes. Conservative dress and a groomed appearance will assure all eyes are on you. Make sure your tie is straight, zippers zipped, and eye makeup is in place before taking center stage.

As a presenter representing your agency, first impressions are critical. What you wear will determine your attitude, confidence, and credibility, so it is important that you project the image you wish to portray. It's not unusual for your audience to have already formed some kind of opinion about you based on your dress, overall grooming, and posture, even before you begin the presentation.

Since you're already the center of attention, while speaking it's best to take a subtler, though still professional, approach to your choice of dress. For men suits in dark colors such as black, navy, or gray are a great choice. Feel free to add a little personality with your choice of tie or shirt. But remember that one should not compete with the other.

Women have a few more options, but the key is to not wear anything that will draw attention to itself and to avoid colors that outshine you. You want the audience's focus on your face, not your dress. Any jewelry that jingles or causes any type of reflection should be avoided. It's distracting. If you must wear jewelry, keep it small, quiet, and unobtrusive.

Avoid overpowering perfumes or colognes. Many people are allergic, sensitive, or find them just downright offensive. In the end, you want your ideas to linger, not your scent.

Business casual has no place in a professional presentation, even if your audience has chosen that type of dress. The best advice is to always dress more professionally or formally than your audience, especially if you are trying to prove your expertise and build credibility.

PHASE TWO: The Opening/Introduction

Open by introducing the members of the presentation team. Introduce them by name, then their title, expertise, and experience. Explain the section they will be covering. Next, let them know what you're going to talk about, why it's important to them, and why your agency is qualified for the account. Also let them know how long you will be speaking, and whether or not there will be time for a formal question-and-answer session.

The opening is critical to building a rapport, establishing credibility, and creating excitement, so it's important to grab your audience's attention in the first three to seven seconds, in much the same way as radio or television commercials must catch and hold attention. Now is not the time to bore the audience by jumping in with details and elaborate discussions. Now is the time to be enthusiastic and show pizzazz, to tantalize and build expectations with glimpses of creative, and reflect just a taste of your strategic and media ideas.

Exposing tiny portions of your visual/verbal solution early allows the creative discussion in the next phase to concentrate more on the strategy behind what is being shown. It also allows you to show how the overall objectives will affect and reach the intended target audience.

PHASE THREE: The Middle or Body

Phase three concentrates on your agency's solution(s) to the client's advertising problem. Focus here will be on the various business, media, and creative solutions. New and existing research will be used to support your main point, determine the best visuals to include, and define the outcomes. The main point is to feature that one idea your agency feels will best solve the client's advertising problem. It is important to tie the main point to its effect on the target audience, the communication objectives, the competition, and overall product positioning.

The middle section is the toughest section for your audience to get through. They have probably sat through several presentations before yours. So be sure to set yourself apart from competing agencies, go beyond expectations, and offer something no one else has, such as testimonials from focus groups or a musical reference that complements your creative direction.

The goal for this heavy, fact-based section is to not only educate, but also entertain by whetting your audience's intellectual and imaginative curiosity.

Consider using some of the following techniques to organize the body of your presentation.

- Stick to the point. You have one major and perhaps two or three smaller points to make, don't go off on a tangent.
- Lighten up. The middle section will bombard the audience with facts and statistics. To keep them listening, here you could introduce an anecdote or a humorous story that of course relates to your main point.
- Build credibility. Using your main point as a catalyst, you could now rediscuss your experience and how it will strategically benefit this client and this product or service.
- Dilute and simplify data. Here is where PowerPoint shines. Focus on a few bullet points for a detailed discussion. Make them more memorable by breaking up complex points with creative or other visuals, even if they are nothing more than charts and graphs.
- Rehash the facts. Each new point should build on the last. Be sure to point it out and often. This is also a good way to segue from one section to another.

- Transition or segue. Use transitions to link sections or main points. For example, if your media discussion emphasizes heavy target use of a particular media, you might consider referring back to it in the creative section when you are discussing consumer benefits and use. Transitions can be either visual or verbal. Show-and-tell techniques are very memorable.

PHASE FOUR: The Conclusion

Donald Parente, Bruce Vanden Bergh, Arnold Barban, and James Marra in their book *Advertising Campaign Strategy: A Guide to Marketing Communication Plans* offer the following options for concluding your presentation:

- The happy ending
- The funnel ending
- The we're-here-to-help ending
- The predict-the-future ending
- The quote ending
- The emotional ending

The happy ending. Make it positive. Show your enthusiasm for the product or service and your ideas.

The funnel ending. Here is where you summarize your presentation down to one, two, or three main points.

The we're-here-to-help ending. This ending promotes what you have to offer, and how you can solve the client's advertising problem.

The predict-the-future ending. This ending does just what it promises. It predicts how your ideas will positively solve the client's problems for years to come.

The quote ending. This ending works best if you opened with a quote; you can now refer back to it and how it positively reflects your ideas for the client's problem.

The emotional ending. This ending gives you the chance to hammer home why you are the best agency to handle this account.

Overall, the choice of ending can be based on either the tone of the presentation or the personality of your key point or theme. During your summation, be sure to end the presentation on a positive note, and if possible, a memorable one. Tell your potential client what you want them to do, and be sure to not only say that you're the best, but review why you're the best, based on your past performance with this type of product, service, or situation. And finally, never be afraid to take the time to show you have a view of the future, and to show how this campaign idea can be expanded to stand the test of time.

PHASE FIVE: Questions

A ninety-minute presentation really means sixty minutes when allowing for questions. If you have properly prepared your presentation and done your research, you should be able to anticipate 99 percent of all questions the client might ask. But, it is important to be pragmatic at the same time and realize that it's impossible to cover the client's product or service in its entirety and solve all of its advertising problems in such a short period of time, so be prepared for questions.

The team can determine when they will accept questions. Traditionally, a question-and-answer session is set aside following the conclusion, rather than taking place throughout the presentation. This is for two reasons: 1) questions that arise during the presentation can throw off timing and prolong the presentation, and 2) it is probable that information will be covered in later phases.

In the off chance a question should arise and the team doesn't know the answer, don't wing it. Tell the client that the question or point of view is interesting and that you will look into it and get right back to them. Be sure that you do; your credibility is riding on it. There is no shame in not having the answer to every question. The client will appreciate your honesty and be happy to wait for an answer. However, remember that the client will hold it against you if you make up an answer or ignore the question.

Jon Steel in his book *Perfect Pitch* sums up the question-and-answer section this way:

> However good a presentation might be, it is often the question and discussion time that makes the difference between good and great. By its very nature, it allows a client to participate in the presentation rather than having it just thrown at them, and it gives the agency the first clear signs of how its communication is being processed. If the ideas presented have been clear, the questions will often be geared toward development of those ideas. Any concerns raised will give both the excuse and valuable direction for following up with the client in the days immediately following the pitch.

It's important to follow up with members of the client's team within the first twenty-four hours by e-mail or, preferably, by phone. This way you can answer any outstanding questions, address any additional concerns, reemphasize your agency's talents, and express your thanks.

How Visual/Verbal Information Will Be Presented

Presentations That Say It Clearly

The presentation software of choice is PowerPoint because of its simplicity and compatibility. As a tool, PowerPoint is only as good as the presentation. It can bore as quickly as it can inform. It can ensure a seamless flow of information or bog the presenter down.

As a rule, PowerPoint is a good tool for projecting all verbal information and most simple visual images such as charts and graphs. It is not a good visual tool for projecting creative. Creative work that is scanned and then projected onto a screen often loses clarity, resulting in text that is blurred and colors that are muted. Projected images also don't provide the personal interaction the audience enjoys when able to actually touch or hold the visual product. Tactile presentations engage the audience and allow them to experience the creative product in much the same way the target audience will, making the experience more memorable.

PowerPoint is great for delivering facts, but unlike tactile techniques, detracts from presenters and doesn't allow them to engage the audience. Too much reliance on technology can distance presenters from their audience as they concentrate on the screened images. Once eye contact is broken, presenters are no longer talking *to* the audience, but *at* the audience, eliminating any two-way communication between buyer (client) and seller (agency). So it is important to remember that technology should never dominate the presentation, but supplement the interaction.

When using PowerPoint:

- Don't clutter slides with verbal points. Keep the visual simple and the center of attention, even if it's nothing more creative than a media flow chart.
- Keep your slides simple and confined to one point or one section of the presentation at a time. When you have too much information on any one slide, you will lose your audience's attention as they read ahead.
- Don't change slides until you are ready to discuss the information presented. Be sure each slide reinforces what you are saying so as not to generate unnecessary and disruptive questions.
- Don't rely on PowerPoint slides to sell your idea.
- Personalize the presentation by projecting only the most important points, and elaborate using a more conversational or one-on-one tone.

- Never read directly from the presentation slides. They were made for your audience's convenience, not yours.
- Don't use too much color or too many different typefaces or styles.
- Don't overdesign or use tacky or amateurish visuals. Each visual should have a point. If it doesn't, it shouldn't be there.
- Don't overuse animation or sound effects. Repetitive movement or sound annoys quickly and everybody.

Presentations That Show It Clearly

Every presentation should include a mixed bag of visual aids to capture the audience's attention both visually and verbally, making the presentation more memorable. Presentation teams can select from two types of visual aids: technology and props. Technology-based visual aids include: animatics, PowerPoint slides, traditional projection slides, and overhead transparencies. Visual aid props include: package designs, product samples, handouts, flip charts, and varied gimmicks, to name just a few.

Imaginative presentations can include dress and a few "clever tricks" to punch your strategy or name and stand out from competing agencies. For example, when one of the authors went to present to a client, she had injured her ankle and had it set in a large pink cast. The entire presentation wrapped around a Major League Baseball theme, so she wore an authentic baseball uniform with the client's name embroidered across the shirt. Not wanting to reveal the entire theme and needing a cane to walk, she wore a trench coat over the uniform and used a baseball bat for support.

When she walked in to the client's building, a national car rental company, she ran into another agency that had just presented. One of the team members said to her, "Oh, nice. So you're wearing a cast just like the client. That ought to score some points." Sure enough, the client had broken her ankle and was wearing a blue cast on the opposite leg. When she saw the client, she said, "Oh, great. We look like bookends!" Although no one believed her, it wasn't set up—it just happened. It certainly set the pace for a fun presentation.

What to Do When You're Not Invited to the Party

Sometimes agencies look for a clever way to get invited to the party. They want to get a chance to present and are hoping to be able to respond to an RFP (Request for Proposal), which is a document that details what the client wants in a presentation. Agencies have to be invited to pitch with an RFP. Well, not having been invited to present for a campaign that was running in the fall, the same author wanted an invitation. So she arranged to have a pair of banner planes do a series of flybys outside the client's window.

Some people don't know that these planes could fly by a specific floor, before 9/11, and even in front of the exact corner the client's offices are facing. Knowing this, she had the planes pulling messages set in red and black type. Plane one said, "We want to *land* the fall *campaign*." The second one added, "We need *clearance* from the *tower*." The italicized words appeared in red.

She arranged to be at the client's office that day and mentioned to her contact how beautiful the day was, as she guided him toward the window. Within a few minutes, the first plane came by. He said, "Gee, isn't that plane awfully close?" She said, "Yeah, and look, there's another one. What do they say?" The message didn't make sense to him at first. She said, "Isn't this building called the Tower?" He said, "Oh, yes." After the second flyby, six people were at the window. By the sixth and final flyby, almost forty people were looking outside. Suddenly, someone said, "Oh, YOU did this! You always have such creative ideas!" The author's art director used a panoramic camera to capture a shot of the planes from the street. The author placed the photos in frames and gave them to people who had missed it. And yes, the agency got invited to pitch a new piece of business, even though it wasn't the fall campaign.

Design for Clarity

Design knows no visual/verbal boundary. It doesn't matter if you are designing an ad or a presentation, the same principles apply. Consider using some of the following techniques to help make your presentation more visually/verbally appealing.

- Create eye flow. Open each slide with a dominant image, whether visual or verbal, and place it near the top. Because it must be read or seen in the back of the room, you will need to know the general size of the room you will be presenting in.
- Keep it simple and get to the point. Highlight only points of importance, and be sure to spend time discussing the details.
- Use upper and lowercase letters. They are easier to read and are quickly recognizable.
- Limit typefaces. When designing, the number of typefaces and type weights used on a PowerPoint slide should be limited. The basic rule of thumb is two typefaces per presentation.
- Choose a readable type size. Be sure the type is large enough to be read from any point in the room.

- Avoid using all capital letters anywhere in an ad. Most people are not familiar with an all-cap format, and as a result must read slower.
- Avoid using reversed text in large blocks of copy. Readability is reduced because the format is unfamiliar.
- Avoid excessive use of italics. Italic type suffers the same readability problems discussed above. Use it sparingly. Its best use is for emphasis and to set off a special word or phrase, quotation, or foreign word.
- Avoid decorative faces. Fancy or novelty typefaces, with all their elaborate flourishes and decorative appearances, make readability and legibility almost impossible under any circumstances.
- Use san serif fonts. San serif fonts are easier to read from a distance.
- Mix it up. Feel free to mix vertical layouts with horizontal ones. It creates visual diversity and eliminates a rubber stamp look.
- Consider using borders. Graphic but simple borders draw the eye in and highlight the copy.
- Add a dash of color. Too much and you've got gaudy, so be careful. Create a color scheme that matches your creative, or the client's packaging. Color helps to grab the viewer's attention. Use contrast. Avoid any light or pastel colors for type. These affect both readability and legibility.
- Use visuals with a purpose. Do not use them for decoration. Be sure they are large enough to be seen. Remember eye flow and the use of white space to increase readability and legibility.
- Use bullet points. A small amount of bulleted information per slide keeps things clean and controls the viewer's eye.
- Use bar graphs and pie charts. Graphs and charts simplify difficult information. Too much complex information can bog down even professionals. This is a good place to show, not tell. Keep it simple.
- Choose the best charting option. Graphs are used when you need to show numbers. Use a graph only if you are comparing data. Bar graphs show growth or loss by comparing similar categories. Use a pie chart to compare the percentage of use or size as compared to a whole. Data must add up to 100 percent; if it doesn't, don't use a pie chart. Use a diagram to explain a relationship or process, or to simplify complex concepts. Diagrams are often used to show how to do something.
- Avoid jargon. Don't use big words, techno lingo, or run-on sentences. Because a presentation is delivered only once, the audience cannot rewind, look up meanings, or reread to clarify.
- Be active. Use the active voice and simple, but descriptive words.
- Use repetition to enhance recall. Use multiple short sentences interspersed within longer statements. Repeat important points often to improve clarity and increase recall.

Visually/Verbally Telling Broadcast's Story

Print ads can be presented tactilely or added to your PowerPoint presentation. Alternative or electronic advertising can also be presented tactilely or via the Internet or alternative device. Broadcast can be presented by projecting one storyboard frame at a time on screen, with the accompanying script being either read aloud or played from a prerecorded sound track. Creative teams can take advantage of technology by producing an animatic of their storyboard. An animatic is a rough version of the hand-drawn storyboard, created on a computer, that uses animated illustrations and a sound track.

Technology often wows, so be careful your little animatic doesn't become too good a visual/verbal solution. If the client falls in love with its simplistic look, you may find the slicker, more professionally produced commercial rejected later.

Presentation Demons

In the days surrounding any presentation, the "presentation demons" usually show up. They come in all shapes and sizes. Printers don't work. Jump drives blow up. Copiers shut down. Computers crash. Highways are jammed with extra traffic or accidents. All of this is to remind you to plan ahead. Don't wait for the last minute to complete a presentation. Prepare early and have double copies of everything you're going to present. Keep all beverages away from presentation boards, computers, and other equipment.

Be sure to go to the presentation with an extra computer, extra copies (with pages numbered) of all presentation materials, and a backup way to present if there's a power or computer failure. Just remember, the "presentation demons" don't use Murphy's Law. They use O'Toole's Law: Murphy was an optimist.

Dealing with Clients

After you've landed the account, dealing with clients is not always easy. Some can be the devil incarnate, while others are cooperative and open to suggestion. But overall, there is very little difference between the good and the bad client. All clients are demanding, will push for good work, want you to read their minds, and want it yesterday. What sets clients apart are their interaction skills. Some yell. Some discuss it to death. Some are indifferent. Some feel they are better businesspeople, writers, or artists than you. These frustrated "creatives" are the most dangerous, often taking a good idea and turning it into something even the garbage disposal won't take. The key to survival both personally and artistically is communication. The more communication, the less chance there is that the idea and design that initially landed you the account will fall apart.

Notes

1. Linda Kaplan Thaler and Robin Koval, *BANG! Getting Your Message Heard in a Noisy World* (New York: Doubleday, 2003), 145.

2. Andrew Jaffe, *Casting for Big Ideas* (Hoboken, NJ: John Wiley & Sons, 2003), 51.

Interview

Eric Springer, personal communication, May 2, 2007.

Presentation Checklist

1. ____ Does your opening include the introduction of the team members, their experience, and your agency's qualifications?
2. ____ Does your presentation have a clear set of objectives?
3. ____ Does the presentation deliver a solid strategy to solve the client's advertising problem?
4. ____ Does the presentation both educate and entertain?
5. ____ Is the idea presented on-target and on-strategy?
6. ____ Did the team create something original?
7. ____ Does the presentation outline long-term communication options?
8. ____ Does the presentation include any attention-getting techniques?
9. ____ Does the presentation build your agency's credibility and instill the client with trust and confidence?
10. ____ Is the presentation simple and does it stay on the main point(s)?
11. ____ Does the middle section of the presentation clearly explain your ideas on how to solve the client's advertising problem?
12. ____ Does each section of the presentation transition easily from one to another?
13. ____ Does each point made build on the last?
14. ____ Do you have examples that will help you to prove any difficult points?
15. ____ Did you remember to keep terms and verbiage consistent throughout the presentation?
16. ____ Did you remember to tie boring facts into a story line to entertain, rather than bore the audience with a lecture?
17. ____ Are all transparencies and papers organized and in the proper order for easy access during the presentation?
18. ____ If using props, are you sure they are in the proper order and easy to reach during the presentation?
19. ____ Did you time out your presentation to fit in the time allowed?
20. ____ Are you prepared for anything, and for anything to go wrong?
21. ____ Do you have an alternative plan, should anything go wrong?
22. ____ Have you visited the presentation site? If so, do you know the layout well?
23. ____ Is there a place to set the computer or projector to avoid anyone's head from blocking the screen?

24. _____ Can all the projected images be seen clearly from anywhere in the room?

25. _____ Is your presentation interactive, mixing slides with discussion or demonstrations to hold interest and attention?

26. _____ Do you offer glimpses of your creative throughout the presentation to whet the client's interest?

27. _____ Are you going to use tactile props, and if so, can they be clearly seen or easily presented to everyone in the room?

28. _____ Have you double-checked to be sure all projected images are centered and aligned properly?

29. _____ Did you remember to show only those parts of the slides you are talking about at the time and cover those not currently under discussion?

30. _____ Are the colors used on individual slides dark enough to be easily seen from any point in the room?

31. _____ Is the type on the slides large enough to be seen anywhere in the room?

32. _____ Is there only one point per slide, avoiding a cluttered look?

33. _____ Do each of your visuals have a purpose?

34. _____ Do each of your slides have a point?

35. _____ Did you remember to bring items such as flip charts, layout pads, markers, and so forth?

36. _____ Did you remember to bring an extra laptop, cords, bulbs, pads, pens, and/or markers just in case they are needed?

37. _____ Do you have someone assigned to equipment maintenance and setup?

38. _____ Do you have someone assigned to attending any lighting issues, making sure the lights are at their brightest level during the introduction and the closing?

39. _____ Did you check the equipment to ensure everything is in place and in good working order before the presentation begins?

40. _____ Be sure to watch your footing. Did you remember to tape all cords to the floor to avoid tripping over them during the presentation?

41. _____ Since exact numbers can be difficult to follow in a presentation, did you remember to round up numbers when possible?

42. _____ Did you create a time schedule for each of your visuals in order to show the correct image at the correct time and in the correct order?

43. _____ Did you clutter your slides with too much detail of art?
44. _____ If the equipment fails or there is a power outage, can you still deliver the presentation?
45. _____ Did you build time into the presentation for questions?
46. _____ Did you repeat what you wanted your audience to remember?
47. _____ Does your closing have a call to action?
48. _____ Did you close the presentation on a positive note?
49. _____ Did you remember to proof the presentation for spelling, grammar, text formatting, layout, accuracy, and consistency?
50. _____ Have you and your team practiced enough?

BIBLIOGRAPHY

Avery, Jim. *Advertising Campaign Planning*. Chicago: Copy Workshop, 2000.

Berman, Margo. *Street-Smart Advertising: How to Win the Battle of the Buzz*. Lanham, MD: Rowman & Littlefield Publishers, 2007, 109.

Blakeman, Robyn. *The Bare Bones of Advertising Print Design*. Boulder, CO: Rowman & Littlefield Publishers, 2004.

———. *The Bare Bones Introduction to Integrated Marketing Communication*. Lanham, MD: Rowman & Littlefield Publishers, 2009.

———. *Integrated Marketing Communication: Creative Strategy, from Idea to Implementation*. Boulder, CO: Rowman & Littlefield Publishers, 2007.

The Designers and Art Directors Association of the United Kingdom. *The Copywriter's Bible*. Switzerland: RotoVision SA, 2000.

Garfield, Bob. *And Now a Few Words from Me*. New York: McGraw-Hill, 2003.

Higgins, Denis. *The Art of Writing Advertising: Conversations with the Masters of the Craft*. Chicago: NTC Business Books, 1965.

Jaffe, Andrew. *Casting for Big Ideas*. Hoboken, NJ: John Wiley & Sons, 2003.

Kaplan Thaler, Linda, and Robin Koval. *Bang! Getting Your Message Heard in a Noisy World*. New York: Doubleday, 2003.

Monahan, Tom. *The Do It Yourself Lobotomy*. New York: John Wiley & Sons, 2002.

Ogilvy, David. *Confessions of an Advertising Man*. New York: Atheneum, 1981.

———. *Ogilvy on Advertising*. New York: Vintage Books, 1985.

Oldach, Mark. *Creativity for Graphic Designers*. Cincinnati, OH: North Light Books, 1995.

Parente, Donald, Bruce Vanden Bergh, Arnold Barban, and James Marra. *Advertising Campaign Strategy: A Guide to Marketing Communication Plans*. Orlando, FL: Harcourt Brace, 1996.

Percy, Larry. *Strategies for Implementing Integrated Marketing Communications*. Chicago: NTC Business Books, 1997.

Rekulak, Jason. *The Writer's Block*. Philadelphia: Running Press, 2001.

Steel, Jon. *Perfect Pitch*. Hoboken, NJ: John Wiley & Sons, 2007.

Vonk, Nancy, and Janet Kestin. *Pick Me: Breaking into Advertising and Staying There*. Hoboken, NJ: John Wiley & Sons, 2005.

von Oech, Roger. *A Whack on the Side of the Head*. 3rd ed. New York: Warner Books, 1998.

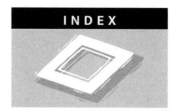

INDEX

ABOUT THE AUTHORS

Margo Berman teaches strategic and conceptual advertising classes with a focus on the creative process at Florida International University. She has won outstanding teaching awards from the state of Florida and from the university. She was named the 2001 AWC Woman of the Year in Communications Education. Her website, www.UnlockTheBlock.com, won a 2003 National AWC Clarion Award. She was named a Kauffman Faculty Scholar in 2005, and developed a new course, *Strategic Entrepreneurship Communication*, which received a 2006 National AWC Clarion Award for Course Development.

Her first book, *Street-Smart Advertising: How to Win the Battle of the Buzz*, has gone global and is in the United Kingdom, India and Russia (in Russian). It was featured in the June 2008 issue of Delta *SKY* magazine, and nationally on Fox Business News. The two six-part CD webinar sets Berman developed expanded on the principles from that book and offer twelve hours of audio and video learning. The two sets, *Street-Smart Advertising* and *More Street-Smart Advertising*, won a 2008 National AWC Clarion Award for Educational Reference. She also produced three audio advertising CDs: *How to Write Killer Copy*, *How to Create Great Ads at Breakneck Speed*, and *Mental Peanut Butter®: Slogans that Stick to the Roof of Your Brain*™.

As an inventor, she created a patented system of learning, *tactikPAK®*, in nine business disciplines from marketing and writing to creativity and design. She has co-authored three books on spirituality, has written articles for national trade journals as well as reference publications, including the *Encyclopedia of Advertising*.

Berman is also a corporate trainer of interactive seminars that focus on creativity, branding, and advertising. In addition, Berman produced and hosted her own radio talk show in Miami on public radio: *Artists About Themselves*.

She brings more than twenty years of experience as an award-winning creative director who founded her own ad agency, Global Impact, which handled clients like American Express, Alamo Rent A Car, and Banana Boat. She has won numerous advertising awards, including Addy, Tellys, Andys, Clarions, Angels, FAME, and International Radio and International Film Awards.

Always looking to showcase innovative ad campaigns, she searches for the most cutting-edge examples. Her tireless desire to feature exciting visual references highlights her passion to enhance the learning experience for all her audiences: students, colleagues, and seminar attendees. She is passionate about sharing what she discovers with others, hoping to simulate more right-brain thinking and create SponBRAINeous Combustion®.

Robyn Blakeman received her bachelor's degree from the University of Nebraska in 1980 and her master's from Southern Methodist University in Dallas, Texas, in 1996. Upon graduation in 1980, she moved to Texas, where she began her career as a designer for an architectural magazine. She next took a position as mechanical director for one of the top advertising agencies in Dallas before eventually leaving to work as a freelance designer.

Professor Blakeman began teaching advertising and graphic design in 1987, first with the Art Institutes and then as an assistant professor of advertising teaching both graphic and computer design at Southern Methodist University. As an assistant professor of advertising at West Virginia University she developed the creative track in layout and design. She was also responsible for designing and developing the first Online Integrated Marketing Communications Graduate Certificate and Online Integrated Marketing Communications Graduate programs in the country. While at West Virginia University she held several positions including: advertising program chair, coordinator of the Integrated Marketing Communications Online Graduate Certificate program and coordinator of Student Affairs and Curriculum.

In 2002–2005 Professor Blakeman was nominated by former students for inclusion in Who's Who Among America's Teachers. In 2003–2006 she was included in Who's Who in America, has received the Kappa Tau Alpha honorary from her peers and was voted P.I. Reed School of Journalism professor of the year for 2001–2002.

Blakeman is the author of three previous books: *The Bare Bones of Advertising Print Design*, *Integrated Marketing Communication: Creative Strategy from Idea to Implementation* and *The Bare Bones Introduction to Integrated Marketing Communication*. Professor Blakeman currently teaches advertising design at the University of Tennessee in Knoxville.

DATE DUE